Dante in Conversation with Contemporary Theorists

Dante in Conversation with Contemporary Theorists

Insights for the Western Secular Cognoscenti

BLAISE CIRELLI

Foreword by Arthur G. Holder

☙PICKWICK *Publications* · Eugene, Oregon

DANTE IN CONVERSATION WITH CONTEMPORARY THEORISTS
Insights for the Western Secular Cognoscenti

Copyright © 2024 Blaise Cirelli. All rights reserved. Except for brief quotations in critical publications or reviews, no part of this book may be reproduced in any manner without prior written permission from the publisher. Write: Permissions, Wipf and Stock Publishers, 199 W. 8th Ave., Suite 3, Eugene, OR 97401.

Pickwick Publications
An Imprint of Wipf and Stock Publishers
199 W. 8th Ave., Suite 3
Eugene, OR 97401

www.wipfandstock.com

PAPERBACK ISBN: 979-8-3852-2065-6
HARDCOVER ISBN: 979-8-3852-2066-3
EBOOK ISBN: 979-8-3852-2067-0

Cataloguing-in-Publication data:

Names: Cirelli, Blaise [author]. | Holder, Arthur G. [foreword writer].

Title: Dante in conversation with contemporary theorists : insights for the western secular cognoscenti / Blaise Cirelli.

Description: Eugene, OR: Pickwick Publications, 2024 | Includes bibliographical references and index.

Identifiers: ISBN 979-8-3852-2065-6 (paperback) | ISBN 979-8-3852-2066-3 (hardcover) | ISBN 979-8-3852-2067-0 (ebook)

Subjects: LCSH: Dante Alighieri, 1265–1321.—Divina commedia. | Dante Alighieri, 1265–1321.—Philosophy. | Hell—Poetry. | Purgatory—Poetry. | Paradise—Poetry. | Deleuze, Gilles, 1925–1995. | Guattari, Felix, 1930–1992. | Lévinas, Emmanuel. | Von Balthasar, Hans Urs.

Classification: PQ4412 C57 2024 (paperback) | PQ4412 (ebook)

12/06/24

Contents

Foreword by Arthur G. Holder   vii

Preface   xi

Acknowledgments   xiii

1   The Divine Comedy as Spiritual Template   1
     1.1 Introduction   1
     1.2 Hell: Deleuze and Guattari   2
     1.3 Purgatory: Levinas   5
     1.4 Heaven: Hans Urs von Balthasar   7
     1.5 Conclusion   10

2   Hell: Deleuze and Guattari and Dante's Hell   11
     2.1 Introduction   11
     2.2 Cosmological Hierarchy vs Immanence   18
     2.3 Social   24
     2.4 Self   33
     2.5 Deleuze and Guattari in Conversation with Dante   41
     2.6 Conclusion   54

3   Purgatory: Levinas's Modes of Being and Dante's Divisions of Purgatory   56
     3.1 Introduction   56
     3.2 The Teleology of Plato and Aquinas   64
     3.3 Levinas and Teleology   66

Contents

    3.4 Plato's Cave Allegory   67

    3.5 Plato's Influence on Neoplatonic Christianity and Dante's States of Being   70

    3.6 Plato's Influence on Levinas's Modes of Being and Encounter with the Other   73

    3.7 History of Purgatory   86

    3.8 Levinas and Ante Purgatory   91

    3.9 Levinas and Purgatory Proper   100

    3.10 Levinas and Earthly Paradise   103

    3.11 Conclusion   108

4   Heaven: Hans Urs von Balthasar's Theory of Beauty and Dante's Heaven   110

    4.1 Introduction   110

    4.2 Heaven: A Christian History in Relation to Dante's Paradiso   114

    4.3 Inner Dynamics of Beauty   116

    4.4 Outer Dynamics of Beauty   140

    4.5 Conclusion   163

5   Conclusion   165

    5.1 Objective   165

    5.2 A Conversation between Past and Present   166

    5.3 Religious and Spiritual Poll Data   166

    5.4 Conceptions of the Afterlife   169

    5.5 Dante for Our Time   176

Bibliography   179

Index   187

Foreword

A GREAT MANY BOOKS have been written about Dante's *Divine Comedy*. You can find any number of historical commentaries, literary analyses, theological interpretations, and guidebooks for the spiritual life based on this fourteenth-century Italian poetic masterpiece. Blaise Cirelli knows about all these scholarly genres and draws on some of them for his own purposes. But in this book, Cirelli is doing something different. The nature of his project is articulated in the book's title, which deserves close attention. Consider three salient phrases in the title that reveal Cirelli's method, his context, and his audience.

First, we have "Dante in conversation." This is not so much a book about Dante or his work as an invitation for Dante to speak about some existential questions: Is there an afterlife, and if so, what difference does that make for life in the present? What are the limits and the possibilities of human agency? How do societal norms function to regulate human behavior and contribute to human flourishing? Can the arts reveal deeper dimensions of meaning and value that lead us to an apprehension of the Good and the True, as well as the Beautiful? To let Dante speak in a manner comprehensible to us today, Cirelli needs to explain some key historical references and theological concepts, which he does clearly and concisely. However, his primary aim is to help us see what Dante saw so that we can truly hear what Dante said. We are not asked to accept Dante's vision as dogma or even as necessarily plausible, but we are subtly enticed into finding it interesting and worthy of our attention. From there, the inquiry develops as any conversation among friends might do—not as a debate or argument, but as a mutual exploration of common interests, with differences of opinion providing just as much food for thought as do the points of agreement. The cosmology of the *Divine Comedy* provides the general structure of Cirelli's explorations as he follows Dante's journey from hell through purgatory into heaven. Along the way, Cirelli invites us to linger on some particularly resonant passages in Dante's text that are pertinent to his chosen themes. Again like a conversation among friends, the desired end of this exploration is insight rather than a tidy list of conclusions.

Another revealing phrase in the title is "contemporary theorists." Cirelli has astutely given Dante different conversation partners for each stage of his journey: Gilles Deleuze and Felix Guattari for Hell, Emmanuel Levinas for Purgatory, and Hans Urs von Balthasar for Heaven. These late twentieth-century philosophers (and one theologian) sometimes share Dante's perspective, but more often challenge it. In either case, they were writing in a context in which Christian faith could no longer be taken for granted as providing a shared worldview. They are "contemporary" theorists not only because they lived in the recent past, but also because they were trying to understand and articulate the peculiar concerns of our troubled times. Even for readers who are yet unfamiliar with their work, an encounter with these four theorists offers intuitions of the postmodern reality of life in an anti-foundationalist, pluralist, and uncertain world. Just as he did for Dante, Cirelli takes care in his discussion of these complex thinkers to set them in context, explain their concerns, and provide definitions for their idiosyncratic (and sometimes abstruse) technical terms. As he imagines and then analyzes intellectual conversations between these theorists and Dante, we are invited to sift through the tangled mass of our own presuppositions and commitments, reflecting with all of them on the great questions that Cirelli is posing for their consideration and ours.

Then we come to the book's subtitle in which Cirelli identifies his intended audience as "the Western secular cognoscenti." While this phrase may well acknowledge that readers of this book will have a certain advantage if they are "in the know" concerning recent developments in continental philosophy, it is primarily intended as an invitation to those readers who are very much aware of the vast distance between Dante's worldview and their own. Unbelievers and skeptics are welcome! Readers of any philosophical school, any religious affiliation (or none), any critical or postcritical perspective, can enter this conversation without having to set their existing commitments aside. Like Friedrich Schleiermacher addressing his book *On Religion* to the "cultured despisers" in Germany at the dawn of the Enlightenment, Cirelli wants to find common ground with his audience

Foreword

by showing that he understands our concerns and speaks our language. Wherever in the world we may live, it is likely that we are influenced by Western ideas and values. However much we may adhere to traditional religious practices and communities, we live in a world that has been secularized to a large degree. And whether we are self-aware of our knowledge or not, we live in a time in which the onslaught of information threatens to overwhelm us with its abundance and its complexity. In a sense, most of us are Western secular cognoscenti now, with varying levels of awareness and varying degrees of resistance to the fact. This book is for us.

Like Dante himself, the author of *Dante in Conversation with Contemporary Theorists* has a spiritual purpose for writing. This book raises deep questions without attempting to provide all the answers, but it does suggest a trajectory for us to follow. As we work through our puzzles and our doubts, Blaise Cirelli hopes that we will be inspired to use the *Divine Comedy* as a "spiritual template" for our own experiences of illumination and transformation. Readers who accept the invitation will find the journey to be well worth the effort.

Arthur G. Holder
Emeritus Professor of Christian Spirituality
Graduate Theological Union
Berkeley, California

Preface

IN THE *DIVINE COMEDY*, the protagonist, Dante, describes the spiritual wisdom one medieval soul acquires through a journey in the afterlife. I will argue that an experience like Dante's can become a template for today's readers in their spiritual journey. Putting Dante's poem into conversation with contemporary philosophers and theologians demonstrates the link between the cultural past and present and at the same time emphasizes spiritual insight that endures into the present secular age.

Although most of us in contemporary Western culture live in a strictly secular realm, we still yearn for authentic spirituality. Many people, including the highly educated and liberal elite, often lack clarity about a credible spiritual path. In 2018, data from the Cooperative Congressional Election Study showed that 30 percent of the US population affiliates with no religion.[1] However, this phenomenon may be less a movement towards secularity than an expression of dissatisfaction with traditional religious denominations and a movement towards spiritual individualism. How can a secular audience for this text approach Dante who is so imbued with a religious outlook? In order to accomplish this task, I want to bring Dante up to date by having him speak with contemporary theorists.

In this book, I engage Dante in conversation with Gilles Deleuze, Felix Guattari, Emmanuel Levinas, and Hans Urs von Balthasar. The purpose of this conversation is to help make Dante's *Divine Comedy* more pertinent to contemporary readers. Since the *Divine Comedy* is steeped in fourteenth-century history, philosophy, and theology, it can be difficult for a contemporary reader to understand the spiritual message that Dante conveys. Dante's medieval readers were people like him, i.e., Catholic and

---

1. Burge, "Growth and Decline in American Religion."

Preface

with a belief in the afterlife states of hell, purgatory, and heaven. They also had a belief in a universal ethical standard that had clear demarcations of what constituted a grave ethical breach. Yet often contemporary readers are secular without attachment to a religious congregation. Some may believe in an afterlife, but many do not. Additionally, some do not believe in a universal ethical standard. Instead, they see each ethical decision as situational and unique. Thus, how could such a reader, who professes to be spiritual but not religious, gain a spiritual understanding of what Dante achieves in the *Divine Comedy*?

In order to help the contemporary reader, this text situates Dante's ideas in comparison with contemporary theorists who either accentuate Dante's ideas or puts them into counterpoint with their own ideas. In either case, the readers may find a new mode of entry into the *Divine Comedy* that either confirms their existing belief or challenges their belief system. The hope is that Dante and these contemporary theorists can help move the reader out of the dark woods and provide an illuminative path to a new spiritual experience.

Acknowledgments

I FIRST ENROLLED AT Graduate Theological Union at Berkeley in 2001. Over the many years at GTU, as I pursued my degree part-time while working full-time, I encountered many wonderful teachers and staff. I cannot thank all of them, but I would like to recognize how important GTU as an educational institution has been to me. In the writing of my book, I am grateful to those who agreed to be on my dissertation committee.

I want first to thank my PhD advisor, Dr. Arthur Holder, for the insightful advice on how to create a book. For most people, authoring a book is a unique event in a person's life. Thus, having an advisor like Dr. Holder with his stature and knowledge of the PhD process was an immense help to me. Additionally, his classes on Christian Spirituality assisted my understanding of how Dante was influenced by the Christian culture of his time.

My initial academic advisor, Dr. Mia Mochizuki provided me with her insightful inspiration concerning the direction of my studies. It was she who intuited that Dante and the *Divine Comedy* might be an area of interest for me. Little did she know when she suggested that I read Dr. Peter S. Hawkins's writings on Dante that I would choose the *Divine Comedy* as my PhD topic.

I would like to thank Dr. Anselm Ramelow for the wonderful classes that I took with him in the areas of modern philosophy and aesthetics. He instilled in me a love of philosophy that I never knew was hidden inside of me. I would also like to thank him for the suggestion of Hans Urs von Balthasar as one of Dante's interlocutors. Balthasar made a deep impression on me, and I will continue to read his large and varied corpus of work.

Additionally, I want to thank two other members of my committee, Dr. Drew Dalton and Dr. Brenda Schildgen. Dr. Dalton challenged me to

Acknowledgments

dig deeper when I was reading Levinas and that as a result extended my knowledge of Levinas's philosophy. His writings on Levinas helped me understand the genealogy of thinkers who influenced him. I also owe a great deal of gratitude to Dr. Brenda Schildgen who helped me not only with the topic of Dante's *Divine Comedy* but also in the writing process itself. She encouraged me to better organize my writing and gave me advice on how to write something that mattered to the reader.

Finally, I would like to thank my mother for her down-to-earth spirituality and her active participation in the Catholic Church. She set an example for me of how to live one's life in a modern world while still maintaining one's faith. She practiced the advice commonly attributed to St. Francis on the subject of evangelization, i.e., preach the gospel at all times and if necessary use words. It matters little if St. Francis actually said those words or not. I doubt my mother even knew about this advice, but she lived her life in a way that mirrored that dictum.

1

The Divine Comedy as Spiritual Template

1.1 INTRODUCTION

WHEN DANTE WROTE THE Divine Comedy, his spiritual world view was commonly shared throughout his Italian society. Yet, with the Reformation and the movement towards secularism, a unity of shared spiritual belief within the western world collapsed. Today, we inhabit a culture that has been categorized as spiritual individualism. Michel de Certeau believed the movement towards spiritual individualism (termed by de Certeau as "mysticism") began in the sixteenth century as Western culture no longer defined itself as a single Christian faith. Spiritual seekers realized an "experimental knowledge that slowly detached itself from traditional theology or church institutions."[1] Yet de Certeau asserted that a mystical experience is always represented culturally. By that, de Certeau means that a mystical experience is embedded in one's historical, cultural, and religious framework. Spiritual insight is not a perennial pool from which diverse religions and cultures draw. Rather, spiritual insight begins within a historical and religious culture. For example, in the *Divine Comedy*, Dante's last spiritual guide is St. Bernard, who for contemporary readers may seem like an odd

---

1. Certeau, "Mysticism," 13.

choice. However, Steven Botterill explains the aptness of Bernard's appearance for a medieval audience:

> By the end of *Paradiso* XXXI . . . Bernard of Clairvaux has been fixed in the reader's mind as a devotee of the Virgin . . . and a contemplative . . . in accordance with the prevailing interpretation of his significance in early Trecento culture.[2]

Botterill's comment indicates that fourteenth-century Christian culture understood implicitly Bernard's role in the *Divine Comedy*. Bernard's dedication to the Virgin was known throughout Italian Christendom and his appearance as a guide that leads Dante to Mary does not come as a surprise. Therefore, a culture's history must be understood so that wisdom from the past can be integrated with insight from the present. The question becomes which wisdom model can be studied that forms a bridge between the two.

This text will advocate for Dante's *Divine Comedy* as a platform for spiritual insight. Of course, one can read it merely as a literary artifact from the past. However, the fact that the *Divine Comedy* has endured for more than seven hundred years indicates that it is more than that. Its power is that it stands as one of the foremost artistic templates for spiritual wisdom within Western culture. While the *Divine Comedy* can impart wisdom, it requires an erudite contemporary reader because it abounds with fourteenth-century history, philosophy, and theology. To clarify its encyclopedic density, this text will put the *Divine Comedy* into conversation with contemporary thinkers. The past can be better understood when presented in counterpoint with the present. The task will be to take Dante's three canticles and interpret them in relation to some contemporary theorists: Hell with Gilles Deleuze and Félix Guattari, Purgatory with Emmanuel Levinas, and Heaven with Hans Urs von Balthasar. The hope is to establish for the reader the conditions for the possibility of a spiritual experience via the intellect. Additionally, the result will be that they will find themselves better spiritually connected with the past and the present.

1.2 HELL: DELEUZE AND GUATTARI

I chose Gilles Deleuze (1925–1995) and Félix Guattari (1930–1992) as the theorists who will be conversational partners with Dante's realm of hell. Gilles Deleuze was a French philosopher whose writings were very

---

2. Botterill, *Dante and the Mystical Tradition*, 85.

influential in the second half of the twentieth century. He spent the first part of his career writing on his own without Guattari and publishing works on various philosophers who influenced him (Hume, Bergson, Nietzsche, Kant, and Spinoza). Deleuze criticized Hegel for his dialectics and the idea that difference would be destined to a kind of unified dialectical system (i.e., the dialectics of opposition, then contradiction, and finally the resolution of contradiction). In Hegel's dialectical philosophy, there is an idea of teleological becoming. Dante, the author, also projects a teleological becoming as his character traverses the afterworld. However, unlike Hegel, Dante's becoming will end with the beatific vision. For Deleuze, teleology is antithetical to his philosophy. Unlike Dante, for Deleuze, there is not an agreed-upon end for which a person strives. Deleuze's philosophy insists on differentiation and multiplicity rather than a defined ending. Deleuze and Guattari also insist on an immanentism that has no hierarchical structure. This kind of immanence argued for by Deleuze was influenced by his association with Guattari. Both men were affected by the radical political activism that was occurring in Paris in 1968. Guattari was a psychotherapist and political activist who had been trained by Jacques Lacan. Deleuze met Guattari through an intermediary, Dr. Jean-Pierre Muyard, who was Guattari's associate. They exchanged letters before meeting in person. Both expressed interest in the other's work. They met together at Deleuze's home during a time when he was recuperating from a serious operation in which he had a tubercular lung removed. Guattari worked at La Borde, an experimental psychiatric clinic that advocated for a more democratic style of administration that gave voice to the patients who resided there. Deleuze and Guattari's major output together consisted of a two-volume work entitled *Capitalism and Schizophrenia*. In the first volume, *Anti-Oedipus* (1972), Deleuze and Guattari posited a different idea of desire than what is found in Dante. For Dante and much of the early and scholastic Christian tradition, desire represents a lack. And disordered desire is what leads human beings to behavior that often breaches ethical standards and results in sin. For Deleuze and Guattari, desire is not lack but production. Deleuze and Guattari do not separate what happens in the economic sphere of life from what happens in the intra-psychic sphere. Desire is production, and production is conducted by desiring-machines. We shall see how specific episodes in Dante's *Inferno* can be examined using Deleuze and Guattari's idea of desiring-machines. This is particularly true in the famous episode with Francesca and Paolo. Deleuze and Guattari refine their concept of desire, along with other new theories, in their second volume of *Anti-Oedipus* entitled *A Thousand Plateaus*.

One concept that Deleuze and Guattari expand upon in *A Thousand Plateaus* is the field of immanence, which serves as a counterpoint to Dante's conception of universal metaphysical order. Dante, the author, perceives his journey in the afterlife as a descent into the depravity of the *Inferno* and then an upward climb through *Purgatorio* and *Paradiso*. Dante's vertical descent through hell represents a journey towards the lowest levels of depravity. Yet I believe that it can be flipped ninety degrees by Deleuze and Guattari's philosophy and equated with a horizontal movement towards freedom. As an example, hell's segmentation into nine circles exemplifies the medieval era's penchant for hierarchies. It presupposes a ranked state of being wherein one finds one's permanent place in a fixed moral universe. Deleuze and Guattari, however, might imagine Dante's traversal through hell as a horizontal "line of flight." Deleuze and Guattari invent that term to emphasize "how things connect rather than how they 'are.'"[3] A line of flight breaks through the rigidity of hierarchical strata to create an emancipatory mode of thought. Reading Dante through Deleuze will challenge the normative reading of hell by reconfiguring Dante as a "Body without Organs (BwO)." This is another Deleuzian term that can be defined as a process "directed towards a course of continual becoming" but which "cannot break away entirely from the system that it desires to escape from."[4] Deleuze and Guattari freely use the term "body without organs" in various ways out of poetic license and to disrupt the idea of the foundational notion of structures both physical and virtual. The body without organs is Deleuze and Guattari's primordial state. I propose that Dante's movement through hell can be interpreted in two ways: first in the traditional manner with hell as a place of punishment for ethical breaches, and second as an escape towards emancipation in a traversal through the desiring-machines of hell. For Dante, the protagonist, the ultimate journey upward must first begin with a downward journey. Dante's education is to see evil firsthand in order to free himself for an ascent through Purgatory and ultimately Heaven. In a Deleuzian reading, Dante's journey can be considered as a freeing escape via a line of flight that allows him to extricate himself from the highly structured strata of hell.

---

3. Lorraine, "Lines of Flight," 147.
4. Message, "Bodies Without Organs," 37.

1.3 PURGATORY: LEVINAS

Emmanuel Levinas (1905–1995) is the philosopher who will be Dante's conversational partner for *Purgatorio*. Levinas was born in Lithuania to an orthodox Jewish family. He began his philosophical studies in Strasbourg, France. Between 1928 and 1929 he was in Freiburg and took courses offered by Edmund Husserl and Martin Heidegger. During the Second World War, Levinas was imprisoned in a German prisoner of war camp for five years. Levinas's major premise is that, contrary to Heidegger who conceives of Being as first philosophy, Ethics, is first philosophy. Levinas, who was a student of Heidegger's, often obliquely critiques Heidegger in his work wherein Levinas conceives of Being as a form of totality. It is these totalities that often are the causes of war. As an example, Levinas will claim that within war, humans are reduced to a totality of the state. The otherness of individuals is taken away through war. Politicians insist that war mobilizes all to become one in the defense of the state. Levinas famously critiques the idea of peace through war by saying that "the peace of empires issued from war rests on war."[5] Levinas's answer to the problem of war is to postulate a radical ethics of being responsible for the Other. According to Levinas, this responsibility to the other is beyond being. The idea of a good beyond being is an idea that both Levinas and Dante share with Plato. In the *Republic*, Plato recounts his famous Cave Allegory. In the allegory, prisoners are held captive in a dimly lit cave and cannot see true images. Instead, they see only shadows on the cave wall. When they are allowed to exit from the cave, they ultimately can see the source of light which is the sun. In Plato's allegory, the sun represents the good wherein the idea of light and goodness become intertwined. The good and intelligence also become related. For Plato, the most elevated state is pure intelligence. Yet Levinas has reservations about intelligibility. He explains that intelligibility leads one to representation, and representation occupies a privileged place in Western thought, especially in literature.[6] Levinas's primary concern with representation is that like intelligence or science it can lead to a closure that does not give weight to ethics. Richard Cohen states that what Levinas demands of both science and art is "that they recognize the supra-epistemological

---

5. Levinas, *Totality and Infinity*, 22.

6. Levinas in *Totality and Infinity* argues that representation is an act that "discovers, properly speaking nothing before itself." Representation acts to subsume exteriority, and in that act it will make the other like the same. See Levinas, *Totality and Infinity*, 124–25.

and supra-aesthetic character of a prior and commanding allegiance to ethics."[7] Thus, while Levinas appreciates art and literature, he maintains that they cannot interfere with the project of ethics. The reason, then, that Levinas is an apt conversational partner with Dante's purgatorial state is because ethics are central to the idea of purgatory. It is the place where souls must correct the tendencies in themselves which often caused harm to other beings during their earthly life. Theoretically, one could surmise that souls who inhabit Dante's purgatorial world could have avoided their time in *Purgatorio* if they would have practiced Levinas's radical ethical philosophy. For this study, I wish to look at how Dante divides his purgatorial states and compare them to Levinas's modes of being found in his text *Totality and Infinity*. The use of different terms (i.e., "states of being" for Dante and "modes of being" for Levinas) is intentional. This is because Levinas and Dante are utilizing them for different purposes and differences in underlying concepts.

Dante divides the purgatorial journey into three stages: AntePurgatory, Purgatory Proper, and the Earthly Paradise. Ante-Purgatory exists for those who were excommunicated or who were late in repenting. Purgatory Proper purifies souls from the seven deadly sins. The Earthly Paradise forms the final stage before Heaven. I wish to compare Dante's purgatorial states with Levinas's modes of being—understanding that there is not a one-to-one congruity between them. Additionally, Levinas's philosophy of responsibility for the other does not presume that there is a preconceived path that all follow in their encounter with the other. Like Deleuze's thought, Levinas's philosophical concepts do not presuppose a teleological force that automatically moves a subject from one state to another. As an example, in Dante's purgatory, a subject who lands in Ante-Purgatory will need to progress to Purgatory Proper. Later, that soul will automatically progress to Heaven. However, the modes of being for Levinas do not have an underlying force (i.e., an external agent like God) that moves the subject from one mode to another as Dante does in the *Divine Comedy*. Still, there are modes of being that Levinas describes in *Totality and Infinity* that can be compared to Dante's states of being. For example, Levinas's *il y a* is a totality—a mode of being that is absent of things, and prior to the being of an existent. While it does not map itself perfectly into Dante's cosmology, the *il y a* comprises an important mode for Levinas since it is from this mode that being emerges through hypostasis. I will compare Levinas's *il y a*

7. Cohen, "Levinas on Art and Aestheticism," 162.

with Dante's Ante-Purgatory because I believe that Levinas can extend for Dante a mode outside of hell and purgatory.

The next topic that I wish to analyze is what Levinas describes as "Living From . . . Enjoyment."[8] In this mode, the self enjoys the contents of life and strives for a home and companionship. Yet existing in enjoyment is limited because it opens nothing beyond the self. I want to compare this mode with Dante's Purgatory Proper to see how one might understand the ethics of both.

Finally, I will compare Levinas's encounter with the Other with Dante's Earthly Paradise. Here Dante transcends the self and experiences a kind of Levinasian Other. Dante experiences a clarity of the intellect and understands his relationship with Beatrice. Beatrice's Face calls Dante into being and allows for his transition to Heaven.

1.4 HEAVEN: HANS URS VON BALTHASAR

The theologian and philosopher Hans Urs von Balthasar (1905–1988) is the person who is Dante's conversational partner for *Paradiso*. Balthasar was born in Switzerland and studied in Zurich. In 1929 he attended a retreat for students in Germany. While walking in the Black Forest, he determined that he had a religious experience that ultimately he attributed to St. Ignatius of Loyola, the founder of the Jesuit order. In that same year, he entered the Jesuit order in Germany. As a Jesuit novice, he studied with Erich Przywara who influenced him on the theological subject of the analogy of being. Later, Balthasar relocated to France where he was influenced by Henri de Lubac and other theologians associated with the *nouvelle théologie* movement. Balthasar developed a keen interest in the early church fathers like Gregory of Nyssa and Maximus the Confessor.

Balthasar is renowned for his seven-volume work of theological aesthetics entitled *The Glory of the Lord*. One of Balthasar's primary objections about modern aesthetics is that true and the good became separated from beauty. Balthasar aims to unite beauty with theology where he feels that it first originated. In the *Divine Comedy*, Dante as well is searching for beauty. For example, at the beginning of the *Divine Comedy*, Virgil informs Dante that Beatrice summoned him to help Dante out of the dark woods. From childhood, Beatrice's beauty attracted Dante. Yet when Dante reaches Purgatory, Beatrice reproaches Dante for pursuing counterfeit beauty. Beatrice's

---

8. Levinas, *Totality and Infinity*, 110.

mission was always to help Dante find True Beauty. Dante's search for beauty becomes corrected in his encounter with Beatrice. He understands that his search for beauty has to become a search for God who is not only beautiful but also true and good.

Analogously, Hans Urs von Balthasar's mission is to explain True Beauty to the contemporary era. Graham Ward calls Balthasar "a Dante composing a *Divina Commedia* for the late twentieth century."[9] In fact, in Balthasar's trilogy *The Glory of the Lord*, he comments extensively on Dante. Balthasar's goal is to establish his own theory of beauty. My goal is to compare Dante's conception of Beauty with Balthasar's. I wish to show contemporary readers how spiritual discernment requires an understanding of Beauty. To do this, I approach Balthasar in two manners. I want to first analyze how Balthasar thinks about the inner dynamics of beauty. This consists of the concept of the analogy of being and the dynamic relationships among the triune God. I also examine the outer dynamics of beauty, which I conceive of as beauty's outward Form, and the idea of beauty's Glory as it is expressed theologically. The expression of beauty is paramount for Dante in his canticle *Paradiso*.

One of the inner dynamics of beauty as expressed by Balthasar is the idea of the analogy of being. This idea is not original with Balthasar but is emphasized by him because it shows how God and God's creatures are related. Within every person, there is an image of God that allows each of us to see a glimpse of God's beauty. Similarly, as Dante progresses through the realms of heaven he becomes exposed to ever-increasing vistas of beauty. Each successive stage allows him to become convinced that he is becoming closer to God. And since in the Christian tradition, God is three persons, Dante's experience of God is trinitarian. Likewise, in Balthasar's theology, he describes the relationships between the persons of God—Father, Son, and Holy Spirit. Balthasar places great emphasis on the dynamic love that each of the persons of God has for each other. One of Balthasar's strengths is to demonstrate how the love among the Trinity can serve as an example of God's love for God's creatures. Additionally, Balthasar talks about Christ's mission as the Logos to redeem humans from their alienation from the true, the good, and the beautiful through his kenotic love for the Father. In Dante's *Paradiso*, Beatrice serves as a bridge between Dante and God. She continues to point Dante towards the triune God that Dante meets at the end of the *Divine Comedy*. In addition to the two inner dynamics of beauty,

---

9. Ward, "Kenosis," 67.

Balthasar expresses two outer dynamics of beauty. These are Balthasar's idea of the Form of beauty and also his ideas about the expressions of God's Glory.

Balthasar's idea about beauty's Form can take many expressions. But one which is pertinent to Dante is the form of language. Balthasar credits Dante for writing in the vernacular. The vernacular allowed those who were not fluent in Latin to still understand God's beauty in the language in which they were knowledgeable. Balthasar also praises the Form of Christ as God who was made man. Christ's passion to serve the Father is an expression of agape love that is a model for how humans should love each other as well as God. This idea of agape love is expressed in many forms by Dante's relationships with Virgil, Beatrice, and St. Bernard who lead Dante along his path through the afterlife. Unlike those poor souls in hell whose disordered desire led them astray, the desire that Dante learns allows him to transform his erotic love for Beatrice into a purifying love for all humankind. Dante's realization of this movement within himself allows him to praise God for God's glory.

God's glory is expressed in two ways. The first is how God reveals his glory to creatures. When God reveals Godself to humans they often become overwhelmed with God's power. It is so immense that they are moved to extol God to others. Yet, because the encounter with God is so overwhelming to the senses, it is difficult to communicate. That is one of Dante's challenges for his *Paradiso* canticle. How can he use human language to praise God when the experience is often incommunicable? In *Paradiso* Dante's poetical powers are put to the test. Yet, he is capable of describing it by elevating his language through the setting of *Paradiso* which is located in the heavenly cosmos. Dante, the character, is often depicted as looking down on God's creation from the heavenly realm and seeing scenes from human history that he attributes to God's power. Dante will also associate the idea of God's glory with human vision. As Dante travels through the heavenly realm, vision and light become the primary means through which Dante expresses the glory of God. Even though Balthasar appreciates Dane's poetic gift to display God's glory through vision, he will challenge Dante about his privileging the sense of vision. Balthasar would like to see a more person-to-person approach to God's glory. Balthasar will also challenge Dante about other aspects of the *Divine Comedy* which he believes would make Dante more relatable to contemporary readers. Balthasar's critique of Dante is interesting to review and valid in certain respects, but

I will defend Dante's vision while crediting Balthasar for new insights into the *Divine Comedy* and admitting certain perspectives that might be interesting for today's readers.

1.5 CONCLUSION

This text is designed to bring new readers to Dante's *Divine Comedy* so that they might have a spiritual experience of the intellectual kind. Dante's *Divine Comedy* remains relevant today for those looking for wisdom from the past that still endures. By putting Dante into conversation with contemporary theorists, my wish is to contemporize the *Divine Comedy* by examining how it relates or does not relate to contemporary philosophical and theological positions. My emphasis is not to privilege contemporary philosophical arguments over Dante's fourteenth-century worldview. This text holds both world views as valid. Certainly, our contemporary knowledge of the cosmos must be acknowledged as being an advance over fourteenth-century science. But Dante's philosophical and theological opinions often can withstand the duration of time. Holding both contemporary and medieval philosophical and theological arguments to the light can often clarify each side of the argument. If the reader comes to a new philosophical or theological understanding as a result of reading this text, it will fulfill my expectations for this text.

2

Hell
Deleuze and Guattari and Dante's Hell

2.1 INTRODUCTION

IN A TIME THAT feels so fragmented, contemporary individuals often cannot accept the idea that there is a divinely ordered plan. Additionally, they may have little faith that God has conceived a universe in which humans are a little lower than angels and a little higher than animals. Perhaps they do not believe in angels, and they are beginning to get a sense that animals should have rights similar to humans. They might have doubts about an afterlife, a hierarchical cosmology, a belief in God, and a transcendent ethical system. Contemporary readers of the *Divine Comedy* may disbelieve in a cosmology with interlocking parts and an existence with a teleological plan. Likewise, they may be dubious of a cause-and-effect ethical system. They may not believe that if they adhere to an ethical code they will be rewarded, if not socially and materially, then by divine forces in the afterlife. Perhaps they have little faith that there is a God. I believe that Dante is still pertinent to a contemporary reader's experience. However, to make Dante more contemporaneous, he needs to be contextualized within a frame that recasts the world into a philosophical system that might be more relatable to today's reader. I choose Gilles Deleuze and Felix Guattari as the philosophical interlocutors with Dante's *Inferno* because I believe that they are well suited to present a case for how contemporary society may conceive of our hellish experiences without resorting to medieval theology or philosophy. Additionally, Deleuze and Guattari often present ideas that are in direct opposition to Dante's beliefs. Therefore, they can illuminate Dante's beliefs by comparing them in stark relief with their own ideas. The way that I want to examine these ideas is to categorize them into cosmological, social, and the self. By cosmological, I mean the overarching system by which one conceives of our ontological and metaphysical state. It is how we might conceive ourselves as being part of a larger picture. By social, I mean how we as humanity are organized in the world. That would include the governance and the ethical code in which we as groups interact with each other. Finally, for the self, I mean how the self is constituted. Are we comprised of various parts and if so what are they and how do they function? What is it that we fixate upon and what motivates us to live our lives in the world?

2.1.1 Cosmological

In the cosmological category, I want to contrast Dante's ideas about hierarchy against Deleuze and Guattari's ideas of immanence. Dante's representation of the afterlife comes from the concept of hierarchy that originated from Neoplatonism and was developed later by Christian philosophers and theologians into a unified and ranked cosmology. This is expressed in how Dante divides hell into nine circles and even additional sub-hierarchies based on his idea of which sins are most egregious and which are less so. My wish is to illustrate how Dante in the *Inferno* put together an ethical system that reflected the medieval conception of hierarchy. In the medieval mindset, the ethical system was created by God, based on Scripture, and was transcendent and universal for all. This ethical system is how Dante decides who will go into hell and where they will be placed. In his own ingenious way, Dante creates a punishment system for each group of sinners that is appropriate to their most egregious sin against God. On the other hand, Deleuze and Guattari oppose Dante's idea that a superior being constructed a world that descends from goodness to evil. Rather than a transcendent ethical system, they speak of a situated ethical choice that opens up to life at each unique moment. Deleuze and Guattari will insist that the cosmology is immanent. Deleuze expresses immanence as something that "cannot be brought back to Some Thing as a unity superior to all things, nor to a Subject as an act that brings about a synthesis of things."[1] Attendant with this idea is Deleuze's call for a univocity of being. Deleuze explains this concept further:

> Equal being is immediately present in everything, without mediation or intermediary . . . all things are in absolute proximity, whether they are large or small, inferior or superior, none of them participates more or less in being.[2]

Deleuze does not conceive of a metaphysics as a tiered space with the lower realm as material and evil and the upper realm as ethereal and benevolent. Instead, the idea of being is flat without rank and without the corresponding qualities of evil and good. Given the contrast between a hierarchical cosmology versus an immanent one, it is important to see how Dante and Deleuze and Guattari conceive of the socius (i.e., how various social groups, religious organizations and governmental institutions function in a society as well as how they impact the individual).

2.1.2 Social

I would like to address how Dante conceives of the socious and how Deleuze and Guattari conceive of it.[3] The reason for examining the social is because it forms the suppositions that Dante had about how institutions and groups should function. These suppositions formed the basis of how he judged people who did not live up to the ideals of their duties towards society. It includes exploitative rulers like kings and emperors and dishonest church luminaries like popes, priests, and bishops. It also includes those who were corrupt in their business practices or those who violated societal sexual taboos. I intend to discuss Dante's conception of governance and how he saw the role of the state and the church in human affairs. The topics I will discuss that are common to Dante and Deleuze and Guattari are the ethical and governing systems. Since Deleuze and Guattari have certain ideas that are outside Dante's paradigm, I will discuss how they affect the

---

1. Deleuze, *Two Regimes of Madness*, 385.
2. Deleuze, *Difference and Repetition*, 37.
3. Surin, "Socius," 258–60. The socious is where desiring machines (humans) have their desire coded and recoded so that they can perform their social roles. Desire is also manifested upon the earth and territorialization is one of the first segments that becomes imbued with meaning. Once desire is coded, social machines can perform their work.

socius. They involve the following: social machines, the regime of signs, faciality, deterritorialization, and nomadism/rhizomes.

Within the topic of social machines are the sub-topics of the regime of signs and faciality. Social machines are Deleuze and Guattari's concept about how humans organize themselves via flows of power or desire. Flows happen in many domains, i.e., in human groups and nature including mineral, vegetative, and animal life forms. The human socius is made up of many different flows which form connections through desire and power. Compared to Dante, Deleuze and Guattari have a much different explanation of the socius. Rather than conceiving society in a fixed and hierarchical manner, Deleuze and Guattari theorize how desire and power move through various social machines. One of Deleuze and Guattari's concepts of a linguistic social machine is what they call a regime of signs.[4] Deleuze and Guattari describe various regimes of signs that explain how power and desire are expressed and abused within the socius. By utilizing the concept of the regime of signs, one can better unpack how Dante is judging a particular social group and why the punishment for them is appropriate. Besides the regime of signs, social machines are constituted by the concept of faciality. Faciality is a means by which Deleuze and Guattari explain how a face can explain the dynamics of a socius. Faces often constitute powerful symbols within a culture, e.g., the face of Christ, the face of a sacrificial animal, the face of a white European male, etc. Facial symbols create a milieu in which different subjectivities and meanings can come to the surface. A certain faciality can point to implicit power structures or biases within a socius. Deleuze and Guattari have two other concepts that affect the socius and those are deterritorialization, and nomadism/rhizomes. While deterritorialization and rhizomes span more than just the socius in Deleuze and Guattari's work, it is within the socius domain that they can be applied to Dante's *Divine Comedy*.

Deterritorialization is a concept that Deleuze and Guattari use to describe a point of instability within a socius whereby a degree of freedom emerges that breaks up the bindings of a socius. This creates what Deleuze and Guattari call a line of flight. As an example, within the late feudal system, a change of power brought on by the new mercantile class

---

4. Murray explains Deleuze and Guattari's idea of a sign as "an expression of quasi-causal relationality of immanent processes in matter [and] is at the frontier between expression and things. Indeed, the intensive sign is for them at the same level as intensive matter and bodies and enters directly into matter and bodies" (Murray, "Deleuze and Guattari," 11).

disrupts the existing social system. In the case of Italian city-states, labor that was previously owned by the manor lords becomes deterritorialized and freed up to leave the land and emigrate to the wealthier cities. Laborers who were bound to the land experience a line of flight that loosens the social stuckness that a particular group or an individual might have felt before a deterritorialized moment. The movement of deterritorialization is usually followed by a reterritorialization where new power structures bind society in configurations that were different from the previous system. Also included in the social realm is the idea of nomadism and rhizomes.

Nomadism and rhizomes are two related concepts that I want to treat together. Deleuze describes the rhizome as the opposite of a tree. Where trees have a hierarchical nature with roots supporting the trunk and a beautiful canopy above, rhizomes are horizontal in nature. Deleuze states that the principal characteristics of a rhizome are that "unlike trees or their roots, the rhizome connects any point to any other point, and its traits are not necessarily linked to traits of the same nature."[5] A rhizome is counter to a system that has a hierarchical structure with a central communication system. Instead, a rhizome is "an acentered, nonhierarchical, nonsignifying system without a General and without an organizing memory or central automaton, defined solely by a circulation of states."[6] Therefore, a rhizome fits in with Deleuze and Guattari's rejection of hierarchy and embrace of immanence. Analogously, nomadism is the concept of a society without a place of spatial concentration. Unlike a kingdom that has degrees of hierarchy (i.e., emperor, king, prince, duke, etc.), a nomadic group is not subservient to an existing ruler. A nomadic distribution is something that possesses "a mobile, immanent principle of auto-unification" and is "radically distinct from fixed and sedentary distributions."[7] The central idea of a nomadic socius is that it exists in open horizontal space rather than concentrated hierarchical space. It operates in what we might understand as an independent cell-like group without a central command and control structure. Tiziana Villani utilizes the character of Ulysses to make her point about Deleuze's conception of nomadism. She states Ulysses, despite his many travels, is not a nomad. Rather he is a predator who gathers his friends for excursions to conquer others. His ultimate goal is to return home to glory. Opposed to Ulysses is the nomad who is "Ulysses's enemy, the figure he fears the most,

---

5. Deleuze and Guattari, *Thousand Plateaus*, 21.
6. Deleuze and Guattari, *Thousand Plateaus*, 21.
7. Deleuze, *Logic of Sense*, 102.

the foreigner without a home country, someone who would never build a nuptial bed out of the trunk of an old family olive tree."[8] Villani's critique of Ulysses being termed a nomad is that movement in and of itself does not constitute the idea of nomadism. Ultimately Ulysses's goal is to appropriate the goods of others and return home. In contrast, nomadism is homelessness itself. As Michael Marder puts it, nomadism is for those who "are at home in a homeless world."[9] For Deleuze nomadism is without enclosure. He describes it in this way: "There is no longer a division which is distributed but rather a division among those who distribute themselves in an open space—a space which is unlimited, or at least without precise limits."[10] Nomadism then is an unusual way that a socius is organized. Rather than a hierarchical system, Nomadism is dispersion in space. As such, Dante the writer experienced nomadism when he was exiled from his home in Florence. While Dante may not have been comfortable with homelessness, he was effective in operating within it. Dante the writer's real life is horizontal movement as a nomadic exile. In contrast to Dante the real person, Dante, the character, does not operate in a smooth space. Instead, he travels through heavily striated space. Each realm of Dante's travel in the afterlife, whether in hell, purgatory, or heaven, is a movement through well-marked levels that are either in a downward or an upward mode. Dante the character's afterlife motion is vertical and his movement is impelled by desire. This is one of the topics that I will examine in the category of the self.

2.1.3 Self

The ideas that I want to use from Deleuze and Guattari to contrast with Dante's ideas of the individual are their conceptions of the self, the function of desire, and their concepts of a body without organs and becoming woman / minoritarian. Deleuze and Guattari conceive of the individual differently than Dante's conception of the self. Dante conceives the self mostly as a fixed identity and as a human composed of body and soul. Additionally, the self is a presence that exists in transcendence to the world or at least a step removed from it. For Dante, while humans have the capability of changing—as Dante does through his progression from hell to heaven—the soul of Dante, i.e., Dante's essence, remains fixed. Deleuze's definition of the

---

8. Villani, "Gilles Deleuze," 520.
9. Marder, "Anti-Nomad," 497.
10. Deleuze, *Difference and Repetition*, 36.

human subject is different. In the "Translator's Introduction" to Deleuze's text *Empiricism and Subjectivity*, Constantin V. Boundas lists three definitions by Deleuze on subjectivity:

> (1) "The subject is defined by the movement through which it is developed." ...
>
> (2) "There are no more subjects but dynamic individuation without subjects, which constitute collective assemblages. . . . Nothing becomes subjective but haecceities take shape according to the compositions of non-subjective powers and effects."
>
> (3) "The struggle for [modern] subjectivity presents itself, therefore, as the right to difference, variation and metamorphosis."[11]

Deleuze's definition of the subject as "the movement through which it is developed" removes the subject as the active agent and instead emphasizes the fluidity of the subject's movement. Additionally, the subject for Deleuze is made up of many different parts which emphasize a multiplicity rather than a single entity. One of the aspects of the self which Dante and Deluxe conceive of differently is how the self is affected by desire. Where Dante might conceive of desire as a lack, Deleuze and Guattari think of it as productive. Desire is a connective function that forms relationships among individuals and groups. Rather than being enchained by desire, Deleuze and Guattari see desire as that which affiliates. In contrast to the connective function of desire is Deleuze and Guattari's conception of a body without organs. A body without organs is an idea that allows a decentered self to emerge. It is a notion that exemplifies how one frees oneself from heavily codified social systems. Finally, the concept of becoming woman or minoritarian is the idea of removing the white male face as the predominant mode of subjectivity. It allows a minority (a woman, a person of color, LGBTQ, etc.) person to assume the role of a prevalent subjectivity, and thereby it subverts what is the "normally accepted" mode of subjectivity.

---

11. Deleuze quoted in "Translator's Introduction," in Deleuze, *Empiricism and Subjectivity*, 12. The translator of Deleuze's text, Constantin V. Boundas, takes three quotes of Deleuze from various texts (including *Empiricism and Subjectivity*; *Dialogues*; and *Foucault*) and assembles them in his introductory chapter.

2.2 COSMOLOGICAL HIERARCHY VS IMMANENCE

In the *Comedy*, Dante systematizes good and evil into a hierarchy. This cosmology reflects his time and place. Now it is true that Dante will rebel often against hierarchy, especially when it is related to those who are in power and corrupt. And sometimes Dante will have moments of immanence in his writing. As an example, in *Inferno* XXIV he opens with a beautiful description of a nature scene about a peasant who rises and sees snow covering the field. He returns to his house in a foul mood. But he goes outside and has his hope restored because the "world has changed its face / in that brief time, and now picks up his crook / and drives his sheep to pasture" (*Inf.* XXIV, 13–15). In this example, the subjectivity of the peasant is changed via his immanence in nature. Likewise, Dante will often eschew hierarchy and embrace simplicity. His affiliation with the Franciscans and his regard for St. Francis's embrace of poverty is an example. Still, Dante will often come back to hierarchy as a means of organizing the *Comedy*. Yet the idea of hierarchy is one of the problems that a contemporary reader will encounter when reading Dante. It may be difficult to accept the idea of an afterlife and a hellish world below. Yet the reader must understand the basis of Dante's hierarchy to appreciate what he brings from the cosmological vision of the Middle Ages. Once one understands the nature of Dante's hierarchy, then one will better appreciate the encounter with Deleuze and Guattari. They will challenge hierarchy with their conception of immanence. But let us set this aside for the moment and understand Dante's hierarchy in the province of hell.

One important aspect that Dante brings to the conception of hell is a more methodological approach to the classification of sins. Dante was aware of the afterlife visions written before him. He understood how they were hierarchically structured. Satan, the most evil of all, exists in the lowest part of hell while the most virtuous personae exist in the highest realms of heaven. Yet the afterlife visions before Dante were not consistent in their taxonomy of evil. For example, Dante avoids having a sin related to sexuality exist in more than one realm. In comparison, the author of the *Apocalypse of Paul* (ca. mid-third century), lists the various sins related to fornication in seven different realms of hell.[12] One could argue about how

---

12. There are numerous afterlife visions that were written before Dante's *Divine Comedy*. An unknown author composed the Apocalypse of Paul in the mid-third century when a community of loosely affiliated entities constituted the Church. The original text is thought to be Egyptian in origin, written in Greek, with a preface added in the year

Dante rates the severity of sins, but he at least has consistency in systematization. Dante lays out the hierarchy of sins in a manner that corresponds with a general medieval view of sin.

2.2.1 Influences on Dante's Idea of Hierarchy

Dante inherited his ideas from the classical and Christian philosophers and theologians that came before him. From a philosophical point of view, the idea of a hierarchy of sins, or of any hierarchy at all, is an idea that goes as far back at least to Plato. According to Plato, at the summit of being is the idea of the Good, also described as the One. The Good produces fecundity and plentitude. The One is both being and substance itself. Everything that the Good creates is analogous to the Good. Humans are not substance, but instead, have substance by virtue of their relationship with the Good. Another word for substance is the soul. Therefore, a human participates in the Good via a soulful analogical relation with the Good.

For Aristotle, ethics comes from pursuing the good, i.e., an end. The good manifests itself in many ways. But morality consists in pursuing an end of good. The end is always better than the activity in pursuit of the end. For Aristotle, lower ends are determined by the higher end. The highest end for Aristotle is living a life of the intellect. Intellectual activities, like thought, are better than sense perceptions because intellectual knowledge is more universal than what can be obtained from sense perceptions.

The Platonic idea of the One and the Good was embellished by Plotinus. He imagined the One not as a static force but as a fruitful and productive force that engenders eternally. In the *Fifth Ennead*, Plotinus writes, "Again, all that is fully achieved engenders: therefore the eternally achieved engenders eternally an eternal being. At the same time, the offspring is always minor."[13] The Good engenders eternally, yet what the Good engenders is less than the good. From that relationship, the Good establishes a hierarchical relationship with what it engenders. Plotinus influenced Augustine and future Christian thinkers to a great extent.

---

388. Succeeding authors revised and redacted the text as it transitioned over time. Readers delighted so much in the narrative that the Middle Ages produced many redactions in a number of different languages. For additional information, see Elliott, *Apocryphal New Testament*.

13. Plotinus, *Six Enneads* 5.1.6.

Augustine was very influenced by the Neoplatonists who came before him. As an example, Augustine states that God helped procure for him "certain books of the Platonists" that instructed him about creation.[14] He understands that these books by the Platonists are very much like what he read in Genesis concerning how God created the world. Augustine also mentions that the Platonists taught him to look for "incorporeal Truth" and that "invisible things are understood through the things that are made."[15]

Pseudo-Dionysius the Areopagite, a Christian theologian of the late fifth and early sixth century, picks up Neoplatonic thought about hierarchy and develops it. Dionysius wrote about hierarchies in two of his treatises, *On the Celestial Hierarchy* and *On the Ecclesiastical Hierarchy*. Filip Ivanovic makes a distinction between the philosophy of Neoplatonism and Dionysius's Christian theology. In Christianity, the soul is not an emanation of the eternal soul but is an image of God. And while in Neoplatonism the return of the soul is "a solitary act of an individual, in which the one does not play an active role," for Dionysius the return "is a process of cooperation between God and man; and not only that—the individual is helped by other beings involved in the process, i.e., other humans and angels."[16] In the *Celestial Hierarchy*, Dionysius describes the hierarchical order of angels who assist in reflecting the glory of God. In the *Ecclesiastical Hierarchy*, Dionysius delineates the hierarchy of the church which serves to illuminate the glory of God. Dionysius defines hierarchy as "a sacred order, a state of understanding and an activity approximating as closely as possible to the divine." He goes on to say that "it is uplifted to the imitation of God in proportion to the enlightenments divinely given to it."[17] The hierarchy's purpose is for all to become alike to God as much as is permitted by their nature. The function of each successive level of the hierarchy is to bring into manifestation the Godhead. The *Comedy* provides the idea of a multileveled hierarchy of the good, with many layers of Heaven spilling down into Purgatory. Yet Dante does not stop there. He lays out various levels of depravity in hell to admonish sinners what their fate will be like if they fail to live an ethical life.

---

14. Augustine, *Confessions* 7.9. Augustine does not specifically state which Platonist books he is referring to, but most authorities agree that they include Plotinus's *Enneads*.

15. Augustine, *Confessions* 7.20, 26.

16. Ivanovic, "Ecclesiology of Dionysius the Areopagite," 29.

17. Pseudo-Dionysius, *Celestial Hierarchy* 3.1, 153.

2.2.2 Hierarchy of Inferno

In this section, I will give a general outline of hell and explain the structure. Dante invents a region, Ante-Hell, for people who stood neither for nor against anything. In circle one are the virtuous pagans who lived admirable lives but never knew Christ. Dante does make exceptions for Old Testament figures like Noah and Moses, et al., and allows them places in *Paradiso*. Virgil explains to Dante that Christ freed them when he made his descent into Limbo during the Harrowing of Hell. Circles two, three, and four are for sinners with an excessive appetitive nature. They are the lustful, the gluttonous, and those who either hoarded or wasted money. In all the appetitive realms, the sinners focused only on their own selfish and obsessive needs rather than extending themselves to others. Circle five is for the wrathful, the arrogant, and those who believe falsely in their greatness. One way of categorizing circles two through five is to say that the inhabitants here sin through their compulsivity or their inability to manage their behavior. They are slaves to their addictions. They are lustful, gluttonous, in constant pursuit of security through financial means, and have lost their spiritual nature. Or they are irascible in temperament and could not establish peaceful relationships with their fellow humans.

Beyond the Gates of Dis, that is, beginning with circle six, we descend into lower Hell, and the nature of sin shifts. Here Dante places the heretics and atheists at a lower level of hell because of their intellectual hubris. These sinners have an additional weight of sin because they use more of their conscious will to rebel against God. The sixth circle is where the notable Farinata inspects Dante scornfully and insults Dante's ancestors. The imperiousness of Farinata is emblematic of the kind of hubris that Dante finds more sinful than those who sinned due to their appetitive or irascible natures. Circle seven is where one will find those who commit violence. Violence is divided into three rings in this order: violence against one's neighbor, violence against oneself, and violence against God. In circle seven, ring one, Dante situates tyrants like Atilla the Hun. In circle seven, ring two, Dante locates those who have been violent against themselves, including those who committed suicide or who squandered their fortunes. It may be perplexing that Atilla the Hun and other tyrants are considered less sinful than those who take their own lives. One explanation is that tyrants act out of passion while the suicides and squanderers act out of a conscious will. As an example, Cleopatra and Dido are both characters who committed suicide but are in the less sinful second circle, rather than the seventh circle. The reason is that they were driven to their demise by a concupiscent passion. However, another character who committed suicide, Pier della Vigna, is in circle seven, ring two, because his self-destruction had a different dimension. Pier was a notary for the Holy Roman emperor Frederick II, and he was accused of betraying the emperor. Anthony K. Cassel maintains that Dante knew the historical Pier was corrupt. Recent scholarship shows that the real Pier enriched himself because he had control over the Emperor's legal and financial transactions. He took advantage of his office to expropriate land for himself and to use his power to gain wealth at the expense of the poor and the less fortunate.[18] After he is sentenced to death, Pier decides of his own volition to kill himself. In this case, Pier's suicide is not an act based on physical concupiscence, nor a sudden act of irrational passion. Rather it is a deliberate act to rebuke Frederick II and as such a premeditated and sinful act of taking his own life. Cassell makes the case that Pier can be compared with Judas Iscariot who was unfaithful to Christ and ultimately committed suicide. Of Judas, it is said that his greatest sin was not covetousness for the money he took from betraying Jesus but the taking of his own life. Judas believed that his betrayal of Christ could never be forgiven. But he should have known that just as Christ forgave those who crucified him, he would have forgiven Judas as well since Christ's forgiveness is forever and absolute. In circle seven, ring three, are those who committed violence against God. These include the blasphemers, sodomites, and usurers. Here Dante encounters Capaneus, who with other kings assaulted Thebes. Zeus killed Capaneus by casting down a thunderbolt while he was scaling the wall of Thebes. In the *Inferno*, Dante has Capaneus lying on the ground saying that even if Zeus hurled lighting at him, Zeus would have no joy in his revenge. Capaneus's outright defiance of God serves as a symbol for those who contumaciously disobey and deny God's authority.

Circle eight is in a pit named Malebolge consisting of ten ditches. Each ditch is reserved for various kinds of fraud. It consists of those who are Seducers, Diviners, and Counterfeiters. The distinction between circle seven and circle eight is that where circle seven consists of those who act wrongly in a willful way, circle eight is for those who sin not only willfully, but also with calculation, thus abusing their rational faculties. These are

---

18. Cassell, *Dante's Fearful Art of Justice*, 38–42. Cassell assembles research from several scholars to make his claim that Pier was guilty of embezzlement, bribery, and other abuses of power to enrich himself.

not irrational characters but rather those who are studiously detached in their commitment to unethical behavior. One of the figures encountered in circle eight, ditch eight, is Ulysses. Dante-poet condemns Ulysses for many counts of fraud and cunning. The most famous example is Ulysses's plan for building the Trojan horse. He deceived the Trojans into believing that the horse was a gift of the Greeks when, in fact, it was a way to get inside the city and attack it. Additionally, Ulysses neglected his family as he went on countless adventures and convinced his crew to do the same. Ulysses's great sin is to be in pursuit of other men's esteem and honor by cunning and dissembling. Ulysses's constant movement in the chase of mundane and worldly matters contrasts with Dante-poet and pilgrim's movement towards higher spiritual realms. Throughout the afterlife, Dante's travel is in service to the lessening of his ego by the honest witnessing of what he finds in his journey. His discovery is not only to help himself but also to help others.

The last circle of hell, circle nine, is the circle for the treacherous. It is divided into four rings. Its most famous inhabitant is Satan. Dante depicts Satan as frozen in ice up to his chest. His wings beat incessantly and create even more frigid wind. In Satan's mouth are three sinners: Judas Iscariot, along with Brutus and Cassius who assassinated Julius Caesar. These characters are guilty of treachery as well as creating religious and social disorder through their acts of perfidy. Dante's gift is the systemization of unethical acts, through a comprehensive hierarchy of evil. This cosmic hierarchy is what Dante inherited as part of his worldview when he wrote the *Divine Comedy*. Opposed to hierarchy are Deleuze and Guattari's views on immanence.

2.2.3 Deleuze and Guattari on Immanence

Deleuze and Guattari insist that the idea of immanence should not be influenced by Neoplatonism. Immanence cannot be thought of as an *immanence to* something. They argue that when immanence is associated to something, "the concept becomes a transcendent universal."[19] By that, they mean that immanence comes to be associated with something to which it is subordinate. If immanence becomes secondary to something else, i.e., to something transcendent, then one creates a hierarchy. To further explain it, Deleuze and Guattari warn about false notions of hierarchy. They say,

19. Deleuze and Guattari, *What Is Philosophy?*, 45.

> There is a hierarchy which measures beings according to their limits, and according to their degree of proximity or distance from a principle. But there is also a hierarchy which considers things and beings from the point of view of power: it is not a question of considering absolute degrees of power, but only of knowing whether a being eventually "leaps over" or transcends its limit in going to the limit of what it can do, whatever its degree.[20]

Deleuze is arguing that deviance or adherence to a transcendental hierarchy is not the correct way of looking at good and bad. Rather, one needs to see what a person can do immanently. Can they transcend their limit? They also warn that Christian philosophy always insists that immanence can be tolerated when it does not "compromise the transcendence of a God to which immanence must be attributed only secondarily."[21] Deleuze calls instead for a univocity of being. In this state, "equal being is immediately present in everything, without mediation or intermediary.... All things are in absolute proximity, whether they are large or small, inferior or superior, none of them participates more or less in being."[22] In other words, immanence levels the plane of being.[23] They insist that "immanence is immanent only to itself and consequently captures everything, absorbs All-One, and leaves nothing remaining to which it could be immanent."[24] Deleuze repeats his description of immanence in *Pure Immanence: Essays on a Life*. He states that immanence is "not immanence to life, but the immanent that is in nothing is itself a life."[25] Deleuze and Guattari's concept of immanence changes the idea of existence and also affects ethics.

2.3 SOCIAL

2.3.1 Ethics

One idea for the rationale of hell is the belief in the need for justice. All civilizations possess an ethical code alongside a means for enforcing it. A

---

20. Deleuze, *Difference and Repetition*, 37.
21. Deleuze and Guattari, *What Is Philosophy?*, 45.
22. Deleuze, *Difference and Repetition*, 37.
23. Of Deleuze's theory of immanence, Agamben talks about the "radical impossibility of establishing hierarchies and separations" (Agamben, "Absolute Immanence," 163).
24. Deleuze and Guattari, *What Is Philosophy?*, 45.
25. Deleuze, *Pure Immanence*, 27.

societal compact generally means that if one disobeys the laws of society, then one deserves punishment. The oppressed could comfort themselves with the idea that those who did not get adequately punished on earth would get punished in hell. In the second century, Tertullian expresses this idea in his diatribe against the pagans who held large circuses and spectacles in the public arena:

> You are fond of spectacles, expect the greatest of all spectacles, the last and eternal judgment of the universe. How shall I admire, how laugh, how rejoice, how exult, when I behold so many proud monarchs, and fancied gods, groaning in the lowest abyss of darkness; so many magistrates, who persecuted the name of the Lord, liquefying in fiercer fires than they ever kindled against the Christians; so many sage philosophers blushing in red-hot flames, with their deluded scholars.[26]

Tertullian expresses a Christian form of *Schadenfreude* where he takes a delight in the idea of seeing those pagans who persecuted Christians suffer in hell. Tertullian believes that the games are blasphemous for several reasons. They honor pagan gods, they engage in lewd and obscene behavior, and they force the poor and the marginalized to fight, sometimes to the death, in gladiator games. Those pagans, especially the powerful organizers of the games, will ultimately have their comeuppance when they are consigned to everlasting torment. In the *Inferno*, Dante develops this idea of punishment as justice more fully than his many predecessors.

When Dante traverses down through hell, he travels further and further away from a transcendent good. Dante's passage in hell is a descending hierarchy with each new ring resulting in a step towards greater depravity. For Dante, every depravity originates from an unfulfilled disordered desire that ranges from immodest to abominable. The gravity of the unethical behavior that an inhabitant of hell committed depends on how much their will and the rational mind were involved. A willful and conscious act of unethical behavior that breaks the transcendent code results in a section of hell that is further away from God. Dante's ethics are based on a set of principles that were developed to account for different degrees of unethical behavior. But suppose the conception of a transcendent moral hierarchy is incorrect. Suppose there is no transcendent hierarchy. If we take that away, what can we say about ethics?

---

26. Tertullian, *De Spectaculis* 30, quoted in Gibbon, *History of the Decline and Fall*, 2:256.

For Deleuze and Guattari, an ethical code that transcends the human plane does not exist. Claire Colebrook says of Deleuze's ethics that if we begin our thinking of ethics from a transcendent code, then ethics are conceived "on the basis of some pregiven unity. The machine by contrast allows for an active ethics, for we do not presuppose an intent, identity or end."[27] In *The Logic of Sense*, Deleuze relates ethics to the event. By this Deleuze means that one cannot presume to know beforehand what is just or unjust. Rather, that question can only be resolved in the situatedness of an event.[28] In *Spinoza: Practical Philosophy*, Deleuze makes a distinction between Good and Evil and good and bad. For Deleuze, there is no such thing as Good and Evil. Instead, good is when something agrees with our nature and bad is when something does not. A bad person lives impotently or foolishly. A good person is one who tries to join with that which increases one's power.[29] A bad person forms relations with that which diminishes one's potency.[30] Deleuze makes a distinction also between Ethics and Morality, stating, "Morality is the judgment of God, the system of judgment. But Ethics overthrows the system of judgment."[31] Therefore, Morality is a judgment that exists outside of life. Morality is a transcendental judgment. Ethics is embodied and immanent rather than transcendent and handed down by God. Of course, this is in direct contrast to how Dante would conceive of ethics. Within the social realm, Dante and Deleuze and Guattari also deal with governance. Governance is the mechanism by which ethics are monitored and enforced. Governance also dictates the organization of the social realm.

2.3.2 Governance

Governance is a topic worth discussing because governance is how ethics are enforced within a socius. Additionally, in the Deleuze and Guattari framework, governance is part of the machinic functions that constitute

---

27. Colebrook, *Gilles Deleuze*, 55.

28. Deleuze, *Logic of Sense*, 149. Of ethics, Deleuze states, "What is really immoral is the use of moral notions like just or unjust, merit or fault."

29. Smith, "Deleuze and the Question of Desire," 125. Smith notes that for Deleuze the question is whether a particular way of existing can deploy one's capacity and go to increase the capacity of what it can do.

30. Deleuze, *Spinoza*, 22–23.

31. Deleuze, *Spinoza*, 23.

how certain forces of power exert themselves within a population. Governance in this sense is not only the secular form of government. In Dante's medieval society, governance also includes personages within the church. In northern Italy during the time of Dante, five competing forces are operating. The first is the papacy that is trying to exert its role in the secular realm. The next is the emperor whom Dante wanted in power. The third is the Italian monarchies of Sicily and Naples seeking to extend their influence north. The next are French incursions in conjunction with the papacy. And the last is the emerging mercantile class that is attempting to wrest control from the more ancient regimes. Dante's reversion to the emperor as the desired ruler and his wish to reestablish the idea of empire is a corrective to what he sees as a church that has not focused on its spiritual mission and has corrupted its power to gain control in the secular realm. The emperor is a reversion to an original power that existed before the church and before the monarchy. It is Dante's dream of a new Roman Empire which aligns with his spiritual vision. Dante's political theory is correlative to his unifying vision in *The Divine Comedy*. The emperor, not the pope, is God's partner on earth who can unite all people into a single and unitive body. Dante's conception of how a ruler forms a socius is different from Deleuze and Guattari's ideas.

Prior to the capitalistic state, which is at the very early beginning of where one finds Dante, Deleuze and Guattari talk about labor being encapsulated within a machinic feudal assembly where labor was encumbered to the manor. Laborers swore their fealty to the manor lord in exchange for land usage and the production of agricultural commodities. In Deleuze and Guattari's terms, the feudal state is considered a despotic state. It disallows labor to build up its own personal labor surplus.[32] Instead, a system is assembled whereby any surplus value is owed to the despotic manor lord. The manor lord overcodes the desiring flows of production. They do that through tax and estate law, landed ownership, and association with the hierarchical church that reinforces both the political and religious notions of lordship and obedience. Much of the tie between manor lords and church

---

32. Deleuze and Guattari, *Anti-Oedipus*, 196–97. Deleuze and Guattari describe the early State acting in a way of fixing residence and forming a pseudo-territory. The earth from a primitive society gets made into an ownership held by the most powerful officials of the state. The state guarantees the property to the powerful. In a despotic regime, the powerful try to prevent decoded flows that would allow for the freer circulation of money. Taxes are levied by the feudal lord on the agrarian populace. Surplus labor value gets sucked up by the feudal lord.

hierarchy was a mutual protection scheme. Manor lords agreed to protect the spiritual authority of the church and not to appropriate church land and in exchange, the church agreed to recognize the legal and property rights of the manor lord. Both the manor lord and the church engage in overcoding. In *The Deleuze and Guattari Dictionary*, one definition provided for overcoding is "where the filiations and allegiances are predicated upon their direct affiliation to the sovereign."[33] In the feudal case, the sovereigns are the heads of the church and the manor lords. Without regard to the people who were subject to them, each sovereign determined their own successor. Unlike in an ideal democratic state where the people determine to whom they will pledge their allegiance, in despotic states, people are subjected to the overcoding of those in power. Those who hold power fear that there will be a decoding of desiring production and the recoding of it into new assemblages. What happens in early capitalistic states is that new mechanic assemblages are formed which deterritorialize labor and decode productive desire. By deterritorializing labor, Deleuze and Guattari refer to the movement of labor away from feudal lands and into urban areas where laborers become "free" to sell their labor to capitalistic enterprises. Capitalism is dependent upon decoded money where money "has become capital and is capable of buying it."[34]

Deleuze and Guattari mean that through decoded capital, money can produce money, via lines of credit and the creation of modern banking institutions. The modern state is born from feudalism. What one finds in the early northern Italian city-states at the time of Dante is the beginning of the formation of an early modern state. Deleuze and Guattari write that the new conception of state "no longer of itself forms a ruling class or classes; it is itself formed by these classes, which have become independent and delegate it to serve their power and their contradictions, their struggles and their compromises with the dominated classes."[35] In the new city-states of northern Italy, a different sense of space gets created. Henri Lefebvre, French philosopher and state theorist, describes the city-state as a place

33. Young et al., *Deleuze and Guattari Dictionary*, 67.

34. Deleuze and Guattari, *Anti-Oedipus*, 225. Deleuze and Guattari note that this phenomenon happens initially in Europe because of the conditions that were available. Unlike Asia which held tightly onto its despotic system that held up deterritorialization and blocked the flow of capital, European states allowed for trade to transpire throughout Europe. Asian states heavily regulated their markets keeping them from freely engaging with the rest of the world.

35. Deleuze and Guattari, *Anti-Oedipus*, 221.

where there is a fixed hub surrounded by peripheral areas. The unboundedness of the previous primitive territorial order transforms and the new space "appears to come under the thrall of a divine order. . . . As image of the universe (*imago mundi*), urban space is reflected in the rural space that it possesses and indeed in a sense *contains*."[36] The idea of space changes from real or absolute space to symbolic space. Space describes not just the terrestrial realm but also the cosmological realm. Jeremy Larkins mentions that from the twelfth century on, the socius decrypts "the subterranean spaces of death. . . . The darkness and descent of tombs and crypts give way to the illumination and elevation of the monumental Gothic cathedrals."[37] In a literary manner, Dante produced in the *Divine Comedy* a Gothic cathedral of the mind. His decryption includes excavating hell and showing it in detail, while also elevating the mind to the symbolic territories of Purgatory and Heaven. Dante is decrypting hell to expose the corruption found in his northern Italian region. The *Comedy* fits Lefevre's theory of how a symbolic space comes under the rubric of a divine order. These spaces become identified with the conditions of the human soul. In lighting up these spaces, Dante is showing how those who have the responsibility for governance have failed in their ethical duties. Dante, the author, assumes the role of the moral leader. He determines who is moral and who is not. For those who failed in their duties, he assigns just punishment.

2.3.3 Social machines, Regime of Signs, and Faciality

For Deleuze and Guattari, what drives the socius are social machines rather than individuals. The background of Deleuze and Guattari's ideas on social machines is a departure from the idea of the transcendental subject. Surin explains that social machines have "humans for their parts and are essential to the generation of cultural forms."[38] Deleuze and Guattari describe three kinds of social machines. They refer to the first social machine as "the savage social machine" because it codes its flows on the physical body.[39] We see that kind of coding enacted in Dante's *Inferno* region where the inhabitants

---

36. Lefebvre, *Production of Space*, 235.
37. Larkins, *From Hierarchy to Anarchy*, 51.
38. Surin, "Socius," 259.
39. Deleuze and Guattari, *Anti-Oedipus*, 188. Deleuze and Guattari use the example of how in primitive societies inscriptions through cutting are made on the body. In the case of a woman a calabash symbol is placed on her body to signify a voice of alliance.

suffer grave indignities to their cosmic bodies. The second of Deleuze and Guattari's social machines is the "transcendent imperial machine," which is manifested in the feudal era. The manor lord and church deterritorialize the previous regime's savagery on the body only to overcode it through feudal serfdom and Christian morality, thus binding the serf to dual despots. Finally, what escapes from notice during Dante's time, but can be seen with historical hindsight within the Florentine socius, is the transition towards the capitalist social machine.

Although Dante lives through the beginning of the capitalist social machine, he does not comprehend its implications because the transition is too new. The third social machine (a.k.a. the modern immanent machine) is the vantage point from where Deleuze and Guattari develop their own implicit ethical system. Capital drives the modern immanent machine. Capital decodes the overcoded flows of the feudal system and deterritorializes the held feudal lands into private property. What also gets decoded is capital itself. One of the miracles of the capitalist social machine is that capital begets more capital. As capital expands within the citizenry, the social hierarchy begins to flatten. As more of the community has money, and along with it power, the governmental structures level and become more democratic. Still, the ancient regime struggles to hold absolute power. Deleuze and Guattari describe the condition which forms the threshold of capitalism:

> Capitalism forms when the flow of unqualified [decoded] wealth encounters the flow of unqualified [deterritorialized] labor and conjugates with it. This is what the preceding conjugations which were still topical or qualitative, had always inhibited (the two principal inhibitors were the feudal organization of the countryside and the corporative organization of the towns). This amounts to saying that capitalism forms with *a general axiomatic of decoded flows*.[40]

"Unqualified wealth" in the Florentine city-state can be thought of as the money coming from the new merchant class. "Unqualified labor" can be thought of as the movement of laborers from feudal manors to cities where they are "free" to sell their labor.

When Deleuze and Guattari note that capitalism forms with a general axiomatic of decoded flows, they refer to how ecumenical capitalism is. Capital has the power to move into almost any society and create its own social organization. Because it can become a global axiomatic, they believe

---

40. Deleuze and Guattari, *Thousand Plateaus*, 453.

that it is a social machine that could practically do without the state. In fact, with a capitalistic model, states are "not at all transcendent paradigms of an overcoding but immanent models of realization for an axiomatic of decoded flows."[41] International corporations can exist across many states without barriers to entry and bring flows of new capital into each state. States do not transcend capital but serve as hosts for the flow of capital. This accounts for a difference between the first two social machines and capitalism. The despotic and the transcendent imperial machines delivered a socius that constituted what Deleuze and Guattari call a "transcendence of a formal Unity."[42] Those older social machines created a hierarchy where the constituent parts fit together as exemplified by Dante's vision of a monarchy and his hierarchical creation of coded realms of hell. In a capitalistic social machine, there is an immanence in the axiomatic of capital. Deleuze and Guattari claim that they have found the most basic law of capitalism, which is that "it continually sets and then repels its own limits, but in so doing gives rise to numerous flows in all directions that escape its axiomatic."[43] In a different way, Deleuze and Guattari are saying what Austrian economist Joseph Schumpeter described as capitalism's propensity for "creative destruction." In Schumpeter's description, capitalism cannot be stationary. It unceasingly destroys old structures and replaces them with new structures that are more fluid, or to use a contemporary term, it replaces them with structures having less friction. In the words of Deleuze and Guattari, capitalism has the effect of smoothing out striated space. Capital flows flatten structures and weaken authority. Previously regimented spaces become more fluid. The important character of capitalism, then, is not the types of capital (i.e., fixed or variable capital costs) but rather "the distinction between *striated capital* and *smooth capital*, and the way in which the former gives rise to the latter through complexes that cut across territories and States, and even the different types of States."[44] Striated capital is capital that is centralized and belongs to a particular regime. An example of striated capital is capital belonging to a single enterprise that funds its own growth by investing profits back into its own business. In this case, capital is bound to a single enterprise. An example of smooth capital would be venture capital used to fund a start-up. It is money put together from a

---

41. Deleuze and Guattari, *Thousand Plateaus*, 455.
42. Deleuze and Guattari, *Thousand Plateaus*, 458.
43. Deleuze and Guattari, *Thousand Plateaus*, 472.
44. Deleuze and Guattari, *Thousand Plateaus*, 492.

variety of sources to fund an enterprise external to any of the originating funding sources. Smooth capital can come from multiple companies that exist in various governmental states. Striated capital comes from a hierarchy. Smooth capital comes from a horizontal multiplicity. The beginnings of the capitalist social machine began in the early Italian city-states.

2.3.4 Deterritorialization

If, according to Deleuze and Guattari, life is machinic and carried out on the immanent plane, then the space of the immanent plane is covered by connective lines that sustain the machine. Since Deleuze and Guattari are speaking of dynamic machines, the connections are usually not permanent. There is no connective network that does not allow the possibility of other more opportune connections. Deterritorialization represents a break or breaks in the existing machinic connections. As an example, during the time of Dante, the northern Italian city-states experienced the beginning of an economic transformation that was co-creative of changes in religious and secular authority. The papacy was attempting to establish more secular power for itself. The monarchies were competing with the emperor for power. And the cities were attempting a form of republicanism but they were still often under the sway of the feudal families of wealth. The northern Italian states were undergoing the seminal beginnings of capitalism. And capitalism accelerates the rate of deterritorialization. If the old regime was attempting to reterritorialize the Italian state, the new dynamics were moving towards deterritorializing. Deleuze and Guattari remark that where the state acts to reterritorialize, i.e., to keep the old regime in power, "capitalism, on the other hand, is not at all territorial, even in its beginnings: its power of deterritorialization consists in taking as its object, not the earth but 'materialized labor' the commodity."[45] Capitalism, unlike early forms of government, does not need to own land. It needs the commodities produced from the land, the resources under the land, or the labor hours of those who work the land. Thus capitalism is not territorial; it is connective and does not require a hierarchical form of governance. The irony of Dante's situation is that although he sought a hierarchical political form of governance, i.e., an emperor who would produce a unified vision of the governmental polis, he instead got exiled from his insular place as a governmental official in Florence. Dante, himself, became deterritorialized. He became a nomad of Italy.

45. Deleuze and Guattari, *Thousand Plateaus*, 455.

2.4 SELF

2.4.1 Nomadism/Rhizomes

Instead of finding himself within a unified governed locale, Dante became an outsider. In the *Divine Comedy*, Dante, the writer, invents a unified system that he wanted in the political realm. He creates a hierarchical and heavily coded realm in the *Inferno* afterlife. Yet in another irony, while the inhabitants of Dante's afterlife are assigned their places in a very circumscribed manner, Dante the pilgrim in the story, as well as the author in his own life, wanders through his literary creation and various towns in his exiled life like a body without organs. As a character, Dante has relatively free movement throughout the story. He is not subject to the hierarchy of the afterlife space. Unlike the characters in hell who are permanently fixed in place because of their ethical breaches, Dante the character can travel freely from one place to another. As Dante, the historical person, became a subject heavily inscribed in the overcoding of various Italian warring factions, the rigidification that he faced conspired to create what Deleuze and Guattari describe as a line of flight. The line of flight allows for Dante, the person, to become "deterritorialized," i.e., to become a nomad and to depart from Florence seeking freedom in other places in northern Italy. As a character in the afterlife, Dante the pilgrim has a similar line of flight that takes him down through hell but later ejects him up through Purgatory and ultimately to Heaven. Dante the character, as well as Dante the person, are imbued with a nomadic nature. As a character, he is not one of the inhabitants of the afterlife; rather he is a nomad traveling through the afterlife.

What Dante was looking to establish was a political vision that was arborescent. This is a hierarchical vision with a structure like a tree. Roots sink down into the ground and a tree rises towards the heaven stretching its beautiful canopy upwards. The emperor rules from above and his citizenry stretches down in a graded hierarchical fashion as envisioned in a Dionysian cosmology. Yet Florence during the time of Dante had no centralized authority. It was not hierarchical; rather, it was rhizomatic. Rhizomes are horizontal in nature. Deleuze and Guattari describe a rhizomatic structure as one that is made of lines stretching out and making connections and then breaking them.[46] During the time of Dante, Florence was in an endless

---

46. In his article demonstrating the influence of Gregory Bateson on Deleuze and Guattari's concept of rhizome, Shaw offers a pertinent description of rhizome that fits for Deleuze and Guattari: "Rhizomes are thus the ever braiding, sinuous paths which avoid

state of warring factions that emerged from existing structures and created connections of the type that Deleuze and Guattari describe as "detachable, connectable, reversible, modifiable and has multiple entryways and exits and its own lines of flight."[47] The White Guelfs became detached from the Black Guelfs and they retreated from the city after being rulers of the government. Dante's exile was a line of flight out of Florence. His exile was the impetus for his *Divine Comedy*. Claire Colebrook describes a line of flight as "where mutations and differences produce not just the progression of history but disruptions, breaks, new beginnings and 'monstrous births.'"[48] These monstrous births have the characteristics of an event where something new is created. Dante's *Divine Comedy* is one of those events. And within the *Divine Comedy* are stories about individuals.

2.4.2 The Individual

Deleuze does not see the individual as an indivisible identity. Oliver Davies states that Deleuze is "able to offer a critique of the Western metaphysical tradition as a system of thinking, predicated always upon operations of identity, and underpinned by a unified theory of the self."[49] For Deleuze, identity never ceases to divide and change its nature.[50] Identity then is a ceaseless expression of differentiation and repetition. Deleuze proposes a changeable and non-subject-oriented ontology as opposed to Dante's idea of subjectivity as a fixed identity having transcendent values.[51] Deleuze and

---

the peaks and troughs of climax or conflict, instead constantly vibrating and negotiating in the middle through continued change" (Shaw, "Bringing Deleuze and Guattari Down to Earth," 158).

47. Deleuze and Guattari, *Thousand Plateaus*, 48.
48. Colebrook, *Gilles Deleuze*, 57.
49. Davies, "Thinking Difference," 76.

50. In a literary example that illustrates Deleuze and Guattari's notion of the self, one can examine how Samuel Beckett expresses it in his story *Molloy*: "The fact was there were three, no, four Molloys. He that inhabited me, my caricature of same, Gaber's and the man of flesh and blood somewhere awaiting me. To these I would add Youdi's were it not for Gaber's corpse fidelity to the letter of his message.... I will therefore add a fifth Molloy, that of Youdi.... There were others too, of course. But let us leave it at that, if you don't mind, the party is big enough" (Beckett, *Molloy*, 155).

51. Deleuze states that all series (e.g., hierarchies) coexist; one is not an originary, as in a divine hierarchy, and one is not a copy, as in a human hierarchy. You cannot privilege one over another. "It is a case in which everything is equal but 'everything is equal' is said of the difference." He believes that the identity of the One is the "greatest and longest

Guattari object to the idea of a fixed being and instead argue in favor of the idea of a being-becoming. For them, every person is a dynamic process. Existence is the infinite set of dynamic processes.

Existence is not an experience of a being. Instead, existence is a multiplicity; it flows from uncountable connections, events, and responses. Colebrook describes the situation, saying, "It is not that there are persons or beings who contemplate the world; [rather] there are contemplations that are passive and impersonal. These contemplations create distinct human bodies and organisms."[52] Deleuze and Guattari upturn the Western tradition that sees the subject or being as the ground of experience. They critique the philosophy of Kant where immanence is immanent to a subject. Instead, they posit that experience is the ground of experience. Deleuze and Guattari call their philosophy "transcendental empiricism." It is critical to distinguish the term "transcendent" from the term "transcendental." When philosophy speaks of the transcendent, immanence usually becomes subject to that which is transcendent. However, what Deleuze and Guattari mean by transcendental empiricism is a field without a subject, a world of experiential flows, wherein human subjects are developed. Subjects, according to Colebrook, "can produce fictions, ideas or assemblages that *seem* to be transcendent, but which are really produced from the very flow of life."[53] How Deleuze and Guattari explain it is that empiricism becomes transcendental when we apprehend "the very being of the sensible."[54] Apprehension of the sensible, according to Deleuze and Guattari, is not a representation of the sensible. An apprehension of the sensible always involves difference in which movement is produced. In Deleuze and Guattari's philosophy, representation is a stagnant form of signification. It abstracts from life and then pretends to simulate life. Instead, Deleuze and Guattari prefer to use the term "apprehension," which signifies production. Production is the way desire becomes enacted in the flows of life, in the differences of affects. Given how Deleuze and Guattari differ from Dante concerning immanence and subjectivity, how can we compare ethics? Deleuze and Guattari's immanentism and subjectivity provide for a different type of ethics. One aspect of ethics that is crucial to Dante is how an individual handles desire.

---

error." Deleuze posits that identity is retrojected onto the series and is a simulacrum. Identity, therefore, is an illusion. See Deleuze, *Difference and Repetition*, 125–26.

52. Colebrook, *Gilles Deleuze*, 87.
53. Colebrook, *Gilles Deleuze*, 89.
54. Deleuze, *Difference and Repetition*, 57.

2.4.3 Desire

One way to examine desire is from a point of view with which Dante would agree. Perhaps Augustine best expresses it when he says in his *Confessions* that even though individuals are only a small part of God's creation, humans have a desire to praise God. Augustine addresses God when he says of humans, "Thou hast prompted him, that he should delight to praise thee, for thou hast made us for thyself and restless is our heart until it comes to rest in thee."[55] Augustine's talk of the heart's restlessness represents what Dante would understand as unfulfilled desire. For Augustine and Dante, desire represents a lack, and sometimes that lack can lead to disorder. Disordered desire is responsible for many of the sins committed by the inhabitants of hell. The desire for money, sex, and power can drive people to attempt to fill the lack. Desire is a sensation that something is missing in this world. Desire causes an irritation that urges us to struggle for its fulfillment. Yet, Augustine and Dante understood that desire could only be fulfilled by a divine power whose love is infinite. They also believed that divine power existed in a plane that was superior to human beings. And in the *Comedy*, Dante's entire passage from hell to heaven is about how he comes to understand what the true nature of desire is and what will satisfy that desire.

Deleuze and Guattari will challenge Dante's notion of desire. Rather than thinking desire is good or bad, Deleuze and Guattari ask if desire works, is it productive or not? Where Dante would describe desire as a lack, Deleuze and Guattari define it as productive life. Desire is not negative; it is positive. Deleuze and Guattari reverse the idea of desire as a lack of something. Likewise, they will not make the distinction that Dante does between caritas and cupiditas.[56] Dante will value caritas as a desire that seeks friendship and amity as opposed to a desire that is acquisitive. Deleuze will not make that distinction when it comes to desire. Claire Colebrook explains Deleuze's notion of desire:

> Desire begins from connection; life strives to preserve and enhance itself and does so by connecting to other desires. These connections and productions eventually form social wholes; when bodies connect with other bodies to enhance their power they

---

55. Augustine, *Confessions*, 1.1.

56. Agamben states that Deleuze's idea of desire is heavily influenced by Spinoza's theory of striving or conatus. Thus, desire, "to desire to persevere in one's own Being is to desire one's own desire, to constitute oneself as desiring" (Agamben, "Absolute Immanence," 166).

eventually form communities or societies. Power, is, therefore, not the repression of desire but the expansion of desire.[57]

Deleuze and Guattari make foundational to their philosophy the idea that desire is productive. Additionally, implicit in the idea that desire is productive is the notion of desire as a connective force that unites things. Desire, however, is not tied to a human subject. A subject does not activate desire because of a perceived lack. Rather desire can be construed as a desiring machine, i.e., as a connective phenomenon. The example that Deleuze and Guattari use is a mother's breast that produces milk and a baby's mouth that attaches itself to it. The machine is productive in that it connects the mouth and the breast. This is different than how Dante and Augustine describe the idea of desire versus productivity using the same concept of mother's milk. Dante, in *De Vulgari Eloquentia*, states that language developed in a prelapsarian state where a person was created by God rather than an earthly mother. Dante expresses that idea using the trope of mother's milk: "We should now begin the pursuit of that language which we believe was used by the man who had neither mother nor mother's milk."[58] Dante is positing the idea that an original language existed in an Edenic-like state not burdened by desire. Augustine, likewise, uses the idea of mother's milk as a desire that represents a lack. In *Confessions*, Augustine states, "For what am I to myself without thee but a guide to my own downfall? Or what am I, even at the best, but one suckled on thy milk and feeding on thee, O Food that never perishes"?[59] Therefore, Augustine poses the idea of desire as something that is a dire lack and which ultimately can only be fulfilled by God. But Deleuze and Guattari contest the idea of desire as lack as they also contest the notion of subjectivity as a fixed entity.

If desire is a productive machine, then a machine requires no subjectivity. Rather, as Colebrook states, "A machine is nothing more than the connections and productions that it makes."[60] If there is no fixed identity that desires and if all desire is machinic, then how does one speak of ethics? If disordered desire produces violations against a transcendent and universal code of conduct, then what can we make of a Deleuze and Guattari ethical system? We will see how that comes about when we examine two episodes from the *Inferno* in section 2.5 below.

57. Colebrook, *Gilles Deleuze*, 91.
58. Dante Alighieri, "De Vulgari Eloquentia" 1.6.21.
59. Augustine, *Confessions* 4.1.83.
60. Colebrook, *Gilles Deleuze*, 55.

2.4.4 Body Without Organs

The term body without organs is something that Deleuze and Guattari borrow from a play by surrealist French playwright Antonin Artaud entitled *To Have Done with the Judgment of God*. In the short radio play, Artaud laments that a person is poorly made; that they are sick and deprived of their freedom. To produce a new person, one must be stripped bare. The pertinent lines Artaud utters are:

> But there is nothing more useless than an organ
> When you will have made him a body without organs,
> Then you will have delivered him from all his automatic reaction
> And restored him to his true freedom.[61]

Artaud's words come in the context of a need for a secular ascesis where one deprives oneself of the materialist secular culture to free oneself from its capture. Deleuze and Guattari pick up the term to mean several things. First, the idea has some resonance with Deleuze and Guattari's notion of subjectivity. For them, Artaud's words about having a body without organs mean to free oneself from an imperialist subjectivity that forms a separation between the me here and the world out there. In the chapter entitled "How Do You Make Yourself a Body Without Organs" from the book *A Thousand Plateaus*, Deleuze and Guattari ask how can we unhook ourselves from what keeps us tied to a dominant reality? They answer that question by stating that the process is "tearing the consciousness away from the subject in order to make it a means of exploration"[62] By that they mean to question our contemporary ideas of subjectivity and to make it more open. Another meaning of a body without organs resounds beyond the human body and is used by Deleuze and Guattari to free oneself from social structures that have become too rigid. Third, it is often used to refer to unformed matter in its pristine state. The state is prior to matter being formed into assemblages of various structures—from the lowest geological level of material particles to the macro level of a modern political state. It is what results after a complete destratification where rigid structures are dismantled and brought back to a simpler form.[63] One of the ways that rigid

---

61. Artaud, "To Have Done With the Judgement of God."

62. Deleuze and Guattari, *Thousand Plateaus*, 160.

63. Schizoanalysis is a process which frees the organism and helps it escape to become a body without organs. According to Deleuze and Guattari, it serves to "explode

structures can become dismantled is by resisting a dominant subjectivity and in the words of Deleuze and Guattari, to become woman or minoritarian. This is particularly true in the realm of literature.

2.4.5 Becoming Woman/Minoritarian

Deleuze and Guattari opt for a literature that deemphasizes the fixed faciality of the white European male and instead embraces the idea of a literature of becoming. The becomings that are particularly important in the analysis of Dante are becoming woman and becoming minoritarian. Becoming woman is a subversion of the master literature that keeps the rigidity of the despotic state in power. Deleuze and Guattari maintain that a girl's voice is stolen from her when she is a child "in order to impose a history or prehistory, upon her."[64] In *A Thousand Plateaus*, Deleuze and Guattari point to Virginia Woolf as an example of an author who embodies becoming woman. Woolf's refusal to be known primarily as a "woman writer" makes their point. According to Deleuze and Guattari, Woolf refused the binaries that would have been imposed on her as the counterpart to man. The "becoming" part of becoming woman implies that there are many different parts of each binary that come into play for all people. As Deleuze and Guattari explain it, "Knowing how to love does not mean remaining a man or a woman, it means extracting from one's sex the particles, the speeds and slownesses, the flows, the n sexes that constitute the girl of *that* sexuality."[65] Their point is that becoming woman is not simply an opposition to man, and certainly not a binary. The idea is to allow many parts of a person to be revealed in one's writing, i.e., male, female, and everything in between and beyond. As we will see later, in the *Divine Comedy*, Dante will utilize the becoming woman idea to undermine Francesca's defense of her adulterous

---

what must explode, make fall what must fall, make escape what must escape, at each point ensuring the conversion of schizophrenia as a process into an effectively revolutionary force" (Deleuze and Guattari, *Anti-Oedipus*, 341). Eugene W. Holland states that the "body-without-organs provides the material basis for the molecular displacement and subversion of identity effected capitalist y and decoding" (Holland, *Deleuze and Guattari's Anti-Oedipus*, 121).

64. Deleuze and Guattari, *Thousand Plateaus*, 276. Deleuze and Guattari maintain that a boy's voice is stolen from him as well, but the girl goes first to act as an example and to point to the girl as an object of desire. This imposes a binary identity of man/woman on to both of them.

65. Deleuze and Guattari, *Thousand Plateaus*, 277.

act. At the same time, by putting Francesca's adultery as one of the least serious offenses within the realm of the *Inferno*, he is in sympathy with her against the male-female binary that forced her into an arranged political marriage. Yet becoming woman is not the only becoming that Deleuze and Guattari promote. Also included is the idea of becoming minoritarian.

Becoming minoritarian is to escape the dominant subjectivity of a culture. In the essay "What Is a Minor Literature," Deleuze and Guattari state that a minoritarian literature by its very nature is involved with the political. Because a minor literature exists in the shadows of a master narrative, by its very nature it appeals to a constituency that has a felt communal nature. They add, "If the writer lives on the margin, is set apart from his fragile community, this situation makes him all the more able to express another, potential community, to force the means for another consciousness and another sensibility."[66] Certainly, Dante was a writer who lived on the margin and his writings challenged those who shaped the master narratives, i.e., those in power in Italy both secular and religious. An additional reason that Dante is considered minoritarian, at least in the *Divine Comedy*, is his decision to write in the vernacular. The vernacular allowed Dante to get his work read by those who were not just in the elite tiers of society. To the masses, Dante's *Divine Comedy* becomes revolutionary for its truth-telling function. It allows Dante to expose the hypocrisy of those in power and at the same time to try them in absentia for their dishonesty. Given that we have covered the general ideas of how Dante and Deleuze and Guattari either agree or contrast with each other, it is time to examine two passages from the *Comedy* that express these ideas in detail. The two passages chosen are the passages involving Francesca and Paolo in *Inferno* V and the Simoniac Popes in *Inferno* XIX. The reason I chose these passages is because they represent many of the ideas that would show the differences between Dante and Deleuze and Guattari. Francesca and Paolo spotlight the nature of desire, the social and political machines that operated in Northern Italy regarding power and marriage, and the idea of becoming woman. The episode of the simoniac popes deals with the religious institutions that held power in Northern Italy. Additionally, it highlights a different form of desire in the realm of money. Also included is the ability to view this passage in the light of Deleuze and Guattari's ideas about the regime of signs and faciality.

---

66. Deleuze et al., "What Is a Minor Literature?," 17.

2.5 DELEUZE AND GUATTARI IN CONVERSATION WITH DANTE

2.5.1 Francesca and Paolo

The story told by Dante of Francesca da Polenta of Ravenna and Paolo of Rimini is a good first start in the contrast between Dante's ethics and Deleuze and Guattari's ethics. Francesca da Rimini may be Dante's best-known character, and her history provides insights concerning her place in the *Inferno*. She inhabits the second circle of hell reserved for those whom lust has imprisoned. In this circle, Dante includes such famous historical figures as Cleopatra, Helen of Troy, and Tristan. In real life, Francesca da Rimini was from a noble Guelf faction who politically dominated the city of Ravenna during the thirteenth century. She married Giancotto Malatesta whose family dominated the politics of Rimini. The marriage was a political arrangement to consolidate power between the cities of Ravenna and Rimini and to maintain peace between the two warring cities. One day Giancotto found Francesca and Paolo Malatesta, Giancotto's brother, in an adulterous act and killed them. Boccaccio, who attempted to redeem Francesca and to embellish the story into a medieval romance, commented that she fell in love with Paolo after being tricked into marriage. Supposedly, Giancotto, who was physically deformed, asked his more handsome brother Paolo to impersonate him to win Francesca's affection. Contemporary scholars believe that the story is fictional, and that Boccaccio may have tried to present Francesca in a more favorable light. Dante, however, has the history more accurately than Boccaccio. In the *Inferno*, Francesca tells Dante that God has abandoned her and Paolo. She proclaims that love afflicted her by seizing her with a force that still affects her. Dante initially feels pity for Francesca and asks how desire overcame her and Paolo. She explains that they were reading a story about Lancelot, presumably his love affair with Guinevere, wife of King Arthur, which caused their eyes to meet. In a single instant, desire overcame Paolo who kissed Francesca on the mouth. Francesca blames the book, most probably *Lancelot du Lac*, as the mediator and cause for the flaming of their inordinate desire. As a result of hearing the story recounted by Francesca, at the end of canto five, Paolo weeps and Dante, the pilgrim, swoons. Dante's grief about the two lovers even continues into the first three lines of canto six until he pulls himself together to continue his journey. Dante's sympathetic grief concerning Francesca and Paolo belies the theological fact that Francesca and Paolo are in hell. Despite Dante, the pilgrim's, emotional pain from hearing the story, the idea of justice for adultery is still maintained by Dante, the author. The historical Dante is strict with Francesca, the character, even though he had a personal connection with the historical Francesca. During a part of Dante's exile, he was sheltered in the home of Guido Novello da Palenta who was Francesca's nephew. Dante's objectivity in the matter shows that he is consistent in his ethical and theological beliefs, i.e., that Francesca committed adultery and needed to be consigned to hell. The decision to do this has split various commentators about whether Dante is too severe in his treatment of Francesca.

Robert Hollander comments that Dante scholars can be divided into Francesca moralizers and sympathizers.[67] I maintain that Dante, the writer, implicitly plays both roles. As a moralizer author, he judges Francesca and Paolo's adulterous actions and places them in hell. As a sympathizer pilgrim, he swoons in commiserating grief over their story. It is not difficult to understand why Dante, as a devout Catholic medieval author, sentences Francesca to hell. Both Francesca and Paolo were married when they committed their adulterous act. Dante sees that the desire they had for each other had gone wrong. As Dante, the author, states, in this realm of hell are those "who make reason subject to desire" (*Inf.* V, 39). Dante, the mature writer, understands the problematic of the courtly love romance. As a reader of Augustine's *Confessions*, he understands that our hearts do not find rest in sensual desire. Our hearts only find rest within God's peace. The restlessness of desire exhibited by Francesca in hell is exemplified by the winds that continually buffet her and Paolo. They are in a squall which never rests and it "sweeps spirits in its headlong rush, / tormenting whirls and strikes them" (*Inf.* V, 32–33). Theologically, Francesca's punishment is just. The theological reading, as expressed by Teodolinda Barolini, is that Francesca's "moral responsibility and personal agency are suspended by an all-consuming sentiment, where passion rules untrammeled by reason."[68] In *Purgatorio* XXI, Dante knows that his own desire is sinful when Beatrice reprimands him for chasing other women out of disordered desire: "Indeed, at the very first arrow / of deceitful things, you should have risen up / and followed me who was no longer of them" (*Purg.* XXXI, 35–37). Dante

---

67. Dante Alighieri, *Inferno*, 111–12. Hollander in the notes to *Inferno* V comments that Francesca's culpability is subject to continuing debate between those who are more rigidly moralizing and those who are more inclined to feel sympathy for Francesca.

68. Barolini, "Dante and Francesca Da Rimini," 9.

understands that he has sinned, perhaps not as egregiously as Francesca and Paolo in the act of adultery, but still, his sins are serious enough that Beatrice forces him to confess. It is not exactly clear to whom his sins of desire were directed. Speculation is that it refers to the *donna gentile* in his *Vita Nuova*. Unlike Francesca, however, Dante admits his sins in *Purgatorio* and has sincere contrition for them. Francesca never really owns up to her sinfulness. Instead, she portrays herself as a victim of Love and as one who has no agency to resist its compelling force. Among various aspects of her sinful behavior is not only her lack of contrition but her inability to see herself as a person having the will and reason to resist the desire she felt for Paolo. Dante's case for placing Francesca and Paolo in hell is clear. They have broken one of the sins of the Decalogue. And given that the sin is mortal and is without contrition on the part of the sinner, and without absolution of the sin by a priest, Francesca and Paolo are designated to hell for all of eternity. Given this situation, it would be interesting to look at Francesca and Paolo's situation from the standpoint of Deleuze and Guattari's philosophical system. In what light can we frame the couple's desire, and what kind of judgment might we make of their behavior?

Deleuze and Guattari speak of courtly love in *A Thousand Plateaus*.[69] In the most elevated form of courtly love, the knight sublimates his physical desire to a more spiritual desire. Deleuze and Guattari, however, would not recognize a value in that sublimation since their philosophy is not metaphysical but completely immanent. Desire is not a metaphysical abstraction. Additionally, they do not see desire as a lack. Desire is productive, by which Deleuze and Guattari mean that desiring machines make connections with other assemblages. Additionally, Deleuze and Guattari would not recognize the idea of a subject that acts unethically out of a transcendental code that is universal and outside of life. Rather, they would see the idea of courtly love as a social machine that is enacted out of various connections that it makes with other areas of life. For example, one theory of courtly love is that it is coded in a way that desire can play out. By this I mean it allows desire to become deterritorialized from the machines that link war with love. Francesca was part of the assemblage that linked two familial dynasties in the territory of Romagna. Her marriage was arranged so that the two families that were antagonistic towards each other could combine with the hope that the combination would provide a politically stable environment. Janell Watson states, "With large inheritances at stake

---

69. Deleuze and Guattari, *Thousand Plateaus*, 156.

for those noble sons who did marry, marriage was too important to entrust to love and was decided by the family. Love thus had to be separated from marriage."[70] Yet within this heavily coded marital world, desire can be productive through other processes. For those sons who were not direct inheritors of wealth, i.e., sons who were not first born, courtly love could be viewed as a way in which desire could be reterritorialized. One way this could be accomplished is by having a knight enact pledges of devotion to an important woman without the relationship necessarily entailing sexual acts. The reterritorialization of a woman's affection by a chivalrous knight provided a way in which a woman, who was viewed as part of marriage property, could express her amorous nature without engaging in socially disapproved behavior. Deleuze's description of this kind of desire is that: Courtly love does not love the self, any more than it loves the whole universe in a celestial or religious way. It is a question of making a body without organs upon which intensities pass, self and other—not in the name of a higher level of generality or a broader extension, but by virtue of singularities that can no longer be said to be personal, and intensities that can no longer be said to be extensive.[71]

If we think of courtly love as a body without organs, then courtly love becomes a plane on which intensities of desire flow without the impediment of the overcoded feudal marital system. For Deleuze and Guattari, what exists on that plane of immanence is just the flow of desire itself. A flow of desire can be a line of flight that allows an exit from the feudal machines that link war and matrimony. Deleuze and Guattari insist that what interrupts the flow of desire is the theological system which they term "the judgment of God." The judgment of God takes the body without organs and imposes "forms, functions, bonds, dominant and hierarchized organizations, organized transcendencies."[72] Although courtly love deterritorializes the marital system, it does impose codes that reterritorialize love. One can only go so far in courtly love because there are codes that bind desire anew. The danger of a line of flight is that it is subject to reterritorialization. Deleuze and Guattari understand that a line of flight has its risks. One must embark on it with extreme care. They warn that lines of flight can be both creative and destructive. A line of flight can be turned against itself by the overcoded structures of society. Deleuze and Guattari pose a question to

---

70. Watson, "Intimacy without Domestication," 85.
71. Deleuze and Guattari, *Thousand Plateaus*, 156.
72. Deleuze and Guattari, *Thousand Plateaus*, 159.

the reader of *A Thousand Plateaus*, "Why [or under what circumstances] is the line of flight a war one risks coming back from defeated, destroyed, after having destroyed everything one could"?[73] The answer that Deleuze and Guattari give is because an unsuccessful line of flight is not capable of making additional connections. It does not have other assemblages that match its valence and add to it to make a new assemblage. Rather, it encounters nothing to augment its productive desire and it spirals into a death flight. When Deleuze and Guattari talk about lines of flight, they provide advice about how to proceed. Their counsel is to start cautiously, to "find potential movements of deterritorialization . . . try out continuums of intensities segment by segment, have a small plot of new land at all times."[74] For Francesca and Paolo, their line of flight was an attempt to deterritorialize the war-matrimonial system. It turned, however, into a death spiral. Deleuze and Guattari would not implicate Francesca and Paolo's behavior as unethical. Rather, they would implicate it as being foolhardy.

As an escape to freedom, how might Francesca and Paolo's line of flight to escape from the overcoded feudal matrimonial system be different from Dante, the character's, line of flight to escape from the rigidly coded political-theological system in which he found himself? Dante's line of flight was a productive desire to express his own ideas about morality. He begins, somewhat unconsciously, by placing himself in a dark wood. He allows himself to connect with a wise partner in the form of Virgil. Both he and Virgil are in alignment with the nature of their journey. Along the way, he becomes more adept at understanding the nature of the afterlife. He understands with whom he can align himself, or in Deleuzian terms, with what other assemblages he can plug into. In the afterlife, Dante learns which assemblages to avoid and to which he should avail himself.

Another way Dante differs from Francesca is how he avoids what Deleuze and Guattari call "signifying and subjective programs."[75] Francesca's discourse is a chapter out of the courtly love handbook. Francesca tells Dante how she and Paolo ultimately sinned: "One day, to pass the time in pleasure / we read of Lancelot, how love enthralled him" (*Inf.* V 127–28). Francesca appropriates Lancelot's subjectivity. She buys into the entire

---

73. Deleuze and Guattari, *Thousand Plateaus*, 229.

74. Deleuze and Guattari, *Thousand Plateaus*, 161.

75. Deleuze and Guattari, *Thousand Plateaus*, 161. Signifying and subjective programs are what Deleuze and Guattari claim keep beings stuck and impede them from making themselves bodies without organs.

courtly love signifying machine. As a woman, a minority within the feudal male-dominated culture, she does the opposite of what Deleuze and Guattari recommend. Instead of becoming minoritarian or becoming woman, she reverts to becoming man. Deleuze's theory is that the European male persona has been the identity through which all have been judged or subjected. Therefore, when Francesca inhabits the persona of the male courtly lover, she is merely developing a binary male/female aggregate. She continues to make herself part of the arborescent or molar system. Paolo, her adulterous lover, inhabits the role of the female courtly lover. Francesca describes Paolo during their illicit interlude as "all trembling" as he kissed her on her mouth (*Inf.* V, 136). During the dialogue between Francesca and Dante, he describes Paolo as one who never speaks but remains in the background weeping. In hell, even though the binary courtly love roles are reversed, Francesca and Paolo are not subverting the courtly love system. Rather they have become merely farcical. Then as Dante, the narrator, completes the scene, Dante the pilgrim faints at the end of the canto. The courtly love scene has completely played out. Neither Paolo nor Francesca nor Dante, the pilgrim, for that matter, have become minoritarian nor become woman. To become minoritarian, Deleuze indicates one must not form a binary or a line that connects two points. Instead, to become minoritarian is "neither one nor two, nor the relation of the two; it is the in-between, the order or line of flight or descent running perpendicular to both."[76] Dante, the writer, is invoking the in-between. He is subverting the courtly love genre. He reverses the male and female roles of Paolo and Francesca. Dante, the pilgrim, assumes the role of the sympathetic audience by fainting at the end of the scene. Dante, the narrator, sees the scene for its banal quality.[77] In a Deleuze and Guattari frame, Dante puts Francesca and Paolo in hell, less for their earthly act of adultery, and more for the superficiality of their affair and Francesca's ridiculous defense of their actions. Dante, the narrator, sees through Francesca's rationale for adultery and judges her on her shallow understanding of love itself. Francesca tries to use the signifying system of courtly love as a reason for her defense. In contrast, Dante, the narrator, does not fall back on a previous signifying system. Dante subverts

---

76. Deleuze and Guattari, *Thousand Plateaus*, 293.

77. Deleuze states that "a minor or revolutionary, literature begins by expressing itself and doesn't conceptualize until afterwards" (Deleuze, *Kafka*, 28). By that he means that it does not rely on past forms. It breaks them. The form then captures the ruptures. Sometimes Deleuze speaks of a "stammering language" as a way of expressing the need to break the conventions of the past.

the genre of afterlife visions to produce a distinctly different form of writing. He elevates the afterlife vision from its overreliance on complete adherence to church doctrine. He mixes classical and Christian cultures and allows sinners into heaven, while he casts popes into hell. He invents a completely new metrical scheme, terza rima, to deliver his tale. He writes in the vernacular rather than scholarly Latin so that the work can circulate among a wide audience. Dante's project in the *Divine Comedy* allows him to formulate a different kind of ethics—an ethics which in part agrees with church moral teaching but often does not. Dante is in alignment with what Deleuze and Guattari would describe as becoming a minoritarian author.

2.5.2 Simon Magus and the Simoniac Popes

Moving further on into the depths of hell, in canto nineteen we encounter Dante's meeting with the simoniac popes. Hell's eighth circle is called *Malebolge* (Evil Ditches) wherein one finds the Fraudulent and the Malicious. Within the eighth circle, there are ten deep trenches called bolge. The simoniac popes constitute the third bolgia which is preceded by the Panderers and Seducers in bolgia 1 and the Flatterers in bolgia 2. In this place, Dante consigns to hell three historical popes of the church. Dante begins the canto with a lament about Simon Magus. He appears in the Acts of the Apostles (8:9-24) as a sorcerer who encounters St. Peter while he is in the act of laying his hands on Christians to bring down the Holy Spirit. After watching St. Peter, Simon offers Peter money so that he might acquire the same power. Peter rebukes him for believing that God's spiritual gift could be purchased with money. Dante himself, at the beginning of the canto, invokes Peter's prophetical voice by rebuking Simon Magus.

> O Simon Magus, o wretches of his band,
> greedy for gold and silver,
> who prostitute the things of God. (*Inf.* XIX, 1-3).

Simon Magus also appears in the apocryphal work *The Acts of Peter*. In that text, Simon and St. Peter have a contest about who can perform the most spectacular miracles. Peter's miracles are derived from God while Simon's are merely tricks and acts of deception. Following a long tradition, Dante associates Simon Magus with those in the church who have focused on acquiring power and material things at the expense of spiritual matters.

Dante wished for a humbler and less avaricious church that was more in line with St. Francis and the Spiritual Franciscans who embraced the idea of poverty and asceticism. In the canto, Dante, the pilgrim, encounters a landscape of rocks pierced with holes. The sinners' heads are sunk in the holes while their legs from the thigh down are writhing. Fire burns their feet. Dante calls out to one of the sinners and asks them to speak. In his address to the sinner, Dante fashions himself as a priest ready to hear the confession of an assassin, "I stood there like a friar who confesses / a treacherous assassin" (*Inf.* XIX, 49–50). The voice who answers is Pope Nicholas III who mistakes Dante for a later pope, Boniface VIII. Boniface is the pope who was instrumental in Dante's exile from Florence. Nicholas, who believes that he is speaking to Boniface rather than Dante, acts surprised that Boniface is just now joining him in hell. He asks the supposed Boniface if he has already been sated with the wealth he acquired by deceit. When Dante clears up his identity, Nicholas asks Dante why he wants to know who he is. Nicholas then goes on to admit that he acted improperly as pope. He describes his avarice, "I filled my purse as now I fill this hole" (*Inf.* XIX, 72). Nicholas tells Dante that when Boniface gets assigned to his place in hell, Boniface will land on top of Nicholas and push Nicholas further down into the hole. And after Boniface, another pope, Clement V, who was a pawn of King Philip IV of France and who was responsible for moving the Papal See to Avignon, will replace Boniface. When Boniface is finished speaking, Dante launches into a lengthy monologue that Giuseppe Mazzota describes as being in the linguistic register of a "prophetic moment."[78] His speech is one of truth to power. He castigates those whose responsibility was caring for the church as the bride of Christ and instead turned it into a prostitute. Dante also blames Constantine who he believes gave control of parts of the Roman Empire to the pope. Dante is still living at a time when the *Donation of Constantine* had not yet been proven a forgery.[79] Dante is incensed that Constantine was complicit in involving the church in the realm of money and power. Dante's critical linguistics include the use of

---

78. Mazzotta, *Reading Dante*, 82.

79. The *Donation of Constantine* was a forged decree wherein the Roman emperor, Constantine, supposedly gave the pope authority over Rome and the western half of the empire. Constantine's largess was purportedly in gratitude for the cure of his leprosy through baptism. The authenticity of the decree was generally accepted until the fourteenth century when it was exposed as a forgery by various personages such as Reginald Pecock (ca. 1393–1461), Nicholas of Cusa (ca. 1400–1464), and Lorenzo Valla (ca. 1406–1457).

apostrophe when he addresses Simon Magus with, "Oh Simon Magus, O wretches of his band" (*Inf.* XIX, 1) and Constantine, "Ah, Constantine, to what evil you give birth" (*Inf.* XIX, 115). The elevated language that Dante uses is part of the prophetic tradition and analogous to the language of prophets like Jeremiah who admonished Israel for its greed and its idolatry. Yet, the seriousness of Dante's language is undercut by the ludicrous inverted posture of the people to whom he is preaching.

Some scholars claim that Dante was influenced by the apocryphal *Acts of Peter*, where Peter requested to be crucified upside down. According to Peter, he was born a man and like the generation after Adam was thrown into the world head down dead with sin.[80] Christ came into the world to reverse down with up and left with right. One interpretation of Peter's words would mean that Peter's crucifixion must be humbler than Christ's. He does not deserve to be upright like Christ but must assume the position of a servant. Jonathan Z. Smith provides a different interpretation of inversion. In his article, "Birth Upside Down or Right Side Up"?, Smith contends that inversion in the *Acts of Peter* could have a different meaning. Inversion could signify a rebellion against the way of the world. Smith says that for Peter to request an upside-down crucifixion was "an *act of cosmic audacity* consistent with an expression of a Christian-gnostic understanding and evaluation of the structures of the cosmos and of the human condition."[81] Smith's interpretation is that inversion is a corrective to the established order and as such is an act of creation—to change the world from what it is to what it should be. Dante's use of inversion with the simoniac popes could be seen as a corrective to their pride, i.e., to enforce a humility on them that they never established for themselves. Additionally, inversion could be seen as Dante's desire to reverse the cosmological order of a sinful world. The contrapasso of inversion is fitting for the popes who polluted the church with their greed. Inversion is a symbol of reversing their destructiveness. Therefore, the theme of inversion is paramount for Dante in this canto. Unlike the scene in the Acts of the Apostles when on Pentecost the Holy Spirit comes and rains down fire on the heads of the disciples, in hell the souls are inverted with fire coming from their feet. Although Dante, the pilgrim, is part of the laity, he plays the hierarch to Pope Nicholas accused of simony. On Pentecost, the disciples speak in their own single language, but they are understood by all who are of different languages and are gathered at

---

80. Schneemelcher, "Acts of Peter," 315–16.
81. Smith, "Birth Upside Down or Right Side Up?," 293.

the scene. By contrast, the language of the simoniac pope is not a language that is universal in its appeal to others. Rather, the language of Nicholas is strictly a language of selfishness. Nicholas admits his guilt and his desire to enrich himself and his family materially without regard to the people of the church and their spiritual needs. Dante is unsparing in his criticism about the corruption in the church. Engaging in the prophetic role, he speaks the truth to the corrupt pope. He tells Nicholas that he still reveres the office of the pope and if it weren't for the respect he has for the ideals of the papacy, "I would resort to even harsher words / because your avarice afflicts the world / trampling down the good and raising up the wicked" *(Inf.* XIX, 103–5). The nature of Dante's language as a critique against a despotic pope can be further developed using Deleuze and Guattari's language theory which they call a regime of signs.

In *A Thousand Plateaus*, Deleuze and Guattari talk about a typology of representation that describes various assemblages of power. They call this typology a regime of signs. A regime of signs is partly a semiotic system, but rather than just a semiotics in itself, a regime expresses "a form of content that is simultaneously inseparable from and independent of the form of expression and the two forms pertain to assemblages that are not principally linguistic."[82] By form of content, Deleuze and Guattari mean that which is material and tangible. By form of expression, they mean that which makes up the semiotic system. A regime of signs, therefore, is a semiotic system and an assemblage of material content.[83] Deleuze and Guattari note that these different regimes are not evolutionary and are not meant to typify a particular historical period. Likewise, more than one regime often operates at the same time. Their typology consists of four different sign regimes: Signifying, Post-Signifying, Pre-Signifying, and Counter-Signifying.[84]

---

82. Deleuze and Guattari, *Thousand Plateaus*, 111.

83. Young et al., *Deleuze and Guattari Dictionary*, 136–37. Assemblages are made from a form of content and a form of expression. Form of content is materiality, corporality. Form of expression is the semiotic system. One form does not signify another. Instead they can be construed as interacting horizontally.

84. Eugene Holland groups Signifying and Post-Signifying as the two most important regimes. The Pre-Signifying regime is for primitive societies while the Counter-Signifying is for the nomad war machine. The despot characterizes the Signifying Regime. They are at the center and rule their empire of concentric circles of power through state functionaries who exists in the rings moving outward. The functionaries are charged with repeating the messages of the despot. Those who fail to obey the despot are either put to death or banished. The regime is characterized by paranoia—on the part of the functionaries who must worry about getting the message correct, on the part of the

Deleuze and Guattari also talk about a Mixed Regime of Significance and Subjectification which combines aspects of the others.

In the chapter "Year Zero: Faciality" in *A Thousand Plateaus*, they describe the Mixed Regime of Signifiance and Subjectification as exemplified by the face of Christ. This regime is marked by what Deleuze and Guattari call faciality. Faciality is an abstract machine that fortifies a regime of power by signification and subjectification. They maintain that an abstract machine

> is neither an infrastructure that is determining in the last instance nor a transcendental Idea that is determining in the supreme instance. Rather, it plays a piloting role. The diagrammatic or abstract machine does not function to represent, even something real, but rather constructs a real that is yet to come, a new type of reality.[85]

They point to the Face of Christ as an abstract machine and an indication of a regime of power whereby faciality comes into its full force. In this regime of signs, full faciality for Deleuze and Guattari means an assemblage of power that expresses a type of politics whereby Christ becomes the face of the power structure. That power structure holds the white, European, male face as the standard by which all others are judged.[86] By contrast, other regimes of signs have either no faces or different faces. A primitive regime of signs has no face but rather a focus on the body. A despotic regime of signs would have the face of the despot (e.g., the Egyptian Pharaoh) as emblematic of the face. The face of the despot is always public and never

---

despot who worries about the loyalty of his officials and on the part of the people who fear the despot's power. The Post-Signifying regime is characterized by passional subjectivity. The face of the despot or God is turned away. The power in the structure is a bureaucracy that is decentralized and immanent. See Holland, *Deleuze and Guattari's A Thousand Plateaus*, 82–84.

85. Deleuze and Guattari, *Thousand Plateaus*, 142. Deleuze and Guattari provide an example from nature of an abstract machine. An abstract machine has two basic movements. The first articulation is when loose particles of sediment within an ocean floor are drawn together through the process of separating like from unlike particles. The second articulation is the hardening of the sediment into strata. Jeffrey A. Bell describes it as a dynamic system. The first articulation "draws chaos (BwO) into a plane of consistency while the second articulation actualizes the consistency into an identifiable state" (Bell, *Philosophy at the Edge of Chaos*, 4).

86. One aspect of Faciality is what Deleuze and Guattari call binarization. That means that a standard is set whereby there are two opposing binaries, and one is judged right while the other is rejected. "At every moment, the machine rejects faces that do not conform" (Deleuze and Guattari, *Thousand Plateaus*, 177).

hidden. If the despot has all power held in the face, then the inverse of the despot is the body of the powerless or the excluded. Deleuze and Guattari point to the tradition of the scapegoat as an example of the excluded in the despotic system. As in the book of Exodus, a goat was released into the desert to carry away the sins of the community. In a Post Signifying regime, faciality would have the face of God and the face of the prophet averted from each other. The example that Deleuze and Guattari give is how Jonah averts the face of God when God orders him to go to Nineveh. Jonah betrays God by fleeing. Ultimately in fleeing, Deleuze and Guattari maintain that Jonah "did exactly what God had wanted: he took the evil of Nineveh upon himself."[87] I maintain that within canto nineteen, one can discern what Deleuze and Guattari would describe as a Mixed Regime of Significance and Subjectification and an abstract machine of Faciality.

Dante, speaking in his own voice and not the pilgrim's, begins canto nineteen speaking from a prophetic voice to indicate a Post-Signifying regime of signs. That regime is defined as having a power assemblage that is authoritarian. In the case of Dante, he is using his position as a prophet to decry the corrupt nature of the church and its leaders. His beginning apostrophe, "O Simon Magus, o wretches of his band" (*Inf.* XIX, 1), invokes his authority to judge the situation. The description of the terrain of this canto with its stony landscape pockmarked with holes is representative of the lunar landscape indicative of the Mixed Regime of signs. The landscape of the simonist popes is described similarly as a landscape that faciality constructs. Deleuze and Guattari state:

> The face constructs the wall that the signifier needs in order to bounce off of; it constitutes the wall of the signifier, the frame or screen. The face digs the hole that subjectification needs in order to break through; it constitutes the black hole of subjectivity as consciousness or passion, the camera, the third eye.[88]

Both the white screen and the black holes depend upon each other. Deleuze and Guattari ask how one can escape the black holes and white walls. They reply that one must find a way to dismantle the face. Deleuze and Guattari suggest knowledge as a way to do that: "Find your black holes and white walls, know your faces; it is the only way you will dismantle them and draw your lines of flight."[89] Dante the author and Dante the pilgrim

---

87. Deleuze and Guattari, *Thousand Plateaus*, 123.
88. Deleuze and Guattari, *Thousand Plateaus*, 168.
89. Deleuze and Guattari, *Thousand Plateaus*, 188.

will define how to break through Faciality by beginning a discussion with Pope Nicholas.

Dante starts by asking the person stuck in the hole who he is. The pope's face is hidden. In fact, half of his body from the waist up is hidden in the black hole. The faces that are visible in this canto are those of Virgil and Dante, who represent the passional face of Christ. The face that should represent Christ (i.e., the pope's face), however, is buried in the black hole. Dante has subverted the faciality abstract machine. The popes in their greed and power grabbing represent what Deleuze and Guattari would call the inhuman in human beings. They cared nothing for the flock they purportedly served and were only interested in their own selfish desires. While in the present, Nicholas is the pope stuck in the hole, Boniface will follow him, and Clement will also be sucked into the black hole. Dante, who inhabits the Hebrew prophetic role of a Post-Signifying passional regime and who subverts the role of the Mixed Regime Face of Christ, has found a way to develop a line of flight that disrupts both regimes. To disrupt the Post-Signifying regime, Dante assumes the role of scapegoat. As the scapegoat, he can play the role of an Everyperson imbued with the courage to walk through hell and witness the suffering of the sinful. In that witnessing, he can be prophetic about those who suffer in hell and how the living can transform their lives to avoid their own suffering.

At the end of canto nineteen, Virgil carries Dante, the pilgrim, in his arms: "Therefore, he caught me in his arms / and, when he had me all upon his breast, / remounted by the path he had descended." (*Inf.* XIX, 121–23). Virgil acts the way in which an animal mother would carry her child. Dante and Virgil, in a Deleuzian way, become animal. Becoming is one of Deleuze's themes in his attempt to express his desire for an emancipatory way of being. He contrasts history versus becoming when he states, "History amounts only to the set of preconditions, however recent, that one leaves behind in order to 'become' that is to create something new."[90] Within the Deleuzian and Guattarian corpus, they propose many becomings: becoming woman, becoming animal, becoming minoritarian, becoming molecule. However, becoming man is not an emancipatory act since man "impose[s] itself on all matter, whereas woman, animal, or molecule always has a component of flight that escapes its own formalization."[91] Deleuzian becoming is also expressed in writing. Literature aids one in freeing

---

90. Deleuze, *Negotiations 1972–1990*, 170.
91. Deleuze, *Essays Critical and Clinical*, 1.

oneself from the imperial "I," i.e., a fixed subjectivity.[92] Becoming animal is another way in which Deleuze and Guattari attempt to subvert the emphasis on subjectivity. Steven Baker describes becoming animal as a situation in which "identity is not the thing to which the participants in the alliance of becoming-animal attend. Separate bodies enter into alliances in order to do things but are not undone by it."[93] As such, Dante and Virgil work together to undo the papal simoniacs' faciality. After carrying Dante up a great steep, Virgil places him down on a rough ridge. Dante describes that journey as something that "would have made hard going for a goat (*Inf.* XIX, 132)." The goat symbol is precisely how Deleuze and Guattari outline a line of flight from a Post-Signifying regime of signs. Dante and Virgil, as pilgrims and witnesses of the sufferings in hell, are the becoming animals. They inhabit that role so that readers of the *Inferno* can understand the transformation that one must make in order to subvert the faciality of an authoritarian regime.

2.6 CONCLUSION

My goal in this chapter is to show how Deleuze and Guattari could be conversational partners with Dante for contemporary readers. Given that many contemporary readers do not believe in an afterlife or hell or possibly God, I wanted to show how Deleuze and Guattari could be used to illuminate Dante's conception of hell. I felt it necessary to show that the origin for much of Dante's representation of the afterlife comes from the concept of hierarchy that originated from Plato and was developed later by Christian philosophers and theologians into a unified and ranked cosmology. My wish was to illustrate how Dante in the *Inferno* put together an ethical system that reflected the medieval conception of hierarchy. In the medieval mindset, that ethical system was created by God, was based on Scripture, and was transcendent and universal for all. I also wanted to explain how a contemporary reader might have doubts about an afterlife, a hierarchical cosmology, a belief in God, and a transcendent ethical system. Those problems can present obstacles for a contemporary reader of Dante's *Inferno*. I believe that Dante is still pertinent to a contemporary reader's experience.

---

92. Deleuze states that literature begins when it "strips us of the power to say 'I.'" Deleuze proclaims that writers are physicians and literature is "an enterprise of health" (Deleuze, *Essays Critical and Clinical*, 3).

93. Baker, *Postmodern Animal*, 133.

However, to make Dante more contemporaneous, he needs to be contextualized outside of a medieval mindset. By that, I mean that the medieval ideas needed to be presented so that Dante could be understood properly within his historical milieu. But at the same time, I wanted to show how he could be read within today's philosophical context. I chose Deleuze and Guattari because of the striking contrast they present to Dante's hierarchical cosmology and his system of ethics. Rather than hierarchy, Deleuze and Guattari insist on immanence. Rather than a transcendent ethical system, they speak of a situated ethical choice that opens up to life at each unique moment. I also believe that Deleuze and Guattari's ideas of assemblages can help to put the cultural and economic forces of fourteenth-century Northern Italy into perspective. It provides a backdrop that can explain how radical Dante was to medieval conventions and leaders (e.g., courtly love and the papacy) so that he could upend them and delineate a line of flight to freedom. Still, Dante was a person of his time and place. He believed in hierarchy. He yearned for an emperor who would unify Italy and its people. He dearly wished for a church that embraced humility and poverty. His hope was for a secular leader and a spiritual leader that could liberate the people of Northern Italy. And although that did not turn out for him, he succeeded in providing a subversive literary work that can still be used today as a means of opening up a line of flight—a line of freedom to escape the overcoding of our present experience.

3

Purgatory
Levinas's Modes of Being and Dante's Divisions of Purgatory

3.1 INTRODUCTION

EMMANUEL LEVINAS, AS A contemporary thinker, can help illuminate Dante's *Purgatorio* for current Dante readers. My project is to examine Dante's purgatorial states of being with Levinas's modes of being. Additionally, I wish to examine how Dante's encounter with the Other as Beatrice in the Earthly Paradise compares to Levinas's encounter with the Other in the idea of Infinity.

In the Dantean system, a soul in Purgatory can progress through the Purgatorial spaces and ultimately ascend to heaven. Dante has an explicit idea of a soul's progression whereby one's sins are purified and removed so that ultimately one can experience a vision of God. In Levinas, there is no idea of progression. As progression often is a function of time, I want to examine Levinas's idea of time as a diachrony to emphasize that Levinas does not posit an idea of progression. Unlike Dante where there is a teological movement from one state to another, in Levinas this is not the case. Since Dante's idea of teleology was influenced by Plato and Aquinas, I will examine Plato's *Phaedo* and *Timaeus* and Aquinas's *De Veritate* in order to better understand it. Then I will examine Levinas's reaction to those thinkers' ideas of teleology as a totality that he opposes. I will also examine Plato's Cave Allegory in the *Republic* to show how Plato influenced Dante and Levinas regarding the idea of the good beyond being. In the Cave allegory, Plato presents three realms of being: the cave or the sensate realm, the realm of light or the intelligible realm, and the realm of the good beyond being. Plato's three realms form a base from which both Dante and Levinas will draw. Dante divides Purgatory into three sections: Ante-Purgatory, Purgatory Proper, and the Earthly Paradise. I wish to compare Dante's purgatorial states with three of Levinas's modes of being: the *il y a* or the *there is*, hypostasis and Interiority and Economy. Within the section of Levinas's *Totality and Infinity* entitled "Interiority and Economy," Levinas covers the mode of Stuckness with the Self, Being in the World and Dwelling and the Feminine. These modes explained in "Interiority and Economy" will also be included in the comparison to Dante's Purgatorial states of being. Finally, I wish to examine Levinas's Encounter with the Other and compare that with Dante's encounter with Beatrice in Dante's Earthly Paradise.

The figures below attempt to depict the ideas that I wish to deal with in this chapter. Since the thoughts of Plato, Dante and Levinas can be exceedingly complex, the diagrams below cannot entirely do justice to all of their conceptions. Yet I believe depicting the ideas below in a graphical format helps more than it detracts from the analysis.

3.1.1 Conceptual Diagrams

Table A: Plato's States of Being

The Cave—	The Light—	The Good—
Sensate Realm	Intelligible Realm	Beyond Being Realm

Table B1: Dante's States of Being

Hell	Purgatory	Heaven

Table B2: Dante's Substates of Purgatory

Ante Purgatory	Purgatory Proper	Purgatorial Earthly Paradise

Figure C1: Levinas's Modes of Being

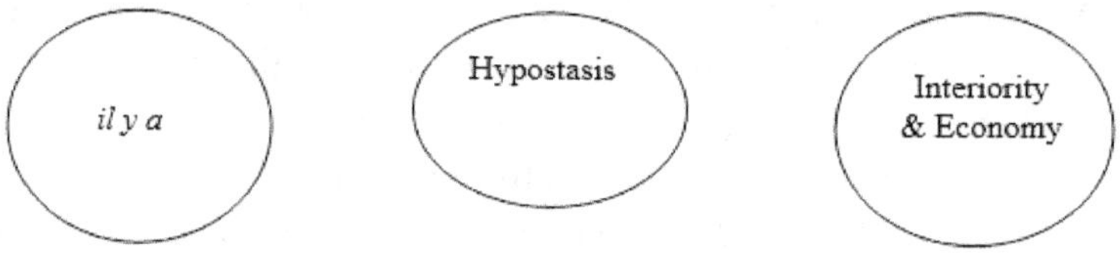

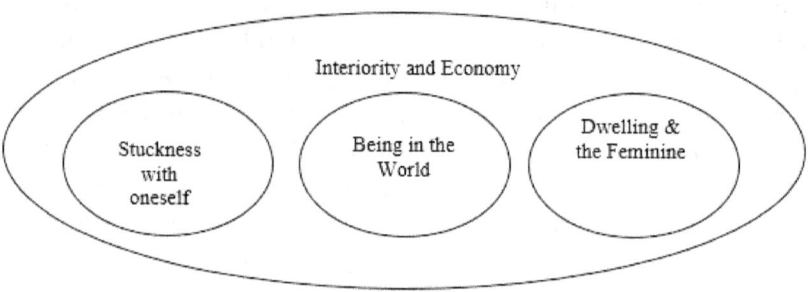

Figure C2: Modes Covered by Levinas in *Totality and Infinity* Section II "Interiority and Economy"

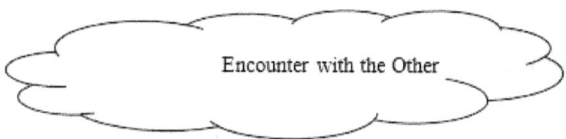

Figure C3: Levinas's Beyond Being / Infinity

Encounter with the Other

Table A shows Plato's states of beings. The idea is that one moves progressively from darkness to light to the good beyond being. Table B is split into two parts. Table B1 depicts Dante's states of being. Hell and Heaven are shown for reference only since this chapter deals solely with Purgatory. Table B2 is a breakdown of Purgatory into substates. In Table B2, those who start out in Ante Purgatory will progress through Purgatory Proper and ultimately be admitted to heaven, as will those who start out in Purgatory Proper. Figure C1 depicts three of Levinas's modes of being. The circle icons, rather than tables, are used for Levinas's modes of being to emphasize that Levinas does not conceive of a progression from one state to another. For Levinas, these modes are always and already part of being and non-being. I include the *il y a* in the model even though it is a mode without existents. The purpose of including it in this study is because in the Levinasian model, the *il y a* remains a haunting experience for the subject. It contains the possibility that non-existence can absorb a subject back into anonymity so that it loses its separateness. Hypostasis is a process that allows a being to become an existent. Figure C2 is based on Levinas's text *Totality and Infinity* wherein Section II, entitled "Interiority and Economy," he discusses the topics of: Stuckness with Oneself, Being in the World among material elements, and The Dwelling and the Feminine. When hypostasis happens, the subject becomes an existent. Once in existence, the subject finds that it is difficult to liberate itself from itself. A way for the self to liberate itself is through action in the material world. An outward focus helps free the self from its stuckness. As a being in the world among the elements, the self strives to find a place of repose, which is the dwelling. Levinas characterizes the dwelling as the feminine because of its gentleness. It affords the self a place of solitude. In contrast to Levinas, in the Dantean model, when Dante, the pilgrim emerges from hell into Purgatory, the existent leaves a place of sinfulness and darkness to assume a fresh start. For Levinas, the existent's hypostasis is not from a state of sinfulness. For both Dante and Levinas, the subject's emergence into Purgatory or the subject's effectuation of hypostasis does signify a break with the darkness and includes a heightened sense of the existent's subjectivity. For Dante, it includes an increasing sense of the need to move past oneself with a concern for a more ethical way of life. For Levinas, a being that escapes from the *il y a* finds itself in the world. In order to remove itself from being stuck, a being must direct its attention outward from itself. It does that by turning its attention to the world, to its material elements and to the construction of a dwelling and habitation with the feminine. In Purgatory Proper the being must ultimately become ready for an encounter with a transcendent Other. The work of beings in Purgatory Proper is to prepare themselves for that encounter the Other. For Dante, an encounter with the other happens in the Earthly Paradise. This is his encounter with Beatrice. Although Beatrice does appear in the guise of the transcendent Other, it is not God, the infinite Other, whom Dante encounters in Paradiso at the end of the *Divine Comedy*. For Levinas, the encounter with the Other is a transcendent experience with alterity. Figure C3 depicts that the encounter with the Other is beyond being or in other words an encounter with infinity.

3.1.2 Progression Through the States

While progression from one state to another is valid for Plato and Dante, it is not valid for Levinas. The genesis of a subject's existence in Purgatory begins after they die. In the Dantean system, a subject after death could enter any domain of the other world, and in the case of the second canticle, either Ante Purgatory or Purgatory Proper. Ante Purgatory is a Dantean invention for the purposes of the *Divine Comedy*. It is a place for those people who lived unethical lives and or were late in repenting. This includes those who were excommunicated, those who committed violence, and those who were purely lethargic in their ethical lives. In the Dantean model, inhabitants of Ante Purgatory will eventually progress from Ante Purgatory to Purgatory Proper. Ante Purgatory is not a required state for everyone who must go to Purgatory. A person after death could enter directly into Purgatory Proper and skip Ante Purgatory altogether, as long as they had confessed their sins and had been absolved before death. In Purgatory Proper, an inhabitant does not need to steadily ascend through all the tiers in *Purgatorio*. Conceivably they can cleanse their soul by inhabiting only one tier in Purgatory and then progress into heaven. Those in Purgatory Proper will eventually progress into heaven after their time in Purgatory. Dante, the character, however, does not progress into heaven without first going through the Earthly Paradise. The Earthly Paradise is not consistent with Catholic theology, but Dante includes it to create a place where he can encounter Beatrice.[1] It is the transitional area that marks Virgil's departure and Beatrice's assumption as a guide to Dante. While progression is a feature of Dante's model, Levinas would not conceive of progression for his modes of being. As a critic of Hegel, he would not agree with an inevitable movement of a spirit through space and time.

Levinas, in fact, is critical of a Western philosophical narrative whereby the subject passes through trials and tribulations and through reason finds its way to its destination home. Levinas states that Western civilization's primary narrative, as influenced by the God of philosophers who received it from the God of the scholastics, is about a subject like Ulysses who through all his adventures returns home from whence he began.[2] This idea

---

1. According to the *Catholic Encyclopedia*, Jewish eschatology developed the idea of a dwelling place similar to the Garden of Eden that would be available for the righteous after death. In Catholic dogma, however, paradise is a heavenly state and not a place in Purgatory. For more information, see Driscoll, "Terrestrial Paradise."

2. Levinas, "Trace of the Other," 346.

of the self who sets out on a journey only to return home is a circularity or a totality which Levinas opposes. It runs parallel to the Hegelian idea of Spirit unfolding and absorbing everything it encounters through the dialectical process. This for Levinas is a totality of violence that has no respect for the alterity of the other. In "The Ego and the Totality," Levinas states that "a particular being can take itself to be a totality only if it is thoughtless."[3] As such, persons have no knowledge of the exterior world. Their inwardness is not concerned with what is outside of themselves. They treat others as essentially the same as themselves. Levinas, in "Language and Proximity," describes how a narrative like the *Odyssey* can divert one from the ethical. He states, "Events which are staggered out according to time and reach consciousness in a series of acts and states also ordered according to time acquire, across this multiplicity, a unity of meaning in narration."[4] Yet this kind of narrative can keep one detached from exteriority and the other. Levinas is opposed to that dominant narrative. Michael J. MacDonald writes, "Levinas proposes another story besides the 'single story' [*monos mythos*]—the quest for the truth of Being 'blazed across the world'—that binds philosophy from Parmenides to Heidegger in the 'unbreakable plot' of ontology."[5] Instead, Levinas argues for a language that acts in a proximity to the other and that is immediate like a caress or a touch.[6] In Levinasian terms, the language of narration is a language of the *said* wherein the said becomes a unity that encloses itself in a totality. On the other hand, a language of proximity to the other is a language of the *saying*. The saying does not produce a theme, or a totality as does the said of narration. Rather the saying "at every moment breaks the definition of what it says and breaks up the totality it includes."[7] Yet this idea of the saying rather than the said is difficult to pull off when one is writing a tome like *Totality and Infinity*. Some scholars have commented that one might think of Levinas's text as a unity. In particular, two Levinas scholars warn readers not to read Levinas as prescribing a serial progression through realms of being. Diane Perpich in her text *The Ethics of Emmanuel Levinas* states:

3. Levinas, *Collected Philosophical Papers*, 26.
4. Levinas, *Collected Philosophical Papers*, 109.
5. MacDonald, "Losing Spirit," 188.
6. Levinas proposes that a neighbor is one who has meaning *immediately* before one ascribes one to him. The contact with another is not a manifestation of knowledge but an ethical event.
7. Levinas, *Collected Philosophical Papers*, 126.

> *Totality and Infinity* exudes the air of a drama complete with protagonist, conflict, and denouement. . . . There is an identifiable plot that might be summarized (a bit hastily, but still accurately) as follows: an ego absorbed in its needs and living in conditions of relative domestic security is confronted by a stranger who disrupts and calls into question its manner of being at home in the world. The result of this face-to-face encounter is that the ego finds itself in an ethical relationship in which it is divested of its egoism and invited to the serious work of goodness and responsibility.[8]

It is true that *Totality and Infinity*, because of its inherent narrative structure, can give the impression of a bildungsroman text. However, Levinas's intent is not to depict the ego's growth over time. Perpich writes, "This tale of 'I meets Other' was not meant by Levinas to be a tale at all, and its narrative structure is importantly at odds with the most original impulses of the work."[9]

Bettina Bergo describes Levinas's modes of being as "levels of sensuous, conative, and reflective experiences as adjuvant preconditions for intersubjectivity."[10] Bergo is speaking of Levinas's modes of being that are in the world and open to the world's pleasures. But Bergo states that these

> first metaphoric "layers" of experience do not precede, temporally or structurally, the face-to-face relationship. The origin of human intersubjectivity thus escapes an explicit grounding because our world and our relationships are, for us, always already human. They are always already imbued with meanings that escape the order of instrumental or mechanistic behaviors.[11]

Bergo admits that Levinas's challenge in *Totality and Infinity* is to create a narrative that explains these "layers of experience" in a way that doesn't present them as a step-by-step series that gives the impression of a formulaic system.[12] One of the ways to understand Levinas's modes of being better is to examine Levinas's conception of time.

---

8. Perpich, *Ethics of Emmanuel Levinas*, 79.
9. Perpich, *Ethics of Emmanuel Levinas*, 79.
10. Bergo, *Levinas Between Ethics and Politics*, 24.
11. Bergo, *Levinas Between Ethics and Politics*, 25.
12. Bergo explains that there are two distinct orders within *Totality and Infinity*. One is everyday being, while the other is transcendence and the Good. These orders cross and are not completely separate from each other. See Bergo, *Levinas Between Ethics and Politics*, 25.

3.1.3 Levinas's Conception of Time

Levinas describes his conception of time as a diachrony. For Levinas, diachrony is the face-to-face relationship with the other. Levinas states that one's responsibility for the other does not start with the subject's decision or commitment. Rather,

> The unlimited responsibility in which I find myself comes from the hither side of my freedom, from a "prior to every memory," an "ulterior to every accomplishment," from the non-present par excellence, the non-original, the anarchical, prior to or beyond essence.[13]

Thus, the responsibility for the other happens in a temporal realm that is prior to the memory of the subject. The responsibility for the other is originary, and this is where time begins. Richard I. Sugarman states that Levinas resists conceiving of the other as entering into my purview at my own discretion. This would place the other as an object in my autobiography. Sugarman explains:

> For Levinas, because time originates virtually with and for the other, the time *of* the other is anterior to ontology. Acknowledging the time *of* the other involves the subordinating of my own sense of temporality to that of the other. This subordination *is* ethics—first philosophy—that leads to a reconfiguration of reason in relation to transcendence.[14]

Levinas's sense of time as beginning with the other is ethical time. In this idea, Levinas was influenced by Franz Rosenzweig. In his text *The Star of Redemption*, Rosenzweig saw eternity as present at every hour. Regarding time, Rosenzweig states, "The future is not anticipation for God; he is eternal and the only Eternal One, the Eternal One absolutely; 'I am,' in his mouth, is like 'I shall be' and really finds his explanation therein."[15] Rosenzweig's influence on Levinas helps disclose how Levinas sees the relationship with the other as a transcendent relationship. Not only is the transcendent relationship a relationship of present and future (i.e., the "I am" in God's mouth is like "I shall be"), but most notably for Levinas, the "I have always been" is like the "I am." The "I have always been" is for Levinas the anterior relationship with

---

13. Levinas, *Otherwise than Being or Beyond Essence*, 10.
14. Sugarman, "Emmanuel Levinas and the Deformalization of Time," 257.
15. Rosenzweig, *Star of Redemption*, 290.

the other that is originary. In Rosenzweig's idea of the relationship between humanity and God, people find themselves outside of the normal time of being. Likewise, Levinas's relationship with the other is beyond being because the other is beyond being. Thus the relationship with the Other is an originary relationship and not a goal to be achieved. To understand this better, it would be appropriate to understand the Western philosophical idea of teleology that influenced Dante and was opposed by Levinas.

3.2 THE TELEOLOGY OF PLATO AND AQUINAS

Dante was influenced by both Plato and the Christian ideas of teleology as described by Aquinas. In Plato's *Phaedo* and *Timaeus* one can see Plato's theory of teleology and time which ultimately influenced Christianity's idea of a human's passage to the Good. In the *Phaedo*, Socrates states that someone he knew read a text by Anaxagoras which asserted that the mind produces order and is the cause of everything. And the operating principle of the mind is to produce an order that

> arranges each individual thing in the way that is best for it. Therefore if anyone wished to discover the reason why any given thing came or ceased or continued to be, he must find out how it was best for that thing to be, or to act or be acted upon in any way.[16]

Yet Socrates is disappointed when he finds that Anaxagoras does not identify the agency that causes what is best. Socrates ultimately works out his own theory in *Phaedo* where he postulates that the cause of something is that it partakes of the absolute form of that thing. Socrates gives an example of beauty. Something is beautiful not because it has a gorgeous color or shape. Rather what makes an object beautiful is the presence in it of absolute beauty.[17] While causation is not explained to Plato's total satisfaction in *Phaedo*, he tries again to understand it in the *Timaeus*. In the voice of the character Timaeus, he explains that the creator made the world because the creator was good. As the Good, God desired all things to be as like Godself as they could be.[18] Therefore, when God created humans, God made them

---

16. Plato, *Phaedo* 97c.

17. Plato, *Phaedo* 98d. Socrates states that he does not insist upon the precise details of the object. Rather he only needs to know that beautiful things are beautiful because they have a relationship with absolute beauty.

18. Plato, *Timaeus* 30a.

as like to Godself as possible, but God could not make humans eternal. Therefore God

> resolved to have a moving image of eternity, and when he set in order the heaven, he made this image eternal but moving according to number, while eternity itself rests in unity and this image we call time.[19]

Plato goes on to relate that before time was created there was no distinction between day and night. When God created the universe, God created past and future. However, these forms of time only imitate eternity.[20] Thus one can argue that Plato's theory of time is that there is an underlying eternity of time that existed prior to the creation of the universe. Before the creation of the universe, what was in existence was not in order. But then God made the universe from the things that were available. God fashioned the material that was available into something that "as far as possible [was] the fairest and the best," although what was available was "not fair and good."[21] Further on, Plato argues that God put together order from disorder. God creates in each thing "all the measures and harmonies which they could receive."[22] Thus God creates order out of chaos and everything for the good. God does not just create an individual good but a holistic good because each thing is created with all the harmonies that it can receive. In his essay on "Plato's Teleology," Thomas Kjeller Johansen states that God's craft for creation

> is not just teleological, it is teleological in a holistic manner. Craft does not just seek to realize the individual good, but where that individual is part of a whole, as in a cosmos, it prioritizes the good of the whole.[23]

Plato's idea that all things created in the universe originate with an idea of the Good, is taken up by Christianity and Dante in a Christian idea of teleology.

Aquinas in *De Veritate* agrees with Plato that all things tend toward the good. He describes humans as part of nature which works towards an end. Humans, unlike inanimate objects, have a knowledge of the end, or the

---

19. Plato, *Timaeus* 37d.
20. Plato, *Timaeus* 38b–c.
21. Plato, *Timaeus* 53b.
22. Plato, *Timaeus* 69b.
23. Johansen, "Plato's Teleology," 35.

good, and they work for the end with a purpose. Aquinas differentiates that which moves through its own agency and that which moves through the action of a director. Aquinas writes, "Created existence is itself a likeness to the divine goodness. So in desiring to be, things implicitly desire a likeness to God and God Himself."[24] Therefore, in a creature there is a desire for God. Aquinas references Wisdom 8:1 when he states that "divine wisdom 'orders all things' sweetly because each one by its own motion tends to that for which it has been divinely destined."[25] Aquinas also mentions that as a thing gets closer to the end, the more vigorous is its inclination. This only happens when that which is moving to its end has the form of the end inside it, but that form is only partial. One might think of this in a spiritual light as humans who have a partial "form" of the divine as their souls and who desire intensely to be with God as their end. Aquinas states, "Any natural motion is intensified near the end when the thing tending to the end is more like that end."[26] Thus a person's desire is heightened as the end is closer to being reached.

3.3 LEVINAS AND TELEOLOGY

In Levinas, one finds a form of anti-teleology. Levinas does not presume that an active and knowledgeable director motivates the individual. In the Christian tradition, the knowledgeable director would be God. One cannot say of Levinas that because of an originary God, a human is motivated to seek a knowable end. In fact, knowledge does not play a role in Levinas's philosophy wherein a human seeks the divine in a pre-established end which is the Good. As Richard Cohen writes, for Levinas, "moral force cannot be reduced to cognitive cogency, to acts of consciousness or will."[27] While Christian theologians can claim that because humans are made in the image and likeness of God, some aspects of God are known, in Levinas's philosophy the other is complete alterity. One does not approach the other purposefully with foreknowledge. Rather, Levinas describes the self as encountering the other in complete passivity. One does not seek the other in Levinas's philosophy. Rather one is commanded by the other. Levinas states that his philosophy "aims to disengage the subjectivity of the subject

24. Aquinas, "Quaestiones Disputatae de Veritate" xx.ii.a2.
25. Aquinas, "Quaestiones Disputatae de Veritate" xx.i.r.
26. Aquinas, "Quaestiones Disputatae de Veritate" xx.i.ad3.
27. Cohen, *Face to Face with Levinas*, 5.

from reflections on truth, time and being and entities which is borne by the said; it will then present the subject, in saying, as a sensibility from the first animated by responsibilities."[28] Levinas opposes the idea that the agency of the subject directs them towards the truth and the good. The said in this context is the idea of a concept or a prescribed action driven by an egoist subject. Levinas will oppose Plato's idea of the beyond being as a conceptual state. Levinas states,

> The beyond being . . . here situated by diachrony, here expressed as infinity, has been recognized as the Good by Plato. It matters little that Plato made of it an idea and a light source. The beyond being, showing itself in the said, always shows itself there enigmatically, is already betrayed.[29]

Thus, Levinas takes direct aim at Plato's idea of the Good beyond being as a philosophical concept. When the Good beyond being is part of the "said," it becomes part of a totality. It loses its ability to be a saying and to show up as complete alterity. Still, Plato's influence affects both Dante and Levinas, even if Levinas objects to some of Plato's ideas. Both Dante and Levinas owe much of their conceptions to Plato and in particular Plato's Allegory of the Cave. To understand how the influence works, it will be necessary to explain Plato's Cave Allegory. After that, I will discuss Plato's influence on Christianity and in particular Dante. Then I wish to show how Plato affected Levinas and his modes of being. Before going through various scenes of the *Purgatorio*, I believe it will be useful to briefly present a history of Purgatory. After that, I will look at particular scenes in Dante's three states of Purgatory, i.e., Ante Purgatory, Purgatory Proper, and the Earthly Paradise. I will discuss the scenes by looking at them through Dante's framework and then through a Levinasian lens. My goal is to show how one can imagine reading Dante through a contemporary interlocutor like Levinas so that it would illuminate Dante better for a modern reader of the *Divine Comedy*.

3.4 PLATO'S CAVE ALLEGORY

Plato's Cave allegory appears in book VII of the *Republic*. In the allegory, Socrates explains a progression of the soul from darkness to the good, and as such, this is a story of transcendence. Before Plato, Greek thought

---

28. Levinas, *Otherwise than Being or Beyond Essence*, 18.
29. Levinas, *Otherwise than Being or Beyond Essence*, 19.

concerned itself with the immanent. Even Greek Gods shared the same cosmological stage as humans. Starting with Plato, ultimate truth is situated in a place beyond the immanent. In the allegory, Plato posits three realms. The first realm is the realm of the sensible, the second is the realm of the intelligible, and the third is a realm of the good beyond being. Socrates asks his audience to imagine humans who for all their lives are chained with fetters around their neck in a subterranean cavern. A fire burns behind them and in the pale enclosure diffused sunlight creeps in. The prisoners can see shadows cast on the cavern wall, but they cannot see the real objects behind them that cast the shadows. The prisoners believe that the shadows they see on the wall are the real objects. When the objects issue a sound, the prisoners believe that the shadows on the wall make that sound. Now if a prisoner was allowed to stand up and turn to see the objects behind them, they would be blinded by the diffused light and unable to discern the real objects. If someone told the prisoners that the real objects were the ones behind them, rather than the shadows on the wall, the prisoners would object. If someone allowed the prisoner outside to look at the sun, the same thing would happen. The prisoners would be blinded by its luminosity.

But with habituation, they would gradually be able to make out forms. At first, they might only be able to look at the sky at night and see the distant stars above them. Or they may only be able to see animals and plants from their reflections in the water, or maybe shadows cast by the sun. Eventually, they would be able to look at the sun. Plato tells us:

> The last thing to be seen is the idea of good, and that when seen it must need point us to the conclusion that this is indeed the cause for all things of all that is right and beautiful, giving birth in the visible world to light, and the author of light and itself in the intelligible world being the authentic source of truth and reason.[30]

A critical aspect of the good is that it generates and sustains life. While the lower two realms are static, the good is productive. As the source of light for all things, the sun provides for the lower realm's generation and sustenance. In a brief but important statement, Socrates adds that while the sensible and the intelligible life forms receive their existence and essence from the good, "the good itself is not essence but still transcends essence in dignity and surpassing power."[31] Hence, Plato alludes to a place that is beyond be-

---

30. Plato, *Republic* 517c.
31. Plato, *Republic* 509b.

ing where the good resides. Sarah Allen interprets Plato's reference to a good beyond being as a source of intelligibility beyond human knowledge.[32] In Plato, therefore, it is possible to distinguish three realms: the sensible realm, the intelligible realm, and the realm beyond being wherein the good resides. What can we make of this allegory and how can we interpret it?

Plato's allegory is a comment on how limited our knowledge is within our earthly existence. In the cave, i.e., the unenlightened existence of our day-to-day lives, the forms that we see are just copies of an original. Those in the cave are deluded. Some scholars believe that Orphic mythology, where rebellious daemons were cast into a dark lower realm for their disobedience, influenced Plato.[33] Putting the Orphic influence aside, the cavernous lower state is the sensible realm wherein the body resides in the darkness of the cave. Humans are subjected to ignorance in their embodied state. What we see are only reflections and not the real. The copies of the ideal forms are fleeting and subject to change over time. Our senses, tied to the body, trap the soul. In order to acquire knowledge, one receives the light and eventually contemplates the ideal forms. According to Plato, the soul has the innate ability to contemplate the good, but it must be educated and trained "to endure the contemplation of essence."[34]

Plato associates the training of the soul with the acquisition of knowledge accumulated through practice. The person who can see the good attains knowledge that others do not have. The knowledge of the good is a form of transcendence. Yet, Plato would not allow the enlightened to stay in that contemplative ecstasy forever. They must return and help others see the truth. For Plato, wise rulers would select who could undergo this training to produce future rulers. Through knowledge, they accumulate wealth—not the wealth of gold, but wealth that makes for happiness. Those who are to be educated must be virtuous. Plato states that those selected must have "bravery and loftiness of soul and all the parts of virtue, we must

---

32. Allen, *Philosophical Sense of Transcendence*. Allen states that one only finds the idea of a "good beyond being" in Plato's *Republic*. But she does mention that there are a group of scholars who take Plato seriously on this idea.

33. The theory is that the source for Plato's cave allegory came from Orphic lure exemplified by Empedocles's poem *Purifications*. The poem describes how the victorious daemons punished the insurrectionist daemons for their involvement with sedition and banished them to a lower realm. The victors required the revolutionary daemons to undergo a lengthy process of purification for thirty thousand seasons before they could ascend back to a divine state. For more information, see Picot and Berg, "Lions and Promoi."

34. Plato, *Republic* 518c.

especially be on guard to distinguish the baseborn from the trueborn."[35] It is no surprise that Plato chooses philosophers as the most capable of learning and acquiring the right virtues for leadership. The allegory shows that one can awaken from the illusion of false images. A person can move from unconscious ignorance to conscious knowledge. In unconscious ignorance, the person lives bound to their deprived and limited sensory experience. But once they can liberate themselves from their own senses and experience the light of truth, they can get a glimpse of true knowledge.

3.5 PLATO'S INFLUENCE ON NEOPLATONIC CHRISTIANITY AND DANTE'S STATES OF BEING

Neoplatonic Christianity adopted and adapted many of Plato's ideas. Its viewpoint is that humans in this world, just like people in the cave, can exist in a state of ignorance. However, for Christians, ignorance is a result of original sin. In the Christian mystical tradition, the classical three stages of transformation that the person must go through in the earthly realm are the purgative, the illuminative, and the unitive.[36] The stages are not always interpreted as being sequential, but the general idea is that one must be purified from sin in order to see the light. A person acquires knowledge as they reform their lives. As one becomes more acclimated to the light, or in Christian terms, as one is purified from sin, one is better able to see the light and receive intimations of the divine. As in Plato, complete union with God could not happen on the earthly plane because God transcends the sensible world. Union happens in the realm beyond being. Still, in the Christian unitive stage, one maintains one's individuality. Of course, differences prevail between Christianity and Platonic thought as expressed in the cave allegory. In Plato, the body is a hindrance to the soul. The weight of the body burdens the soul, and it struggles to free itself from the darkness of the cave. In Plato, one frees oneself through knowledge of the good. Yet in Christianity, the good comes into the world incarnate in the form of Christ. The Word of God is embodied in the world, and it is he who has both knowledge and wisdom. Augustine writes that Christ as the Word of God

> possesses the treasures of wisdom and knowledge. . . . Christ is our knowledge, and the same Christ is our wisdom. He Himself

---

35. Plato, *Republic* 536a.
36. Garrigou-Lagrange, *Three Ways of the Spiritual Life*.

> implants in us faith concerning temporal things. He Himself shows forth the truth concerning eternal things. Through Him we reach on to Himself: we stretch [rise] through knowledge to wisdom.[37]

Christ incarnate is the source of knowledge and wisdom. He allows humans to see past the false images found in Plato's cave. He is the light that draws humans out of the cave. He is the one who enables beings to rise from knowledge to wisdom. One moves from recognizing objects outside of the cave to seeing beyond the heavenly canopy to the true source of good, which is God located beyond being. Yet not everyone completely finishes the purgative stage while they are alive. As such, the faith of the church provides a place for that purgation to take place.

Through his influence on Christian theology, Plato also influenced Dante's conception of Purgatory.[38] Dante divides Purgatory into three realms. Ante Purgatory is at the lowest level of Purgatory's mountain. It is a state for those who were late in repenting or barely repentant at the time of death or for someone whom the church had excommunicated. The first eight canti in *Purgatorio* are set in Ante Purgatory. The characteristics of the first people we meet in this state are that they are consumed by either indolence or distraction. From a Platonic perspective, one might say that they understand that the shadows on the cavern wall are not images of the real, but they are not yet ready to embrace the light outside of the cavern. Ultimately, in canto IX Dante makes the transition from Ante Purgatory to Purgatory Proper. When he wakes at the doorstep of Purgatory Proper, he experiences great anxiety. From a Platonic perspective, Dante's fear is the overwhelming encounter with the blinding light outside of the cave. Yet as Virgil comforts him, he becomes acclimated to it and his fear lessens.

> Like when a man who comes to see the truth
> When he has been in doubt and now is reassured,
> Confidence replacing what in him was fear. (*Purg.* IX, 64–66)

Dante has become habituated to his new surroundings. The light and Virgil's assurance persuade him that what he sees are the true forms. He is becoming educated as he ascends from a lower level to a higher one.

37. Augustine, "On the Holy Trinity" 13.19.24.

38. Lafferty, "Philosophy of Dante." Lafferty notes that Plato's influence on Dante was chiefly indirect. Plato's *Republic* had not been translated during Dante's lifetime and Dante did not know Greek. Therefore, Dante's knowledge of the *Republic* was through intermediaries. It is clear, however, that Dante had read the *Timaeus* since it is referenced in *Paradiso* 4.49.

Dante in Conversation with Contemporary Theorists

At the gate of Purgatory Proper, an angel greets Dante. His sword reflects light so bright that Dante needs to avert his eyes (*Purg.* IX, 82–84). Dante needs to climb three steps to get through the gate.[39] The first step is made of marble which is so clear that his "image was reflected in true likeness" (*Purg.* IX, 96). One can equate Dante's first step to Plato's realm of intelligibility. The first step is where one begins to see the true forms. The second step for Dante is darker. It is purple and cracked. The traditional explanation of this step is the acknowledgment by Dante that he is a sinner who in crossing this step recognizes his broken state. In the Platonic framework, the second step is where the captive out of the cave realizes that the cavernous images were false. The third step that Dante crosses is made of porphyry and is flaming red like blood. The explanation for this step is that it is reminiscent of the sacrifice of Jesus.[40] In the third step, Dante understands Jesus's love for all of humankind when he underwent his great passion. In the Platonic framework, one can say that Christ's salvific mission is analogous with Plato's requirement that the truth seeker cannot remain in ecstasy contemplating the ideal forms. Rather, the person must make a sacrifice and return to the cave to help educate others. Taken together these three steps mark a transition that allows Dante to move from Ante Purgatory into Purgatory Proper. While Dante's movement from Ante Purgatory into Purgatory Proper has Platonic elements, Plato's idea of ascension differs from Dante's idea of ascension. Dante's passing through the portal between Ante Purgatory and Purgatory Proper is the beginning of the ladder that will strip away ego and pride. That is necessary so that one can attain the state of humility required to begin the journey of purification. Since pride is the worse sin, it is the first tier in Purgatory Proper. The virtue of humility is an antidote to overcome the deadly sin of pride. In the Platonic framework, humility is not the focus as one rises. Rather, it is knowledge of the true forms. While Plato does discuss the need for virtue for those who are to rule, it is not as pronounced as what Dante emphasizes for a person to ascend. Dante departs from Plato in this matter. Since Plato and Christianity were influences on Levinas, it is necessary to see how Levinas takes those models and modifies them for his own purposes. What can we

---

39. Hollander's notes explain the traditional interpretation of these three steps. See Dante Alighieri, *Purgatorio*, 201–3.

40. Moore, *Studies in Dante*, 47. Moore claims that Dante changes the normal scholastic idea of the purgative process, which is Contrition, Confession, and Satisfaction—in that order. Instead, Dante's three steps would suggest Confession, Contrition, and Love.

make of the similarities and differences among the states of being for Plato, Christianity, Dante and the modes of being for Levinas?

Where Plato's states of being consist of the sensible, the intelligible, and the good beyond being, and Dante's states of being are Hell, Purgatory, and Heaven, Levinas, by contrast, will divide his modes of being into the *il y a*, hypostasis and Interiority and Economy. The first phase in the model I am describing would be Levinas's *il y a*, vs. Plato's Cave vs. Dante's Hell.

3.6 PLATO'S INFLUENCE ON LEVINAS'S MODES OF BEING AND ENCOUNTER WITH THE OTHER

3.6.1 Levinas's il y a

In philosophical terms, the *il y a* refers to existence without existents or being without beings. Levinas tries to explain the difficulty of this concept by using figurative language. Sometimes he describes it in ominous and anonymous terms. In *Totality and Infinity*, he refers to it as an "absurd rumbling" or as an "anarchy."[41] In *Otherwise than Being*, he describes it as "the overflowing of sense from nonsense."[42] In *Existence and Existents* he says, "Rather than to a God, the notion of the *there is* leads us to the absence of God, the absence of any being. Primitive men live before all Revelation, before the light comes."[43] Levinas often uses darkness to characterize the *il y a*. His use of religious language (e.g., "before all Revelation," "before the light comes") expresses the *il y a* as a mode devoid of hope. The darkness expressed by the *il y a* is different from the darkness of Plato's cave. In Plato's cave, beings exist, and shadow images appear. In the *il y a*, however, there are no beings, there are no shadows; it is without life. The *il y a* is different from the Christian idea of hell. Even though in hell darkness prevails, one encounters beings and images. Another significant difference is that unlike the *il y a*, beings are punished. Yet, the *il y a* provokes a fear that is analogous to the Christian idea of hell. In day-to-day earthly existence expressed by Levinas and Christianity, beings experience an anterior anxiety that resides in their unconscious memories. The term anterior anxiety refers to an ontological mode without existents. In the Levinasian model, beings fear that they can be absorbed into the dark, infinite anonymity of

---

41. See Levinas, *Totality and Infinity*, 261, 281.
42. Levinas, *Otherwise than Being or Beyond Essence*, 164.
43. Levinas, *Existence and Existents*, 61.

the *il y a*. For Christians, humans fear that after death they could be consigned to the everlasting punishment of hell. The "punishment" for beings who are absorbed into the *il y a* is nonexistence. But the *il y a* is not a place one goes to for punishment after death. In fact, Levinas describes the *il y a* as a mode with the impossibility of death—since it is without beings. The *il y a* has some aspects of the Platonic cave and some of the Christian hell. If we acknowledge the Orphic influence on Plato, the cave is a punishment for those daemons who defied the deities. In the *Divine Comedy*, Dante explains that when God cast Satan out of heaven, his fall was so cataclysmic that it created a hole in the earth where Satan resides in the lowest depths of the *Inferno*'s darkness. One of the differences among Christian hell, Plato's Cave, and Levinas's *il y a*, is that in Christian hell one has no escape. Beings are consigned to hell for eternity. In Plato's allegory, the inhabitants of the cave have the capability of escaping from their fetters and entering into the intelligible world. In the Levinasian model, beings escape the *il y a* through the process of hypostasis.

3.6.2 Levinas's Hypostasis

Levinas describes hypostasis as when an "anonymous being loses its *there is* [*il y a*] status."[44] From the *il y a*, a subject finds itself out of anonymity. Levinas describes it as "a rip in the infinite beginningless and endless fabric of existing."[45] Through hypostasis, a being escapes from anonymous being and totality. Drew Dalton states that the hypostatic act is "the demarcation of being as a whole into separate and singular particular beings, beings who do not derive their meaning from their conjugation of universal being but derive their meaning from themselves."[46] Hypostasis from the darkness of the *il y a* can be compared to the light experienced by a being who emerges from Plato's Cave. Likewise, it can be compared to Dante's escape out of hell in the last canto of the *Inferno*. Dante describes the climb of the passageway of hell "to find again the world of light" (*Inf.* XXXIV, 134). Virgil and Dante go through a circular opening that leads out of hell. Dante concludes the *Inferno* with the last line, "Then we came forth, to see again the stars" (*Inf.* XXXIV, 139). Dante feels tremendous relief from exiting hell. For Levinas, one finds the opposite. The being who appears through hypostasis incurs

---

44. Levinas, *Existence and Existents*, 83.
45. Levinas, *Time and the Other*, 52.
46. Dalton, *Longing for the Other*, 183.

anxiety about being swept back into the *il y a*. Yet in both cases, Levinas and Dante would describe the *il y a* and hell as terrifying realms. In Plato's cave, one would not necessarily describe the realm as evil. Rather, it is a place of ignorance. It is true that as in hell beings are enchained without the capability of moving. Still, one would not say that the primary purpose of the cave is punishment—unless of course, we want to invoke the idea of Plato's Orphic influence. However, if we bracket the Orphic influence, the cave is an unfortunate place for beings who have not yet learned the true nature of the forms. Another difference between hypostasis, Plato's Cave, and Christianity's hell is that the latter two contain beings. Additionally, in hell, beings are there because they did not live ethical lives. The *il y a* is not a destination determined by an individual's past ethical life in the world. Likewise, Plato's cave, sans Orphic influence, is not determined by a being's past ethical behavior. For Levinas, hypostasis does not come from the past. He describes hypostasis as a function of the present. It does not have a heritage. Rather "it is something that comes from itself. One cannot come from oneself otherwise than by receiving nothing from the past."[47] Coming into being is coming into the present from nonbeing. Nonbeing does not have a heritage for a being.

3.6.3 Levinas's Interiority and Economy

3.6.3.1 *Levinas's Stuckness with Oneself*

Levinas maintains that as a result of hypostasis, the self finds itself ineluctably with itself. He describes this existing as "closed up . . . a monad and a solitude."[48] Roger Burggraeve describes the situation as how when a being comes into existence the self contracts with itself and "in so doing, the 'I' poses itself under being such that it becomes mine."[49] Now although the I tries to take possession of the self, it does not have complete freedom. Levinas says the freedom it does have "does not save me from the definitive character of my very existence, from the fact that I am forever stuck with myself."[50] Levinas describes the paradoxical nature of the existent as the self's enfolding back into itself. The self experiences a form of suffering as

---

47. Levinas, *Time and the Other*, 53.
48. Levinas, *Time and the Other*, 52.
49. Burggraeve, *Proximity with the Other*, 11.
50. Levinas, *Existence and Existents*, 84.

a result of this self-enfolding because "the price paid for the existent's position lies in the very fact that it cannot detach itself from itself."[51] The self experiences a kind of eternal return that keeps it in a recurring loop. But Levinas does prescribe a solution to this impasse by saying that "it is necessary to begin with the concrete relationship between an I and a world."[52] The subject must have a relationship with something exterior to itself. As a result of hypostasis, the self not only finds itself with itself but also finds itself in the world. Levinas's description of this experience is:

> By connecting solitude to the subject's materiality—materiality being its enchainment to itself—we can understand in what sense the world and our existence in the world constitute a fundamental advance of the subject in overcoming the weight that it is to itself ... in loosening the bond between the self and the ego.[53]

It is this recognition of being in the world that allows the person to move out of "enchainment." Levinas's language of being shackled in a confining realm of existence is similar to Plato's Cave allegory where those in the caves are in fetters. They are in the lower realm of the sensate and bound to it without freedom. When they initially come out into the light, they are blinded, with little capacity to understand what is true. It is a form of stuckness until they can become habituated to the realm of intelligibility. In the Dantean model, imprisonment is the constitution of hell where most of the inhabitants are fixed in place with little capacity to move. In Ante Purgatory, beings have more freedom, but stuckness persists. Ante Purgatory is a place where individuals wait to enter Purgatory Proper. Because they lived sinful lives and repented only at the moment of death, Dante keeps them out of Purgatory Proper. Beings can do nothing to improve their situation. They must wait until their souls are sufficiently purified before they can enter Purgatory Proper. In fact, when Dante hurries along in Ante Purgatory, the beings there question his quick movement. Because they take him for one of their own, they initially believe that he is wasting his time in his haste to advance. The stuckness that the inhabitants of Ante Purgatory experience is similar to the stuckness that Levinas describes as part of the newly hypostatized subject. However, in the Levinasian formulation, the subject does have agency in moving out of its stuckness by becoming involved with the world.

51. Levinas, *Time and the Other*, 55.
52. Levinas, *Totality and Infinity*, 37.
53. Levinas, *Time and the Other*, 62.

3.6.3.2 Levinas's Being in the World

Being in the world has two primary characteristics. The first is increasing freedom and light, which results in a form of secular salvation for the self. The second is enjoyment through an engagement in the sensate world that results in a form of affective knowledge for the subject. Levinas states that the light of the material world is not the ultimate transcendent experience, but it does allow the subject to forget the horror of the *il y a*.[54] Being in the world is where the person utilizes the material objects of the world to constitute the self's existence. Levinas says, "In everyday existence, in the world, the material structure of the subject is to a certain extent overcome."[55] By that, he means that a space is created that loosens the stuckness with the self and the ego. Levinas describes the involvement of the subject's action in the world as on an equal footing "with the struggle for salvation because it [economic activity] is founded in the very dialectic of hypostasis through which the first freedom is constituted."[56] The first freedom for Levinas is breaking free from stuckness with the self. Levinas sees the material world as a place of light for the subject. Levinas argues that for the subject to separate from itself, "light is the requisite for such a possibility."[57] One can make an analogy to Plato's Cave allegory where the prisoner makes a transition to the light of the intelligible world outside the cave. Once outside, they have the freedom to see the forms in the natural light. It is not the ideal form in Plato's transcendental realm. But it is a first step towards the ideal form. From a Dantean model, Levinas's suggestion that freedom from the self is the first step towards salvation is analogous to the soul in Purgatory Proper. Unlike Ante Purgatory, the being is no longer stuck, and it wishes to undergo the required purification behavior to achieve salvation.

For Levinas, being in the world is enjoyment, i.e., the enjoyment of corporeal existence. It is being in the material earthly elements. One feels the rain on one's shoulders, the heat of the sun on one's back, and the earth beneath one's feet. Levinas says that "to-be-in-the-element" means that one experiences "an incessant movement of afflux without respite."[58] This

---

54. Levinas asserts that the light does not completely drive out the darkness of the *il y a*, but it does allow one a temporary diversion from its presence. See Levinas, *Totality and Infinity*, 190.

55. Levinas, *Time and the Other*, 62.

56. Levinas, *Time and the Other*, 61–62.

57. Levinas, *Time and the Other*, 63.

58. Levinas, *Totality and Infinity*, 135.

is what he designates as enjoyment. Levinas sees living "not as a bare existence" but rather as nourishment and that the labor required to become nourished is how we occupy life, it is that "which 'entertain[s]' it, of which it is enjoyment."[59] While a being in the world desires the objects they find in the corporeal world, utilization of those objects is not the same as Plato's idea of desire as a lack of something. Levinas will disagree with Plato's assumption that being affected by the earthly elements is on a lower plane than intellectual pursuits. For Levinas, "'earthly nourishments' is the first morality, the first abnegation. It is not the last, but one must pass through it."[60] Plato, on the other hand, would consider being in the world as a lesser realm than the world of intelligibility. The material elements are less refined than the higher forms of his idealist ontological structure. For Levinas, being in the world has a purpose, and that purpose is to deliver us from ourselves. In Levinas's philosophy, the self utilizes the world and its elements to create a space for itself. The idea of living as enjoyment is somewhat counter to the Christian idea of Purgatory as a place of purification. Yet, as Levinas has stated, being in the world is a salvation because it leads to freedom. In Purgatory Proper, Dante's characters voluntarily take on the discipline of purification because that purification will lead to salvation.

Levinas's being in the elements is similar to Plato's being in a sensate world. Yet Levinas's evaluation of the sensate world is different from Plato's. For Plato, the sensate world is a world lower than the intelligible world. In Plato's world, one is enchained to a faulty representation of forms compared to the intelligible world. Levinas would agree with Plato that the sensate world is different from thought:

> The sensibility that we are describing starting with enjoyment of the element does not belong to the order of thought but to that of sentiment, that is, the affectivity wherein the egoism of the I pulsates. One does not know, one lives sensible qualities: the green of these leaves, the red of this sunset. Objects content me in their finitude without appearing to me on a ground of infinity.[61]

For Levinas, being in the world is being in the realm of affectivity. The world of affectivity is not infinite. Levinas describes the elemental as that which stops the infinite and blocks it from thought.[62] Thus Levinas's el-

59. Levinas, *Time and the Other*, 111.
60. Levinas, *Time and the Other*, 64.
61. Levinas, *Totality and Infinity*, 135.
62. Levinas, *Totality and Infinity*, 132.

emental is analogous to Plato's sensible world but in a more benign manner. And even though the elemental is not the infinite, the sensible world is not inferior knowledge. One need not struggle to understand the sensible world. Sensibility is naïve consciousness, and by naïve Levinas means acting in a childlike way, such as how a child might enjoy the beauty of a flower without needing to know how it is constituted. To continue with the child metaphor, enjoyment is a step in which a child can separate itself from its parents. The child in its enjoyment of a flower has an experience of its own and as such establishes a separation from its parents. In like manner, enjoyment for Levinas is the way for the self to separate from the self. Thus, enjoyment as being-in-the-element is for Levinas a mode somewhere like Plato's cave and emergence from the cave. One is grounded in the sensible world but without the oppression that constitutes the world of the cave. One is outside of the cave, but without the benefit of knowledge in Plato's intelligible sphere. Perhaps, one can think of the fresh experience of one emerging from the cave, still possessed by the senses, but prior to the incorporation of knowledge. From a Platonic perspective, we might imagine the captive who emerges from the cave, sees the light for the first time and experiences a sensibility of wonderment upon looking at the things of the world. It is prior to the acquisition of knowledge, i.e., a step preceding it. From a theological point of view, one might compare Levinas's description of the self's enjoyment to a Christian pre-lapsarian state where Adam and Eve enjoyed creation in a child-like and naïve manner. The difference between the Genesis story and Levinas's account of the self's creation is that in the former an active divine agent creates humans ex nihilo. In Levinas's philosophy, he does not ascribe a divine agent to the self's hypostasis into being. In the *Divine Comedy*, we will see that Dante's emergence from hell and his journey to Purgatory imagines a similar experience of enjoyment. Dante senses a light that breaks through the horizon, a light that he had never seen in hell. Dante's experience is contentment for leaving behind hell's infernal darkness. He has a naive hope that his life will become transformed. Still, he does not yet know what he will experience on the other side when he reaches the mountain of Purgatory.

3.6.3.3 *Levinas's Dwelling and the Feminine*

An additional mode for Levinas within the realm of Interiority and Economy is the Dwelling and the Feminine. While the subject as a being in the elements experiences enjoyment, that experience provides little safety for the subject. The elements press up against the subject with scant protection for itself. Levinas describes the self in the elements as a mode of paganism. The elements are "faceless gods, impersonal gods to whom one does not speak."[63] The faceless gods are impersonal elemental forces like the wind, the sky, the sea. They do not have meaning. The elements are opposed to the Other that comes in transcendence. To protect oneself from the elements, the subject builds a dwelling. The subject seeks a refuge from the world where it can recollect after labor. The way of making the dwelling is through labor. The importance of labor is that the subject can conform the elements and master them. In the act of labor, the subject can remove the elements of their anonymity. Labor "stills the anonymous rustling of the there is."[64] Labor takes the elements and removes them from the *il y a*. Labor uses the elements as a protective shield from the impersonal anonymous mode of being. The dwelling becomes concretized in a work of separation. In his section on "Interiority and Economy" in *Totality and Infinity*, Levinas uses the word "Interiority" to mean the dwelling. Levinas states, "Interiority [is] concretely accomplished by the home."[65] In the dwelling, the person can pull back from the elements. If we can compare this to the cave allegory, the home is the subject coming out of the cave and familiarizing himself with his environment. This is a mode where the subject is still involved in the sensate world. Their faculties have not been sharpened and they have barely reached a semblance of intellection. They have begun to remove themselves from the darkness and have constructed a dwelling that will allow them to recollect. The recollection is essential for them for the experience of transcendence. In the Dantean model, Virgil is a guide and a calming influence in Dante's life. He is the wise pagan of rationality. He helps Dante become comfortable in the dwellings that Dante inhabits. Virgil is a gentle force who provides a welcome to Dante. He is not the transcendent other. He resembles the other who enables Dante to feel comfortable in his habitation. The next Other is Beatrice, whom Dante meets in Purgatory. For Dante, the ultimate Other is Godself. In his *Summa Theologica*, Aquinas utilizes some of the same light imagery as Levinas and Plato and also talks about an inward movement:

---

63. Levinas, *Totality and Infinity*, 142.
64. Levinas, *Totality and Infinity*, 160.
65. Levinas, *Totality and Infinity*, 155.

> Hence Dionysius says (*Div. Nom.* iv) that "God turns all to Himself." But He directs righteous men to Himself as to a special end, which they seek, and to which they wish to cling, according to Ps 72:28, "It is good for Me to adhere to my God." And that they are "turned" to God can only spring from God's having "turned" them. Now to prepare oneself for grace is, as it were, to be turned to God; just as, whoever has his eyes turned away from the light of the sun, prepares himself to receive the sun's light, by turning his eyes towards the sun. Hence it is clear that man cannot prepare himself to receive the light of grace except by the gratuitous help of God moving him inwardly.[66]

Unlike Aquinas's inward theological turning, in the Levinasian model moving inwardly is an essentially secular function. It creates a separation between the self and the elements. Moving inwardly is one of the steps required to maintain separation. Thus separation is necessary not only to keep the self separated from the *il y a* but also to prepare for the welcome of the other. Levinas associates the dwelling with a gentleness and an intimacy with a someone, i.e., the other. Yet, it is not that the other requires the dwelling before it can appear. Rather it is the feminine Other that is the condition for the dwelling. Levinas maintains that "the woman is the condition for recollection, the interiority of the Home and inhabitation."[67] Levinas associates intimacy with a someone as intimacy with the feminine. Although many scholars have written about Levinas's use of gendered language, his association of the feminine as the Other remains problematical.[68] Yet, to elaborate on all the critiques about Levinas's use of the feminine would be beyond the scope of this work. One interpretation to account for the feminine Other is that the other is an alterity that Levinas uses so that he can maintain the requirement of separation—even in the encounter beyond being with the erotic. The erotic is necessary for fecundity. But even in the generative nature of love, the self and the Other remain separate and never one totality. Speaking of the feminine, Levinas praises Dante for the "exceptional position of the feminine in the economy of being" and says, "I willingly refer [the reader] to the great themes of Goethe or Dante, to

---

66. Aquinas, *ST* I–II, 109.6.4.ad.
67. Levinas, *Totality and Infinity*, 155.
68. Simone de Beauvoir critiqued Levinas in her 1949 work, *The Second Sex*, for labeling the female as the Other and the male as the subject. For a more recent collection of essays, see Chanter, *Feminist Interpretations of Emmanuel Levinas*.

Beatrice."⁶⁹ Levinas's reference to Dante is apt because Dante's journey was spurred by the actions of three women, as recounted by Virgil in *Inferno* 2. *Purgatorio* culminates with the encounter with the feminine in the form of Beatrice. In fact, *Purgatorio*'s subtitle could be the title of Charles S. Singleton's text *Journey to Beatrice*.⁷⁰

3.6.4 Levinas's Encounter with the Other

Singleton calls Dante's movement towards Beatrice in *Purgatorio* a process of justification.⁷¹ By that, he means the movement of Dante in *Purgatorio* is a movement towards justice. In the process of justification, souls can transform themselves. In *Purgatorio* X, Dante asks his readers:

> Do you not see that we are born as worms,
> Though able to transform into angelic butterflies
> That unimpeded soar to justice? (*Purg*. X, 124–26)

Singleton asks rhetorically where in the *Divine Comedy* does Dante turn from worm to butterfly?⁷² His answer is when Dante passes from Virgil to Beatrice. It is not possible, however, to use Singleton's worm to butterfly metaphor when one speaks of Levinas's encounter with the other. The encounter with the Other for Levinas is not a developmental stage of progress. For Levinas, the self does not go on a journey to seek out the Other. Rather, as Drew Dalton mentions, "For Levinas, the Other fundamentally precedes the I."⁷³ The Other is always and already anterior to the self. The self's encounter with the face of the Other is according to Levinas "a movement that proceeds from the other."⁷⁴ Therefore, the encounter with the Levinasian other is not a prize at the end of a hero's journey. Rather, the encounter with the Other is a precondition for the very ground of the subject's being.⁷⁵ Likewise, the encounter with the infinity of the other is not like an encounter by a subject with an object. Levinas states that the encounter with the other is a relationship which the subject

---

69. Levinas, *Time and the Other*, 86.
70. Singleton, *Journey to Beatrice*.
71. See Singleton, *Journey to Beatrice*, 57–71.
72. Singleton, *Journey to Beatrice*, 61.
73. Dalton, *Longing for the Other*, 159.
74. Levinas, *Totality and Infinity*, 196.
75. I am grateful to Professor Drew Dalton for his assistance on this point.

can therefore not contain. . . . It is not equivalent to the distance between a subject and an object. An object, we know, is integrated into the identity of the same; the I makes of it its theme, and then its property, its booty, its prey or its victim.

Thus the encounter with the other is something that the subject cannot assimilate into itself. While the subject may have desire for the Other, the subject's desire is a desire without satisfaction because as Levinas states, it is a desire which "precisely, *understands* [*entend*] the remoteness, the alterity, and the exteriority of the other."[76] Levinas describes the alterity and exteriority of the other as "the very dimension of height [that] is opened up by metaphysical Desire."[77] The description of the Other as that which comes from height is further explicated by Levinas when he describes metaphysical movement as a combination of transcendent and transcendence or a neologism that he borrows from Jean Wahl, a movement of transascendence.[78] An encounter with the Other is defined by Levinas as judgment. The judgment that Levinas means is not an impersonal judgment or a verdict that comes "implacably out of universal principles."[79] This is because it would silence an apology from the subject who is under judgment. For Levinas, the act of judgment summons the subject to respond. How does Levinas's idea of an encounter with the other compare with Dante's encounter with Beatrice in Purgatory Proper?

In Levinasian terms, Beatrice is the Other who comes to Dante from a great height. The relationship between Dante and Beatrice is an asymmetrical relationship. This is not to discount Virgil's moral assistance to Dante. Virgil does help Dante's journey towards justice. He advises Dante all along the way throughout hell and purgatory. But because he is a pagan, Virgil is limited in how far he can assist Dante. Within the Platonic states of being (i.e., sensibility, intelligibility, and good beyond being), Virgil can help Dante through the first two realms. His efficacy, however, cannot get

---

76. Levinas, *Totality and Infinity*, 34.

77. Levinas, *Totality and Infinity*, 34. In a footnote to the passage above, Levinas quotes Plato, *Republic* 529b: "In my opinion, that knowledge only which is being and of the unseen can make the soul look upwards." In the reference to Plato's *Republic*, Plato is discussing the necessity of studying astronomy. The discussion refers to the need to study not just the material heavenly bodies, i.e., the things of sense, but what admits of true knowledge.

78. Levinas, *Totality and Infinity*, 35. In a footnote for this term, Levinas refers to Jean Whal's text *Existence humaine et transcendance*.

79. Levinas, *Totality and Infinity*, 244.

him beyond those two states. Beatrice is the person who helps lift Dante into the good beyond being. She is not the good beyond being. Dante does not experience that until the last moments of the *Divine Comedy* when he encounters God as the infinite. Still, Beatrice calls Dante to account and asks him to justify himself.

What is the justification that Dante undergoes in *Purgatorio*? Dante's movement in Purgatory Proper is the stripping away of the seven vices: pride, envy, wrath, sloth, avarice, gluttony, and lust. Dante's movement is from the most serious vice upward through lesser vices. Unlike the ascent in Plato where movement results in knowledge, the movement upwards for Dante is both an intellectual and an ethical movement. Plato's movement results in a person who can rule within Greek society. Plato in the *Republic* asks Glaucon, "Could men who are uneducated and inexperienced in truth ever adequately preside over a state"?[80] The answer of course is no. Still, the educated elite cannot linger in the light. They must return to the cave and educate the ignorant. Similarly, Beatrice encourages Dante to write about his experience after his journey is finished. Likewise, Cacciaguida tells Dante to go back and reveal all. However, Dante and Plato have different primary goals concerning their mission to educate others. Dante's primary goal in the *Divine Comedy* is individual morality while in Plato's cave allegory, the primary goal is to produce not just an educated person but an educated society. However, both are interested in civic society and its reform. In Plato, the educated person must undergo the study of calculations, geometry, astronomy, and dialectics. It is this course that leads to the development of one who is capable of ruling. Thus, the person who has seen the light and gathered the knowledge that he needs must then educate his fellows. The course of studies that Plato lists is a study of knowledge, whereas Dante's course is a study of a much different kind. Virgil directs Dante's study and helps him understand how one becomes a person worthy of being justified. The study that Dante takes up in Purgatory has justification as its end. One must become ethically pure enough to encounter the Other. According to Singleton, Dante's progression to justification encompasses two steps. The first step is "justice according to the Philosophers."[81] The second step is "justice according to the Apostle" (referring to St. Paul). By justice according to the Philosophers, Singleton means that Dante purifies his vices through an ethical correction, and that allows him to live an ordered life.

80. Plato, *Republic* 519c.
81. Singleton, *Journey to Beatrice*, 68.

These vices do not require a belief in a theistic God, and thus Virgil can help him here. However, once Dante moves into the realm beyond Virgil, i.e., justice according to the Apostle, Dante must surrender to Beatrice who acts somewhat like a Levinasian transcendent Other. Levinas says, "The relation with the Other alone introduces a dimension of transcendence, and leads us to a relation totally different from experience in the sensible sense of the term, relative and egoist."[82] For Levinas, a relationship with the Other is beyond the Platonian sensible realm. His use of the term "egoist" indicates his disagreement with Plato about the idea that knowledge alone makes one a better person. In Levinas's encounter with the Other, not only must the subject not be egotistical, but the subject, according to Levinas, should consider itself a hostage. The subject must be responsible and just to the Other. The subject incurs such a responsibility that "the more just I am the more guilty I am."[83] The taking on of responsibility and guilt is counter to what Plato would consider being the work of an educated leader in the *Republic*. Yet the idea of justness, responsibility, and guilt does strike a chord of resonance within Dante. Dante must take responsibility for his sins. He must assume guilt for what he has done in the past. All this is necessary for him to encounter the Beatrice Other, before he can pass into *Paradiso*. In effect, Dante is a hostage to Beatrice. And what he is presenting to Beatrice is a complete sacrifice of himself. Levinas describes the approach to the infinite as an approach to a someone

> who is my contemporary, but, in the trace of illeity, presents himself out of a depth of the past, faces and approaches me. I approach the infinite insofar as I forget myself for my neighbor who looks at me; I forget myself only in breaking the undephasable simultaneity of representation, in existing beyond my death. I approach the infinite by sacrificing myself.[84]

The term illeity that Levinas uses is his own neologism that indicates how the infinite remains detached by a subject whose thought is trying to thematize it. Levinas's approach to infinity can be related to Dante's approach to Beatrice. He presents himself to Beatrice who was his contemporary but now is Other. Dante can only approach Beatrice if he does not bring Beatrice into his awareness through representation. The critique of representation for Levinas means the way that the subject brings the world to

---

82. Levinas, *Totality and Infinity*, 193.
83. Levinas, *Otherwise than Being or Beyond Essence*, 112.
84. Levinas, *Collected Philosophical Papers*, 72.

itself so that the world becomes part of the subject. Levinas explains that "the subject that thinks by representation is a subject that hearkens to its own thought."[85] The error of a subject that thinks by representation is that the subject takes the I of representation and makes it into a universal. The universal aspect of representation is that the subject cannot encounter the particularity of the Other. Levinas's encounter with infinity would need a subject with enough humility to offer itself as a sacrifice. This is what Dante does when he encounters Beatrice. He must humble himself, confess his sins, and transform his life. In Levinasian terms, the transformation happens through the surrender that the subject performs when it encounters the infinite. In Dantean terms, it is the removal of the vices that beset the subject while they were on earth. And that is in fact the nature of Purgatory itself: to purge the sinfulness accumulated from a lifetime of living in a manner that was outside the wishes of the infinite. To understand further the nature of Purgatory, especially during Dante's time period, it will be helpful to provide a brief history of how it came to be in Catholic medieval thought. This will help when I later analyze various scenes in *Purgatorio* through a Levinasian lens.

3.7 HISTORY OF PURGATORY

The beginning of a formal status for Purgatory by the church occurred in 1254. On March 6, 1254, Pope Innocent IV issued a letter to his legate in Cyprus which established Purgatory as a matter of the faith. In Jacques Le Goff's text, *The Birth of Purgatory*, he provides background to the issue that initiated the Innocent's letter. Le Goff's focus in his text was to understand and trace the concept of *purgatorium*.[86] In the letter, Innocent attempts to mediate between the Greek and Latin factions of the Church concerning the fate of souls who were not seriously depraved enough to be banished to hell nor sufficiently pure to be allowed entry into heaven. Innocent allows that there is a middle place where purifying fires can cleanse the dross from souls. Later, in 1274, the church authenticated Purgatory as part of its official doctrine at the Second Council of Lyons.[87] However, before the thirteenth century, Catholic theologians imagined a place like Purgatory. Isabel

---

85. Levinas, *Totality and Infinity*, 126.
86. I am grateful to Professor Arthur Holder for his assistance on this point.
87. Le Goff, *Birth of Purgatory*, 284. Le Goff credits the Second Council of Lyons as the official recognition of the Catholic church on the existence of Purgatory.

Moreira claims that ideas of Purgatory "burst on to the eschatological landscape in the eighth century."[88] Yet Moreira allows that the idea of an afterlife place for purification dates back even before Christianity. Moreira's focus in her text is Christianity and late antiquity. In her text, *Heaven's Purge*, she investigates the writing of early church fathers and how they described a place in the afterlife that could help those souls who either had not sinned egregiously, or if they had, subsequently repented and were absolved from their sins. These souls would be spared from everlasting punishment. But although God will forgive those who are sorry for their sins, forgiveness does not obviate divine justice. In the spiritual economy, one must address a wrong committed. Thus Purgatory is the place of purification. In Purgatory, the soul will do what it should have done when it was among the living.

Of the three Catholic after-life states, Purgatory most resembles natural life, especially from a theological perspective. Purgatory is the afterlife state for fallible and sinful beings. Teodolinda Barolini explains that "the narrative of the second canticle [i.e., *Purgatorio*] is most akin, in its rhythm, to the narrative of life."[89] Barolini goes on to compare the rhythm of the *Purgatorio* narrative to a journey wherein the soul discovers that its true destination is return to God.[90] Yet Purgatory time does possess a different aspect from earthly time. According to medieval church teaching, how much time a being must spend in Purgatory is determined by several factors: the initial state of a person's soul immediately after death, acts of indulgences committed by the person on earth, and prayers for the purgatorial soul by the living. Indulgences could be good works that a person performed during their lifetime. In the spiritual economy, those works would reduce one's time in Purgatory. Likewise, prayers by the living for a soul in Purgatory could cause a reduction of time.

---

88. Moreira, *Heaven's Purge*, 5.

89. Barolini, *Undivine Comedy*, 99.

90. Barolini, *Undivine Comedy*, 99–100. Barolini refers to the text found in *Convivio* 4:12.14–16, wherein Dante describes a pilgrim who is travelling on a road that they have never taken before. They see various buildings that seem like an inn where they can find repose. Yet as they come closer, they find that it is not what they thought. So they must redirect their energy to the future until they find they have come to the beginning of their original nature. That original nature is a state of innocence and where one is in harmony with God.

Augustine in *Confessions* asks God's mercy for his mother. He reminds God that his mother throughout her life practiced mercy and forgave her debtors, he requests from God:

> I beseech thee also to forgive her debts, whatever she contracted during so many years since the water of salvation. Forgive her, O Lord, forgive her, I beseech thee; "enter not into judgment" with her.[91]

In his prayers for his deceased mother, Augustine asks the Lord for forgiveness and mercy rather than justice. He hopes that because his mother was merciful that the Lord will have mercy on her.[92] Augustine was not the only theologian to discuss justice for less egregious sinners. Gregory the Great mostly agreed with Augustine that at the last judgment even slight sins would be punished. He states, "Yet for some slight sins we should believe that there is before the judgment a purgatorial fire."[93] The idea of Purgatory in the period after Gregory becomes less a subject of theology and more an expression of after-life visions. Aaron Y. Gurevich states:

> Between the fourth and the twelfth centuries, theologians did not further investigate the problem of purgatory. It was, however, spontaneously emerging in ideas about the other world which were being outlined in narratives about wandering souls of the temporarily dead in the next world.[94]

When the idea of Purgatory became more established, the requirements for avoiding hell and making it into Purgatory became clearer. For those who were not spotless from sin (the majority of people), penance was a way in which one could avoid hell. After examining earlier theologians like Ambrose, John Chrysostom, and Augustine, the twelfth-century canonist Gratian states, "No one can be cleansed of sin without confession of the mouth and satisfaction of good works, if time is available for such works."[95] The decision that Gratian came to regarding the necessity of a priest to hear oral confession was not without disagreement. Some theologians believed

---

91. Augustine, *Confessions* 9.15.35.

92. Le Goff, *Birth of Purgatory*. Le Goff believes that Augustine's prayer for his mother was sincere but not a treatise on doctrine. In the *City of God* 21.24, Augustine set a limit to how effective prayers for the dead could be. The prayers could have efficacy only for a certain set of admirable sinners.

93. Gregory, *Dialogues* 4.41, quoted in Atwell, "From Augustine to Gregory," 176.

94. Gurevich, "Popular and Scholarly," 72.

95. Gratian quoted in Firey, *New History of Penance*, 223.

that confession to a priest was not necessary if the penitent had sincere contrition for his sins. Except for extraordinary circumstances, however, the doctrinal consensus sided with those who stipulated that only confession to a priest could remit sins. The extraordinary circumstances include the impossibility of confessing to a priest at the time of death. A person could say a perfect act of contrition and that would remove the stain of mortal sin. A perfect act of contrition requires that a person repents through a sincere sorrow for their sins. By contrast, an imperfect act of confession would be one in which the person repents because they are afraid of eternal punishment. Although a person might repent late in life, and maybe even moments before death, sincere contrition of this type is valid. And it is significant in the realm of Ante Purgatory because many of the sinners there had confessed at the time of death without the benefit of a priest hearing their confession.

Aquinas in *Summa Contra Gentiles* talks about the necessity for purification in the afterlife if a soul is not completely purified. He states that after death a judgment takes place, and a soul receives either reward or punishment based on the merits or demerits of their lives on earth. The ultimate reward is the beatific vision. However, in order for the being to unite with God, the soul must be pure. If one dies in a state of mortal sin, then a being has no hope of attaining the eternal reward. If a soul is free from mortal sin, but not completely purged, then one must undergo punishment until their debt is satisfied.

> They must be purged after this life before they achieve the final reward. This purgation, of course, is made by punishments, just as in this life their purgation would have been completed by punishments which satisfy the debt.[96]

Le Goff examines an assortment of texts by Aquinas or by those whom he calls the disciples of Aquinas in *The Birth of Purgatory*. Le Goff argues that Aquinas dealt with Purgatory reluctantly.[97] The ultimate goal for the soul was the beatific vision. Still, Thomas does allow that the living can help the souls in Purgatory. As proof, Aquinas cites 2 Maccabees 12:46 and thereafter comments on it:

---

96. Aquinas, *Summa Contra Gentiles* 4.91.6.
97. Le Goff states that Thomas covered Purgatory because it was obligatory and because it was "'in the syllabus,' not because he thought the issue was a crucial one" (Le Goff, *Birth of Purgatory*, 268). For Thomas, the most key point was the soul's return to God and Purgatory was a short interval in that lengthy process.

> "It is . . . a holy and wholesome thought to pray for the dead that they may be loosed from sins." But this would not be profitable unless it were a help to them. Therefore suffrages of the living profit the dead.[98]

Even today the Catholic Church acknowledges the benefits of prayers from the faithful for the souls in purgatory. The *Catechism of the Catholic Church* states that "through indulgences the faithful can obtain remission of temporal punishment resulting from sin for themselves and also for the souls in Purgatory."[99] Love, according to the church, knows no bounds and can work for the good even if death separates the two people. In *Purgatorio*, many of the characters that Dante meets ask him to have their living relatives pray for them.

In Dante's time, many people imagined Purgatory as a place on earth. Dante, in the *Divine Comedy*, however, imagined purgatory as an island in the southern hemisphere at the antipode to Jerusalem. Dante, the character, spends four days traveling through purgatory: a day in Ante-Purgatory, two days in Purgatory proper, and the last day in the Earthly Paradise. At the start of *Purgatorio*, while Jerusalem is experiencing night, Dante the character is situated at the dawn of Easter Sunday. Dante, of course, wanted to use the concept of Purgatory as a new start where humans could have hope for the future.

One can think of the first canto of *Purgatorio* as an overture to the entire canticle. The overall feeling is a newfound sense of hope. Dante, the character, leaves the darkness of hell behind and anticipates that his journey will be brighter when he reaches Purgatory. From a Levinasian perspective, one might say that the subject is emerging from non-being, out of the anonymity of the *il y a*. As Dante finds himself delivered from *Inferno*, a nascent feeling of hope envelops him, and he extols that hope at the beginning of Canto 1:

> Now I sing the second kingdom,
> there where the soul of man is cleansed,
> made worthy to ascend to Heaven. (*Purg.* I, 4–6)

Dante finds himself metaphorically in a boat sailing through calmer waters, and asks the muse Caliope, the goddess of music and epic poetry, to join him in song. The cause of Dante's elevated feelings is his knowledge that

---

98. Aquinas, *ST* Suppl., 71.2.4.
99. Catholic Church, *Catechism of the Catholic Church*, 1498.

he is putting the extreme suffering of the *Inferno* behind and coming into a realm where he has hope of redemption. Using more symbology, Dante, upon traveling to Purgatory, sees four stars as he looks up into the sky. Dante explains that these are stars "not seen but by those first on earth" (*Purg.* I, 24). Dante scholars have interpreted the four stars to signify the four cardinal virtues of prudence, justice, fortitude, and temperance.[100] The cardinal virtues have a long history beginning with Plato and continuing with the early church fathers through to Dante's medieval era.[101] The four cardinal virtues are virtues upon which all the other virtues hinge. God infuses the virtues in the human person. When God created Adam and Eve, they had these virtues fully infused into their souls. No other humans had these virtues as fully as they did. Therefore, the four stars symbolizing the four cardinal virtues are a portent of what will happen to Dante when he finishes his journey in Purgatory. He will enter into the Earthly Paradise at the peak of the Purgatory mountain and his soul will be restored to an unfallen state prior to original sin. But Dante still needs to start at the lowest level in Purgatory—in the realm of Ante Purgatory.

3.8 LEVINAS AND ANTE PURGATORY

The first realm that Dante reaches from the depths of hell is Ante Purgatory. In *Purgatorio*, the first nine canti take place in Ante Purgatory. Scholars describe Ante Purgatory as a realm for those who are late in repenting. Yet late in repenting does not really capture all of the categories of people who Dante meets there. Most of these sinners lived lives of heresy, indolence, violence, and willful neglect of duty. In Dante's mind, these people did not even qualify for direct entrance into Purgatory Proper. Instead, they must remain outside of Purgatory and spend many years of their afterlife in suspense to atone for their long lives of immorality. The first character in Purgatory that Dante meets is Cato, who gives a sense of the place. Ante Purgatory is at the lowest level of the mountain of Purgatory. Cato describes the dismalness of the place where at its lowest point, hardly any "plant can

---

100. Dante Alighieri, *Purgatorio*, 17. Hollander in his notes explains that "from the earliest commentators: they [the four stars] represent the four moral (or cardinal) virtues: prudence, justice, fortitude, and temperance."

101. For an extensive overview of the history of the cardinal virtues, see Houser, *Cardinal Virtues*. In the introduction to this volume, Houser outlines the development of cardinal virtue theory, from Socrates to Aquinas.

leaf / or endure / without succumbing to the battering waves" (*Purg.* I, 103–5). The description by Cato implies that those who reside there made it only through the most precarious and fortunate manner. Even though Dante is in Purgatory, memories of hell still shake him. He describes the stunned feeling he and Virgil have as they go "along the lonely plain, / like someone who has lost the way" (*Purg.* I, 119). Those haunting memories do not elude him. He states that "I saw and knew the distant trembling of the sea" (*Purg.* I, 116–17). Dante's words paint a tonal picture of what preceded Purgatory with the words "distant" and "trembling." While the memory may be of the past, it still plagues him. That tormented memory symbolized by the trembling sea conjures the *il y a*. Levinas describes it as "where the absence of everything returns as a presence, as the place where the bottom dropped out of everything . . . the murmur of silence."[102] Levinas's description of the *il y a* as where the bottom drops out is like Dante's pervading feeling of being stunned and trying to recover from the trauma of hell. That trauma is reflected by some of the souls in Ante Purgatory as procrastination.

The idea of waiting, of procrastination, is endemic to the afterlives of those who inhabit Ante Purgatory. Dante talks about lingering by the shore "like those who think about the way and in their hearts go on / while still their bodies linger" (*Purg.* II, 10–12). The feeling of dawdling, not taking one's repentance seriously, is echoed by Dante's words. It is similar to what Beatrice will accuse Dante of when she meets him in the Earthly Paradise. It is similar to the state in which Dante found himself at the beginning of the *Divine Comedy*: in the deep dark wood. As Dante is lingering in Ante Purgatory, he sees a boat piloted by an angel. The pilgrims in the boat are singing *In exitu Isräel de Aegypto*, which is the song from Psalm 113 of the Vulgate, a celebration of Israel coming out of Egypt and having God as their sanctuary. After the boat flings the pilgrims onto the shore, they search out Virgil and Dante and ask in earnestness where to find the road that leads up the mountain. However, when they see that Dante is not a shade, but a real person, they crowd around him "as though forgetful of the road to beauty" (*Purg.* II, 75). The pilgrims, who were initially so focused upon finding the road up the mountain, turn forgetful and delay their travel. And Dante prolongs the encounter by introducing the character of Casella, a musician that he knew from the past. Dante asks Casella why it took him so long to get to this place in Ante Purgatory, and Casella answers that his delay was not due to any wrongdoing of the boat pilot even though he waited three

---

102. Levinas, *Time and the Other*, 46.

months on the shore. The implication is that Casella did not deserve to come immediately and was required to wait for the good judgment of the person who decides when they can take a soul to Purgatory Proper. The delay might have been due to the person's lukewarm faith in his earthly life. Indolence marks the character of the inhabitants and is constitutive of Ante Purgatory. Dante prolongs the delay by asking Casella to sing a song which in the past had soothed his soul from sorrow. Casella complies and sings a song from Dante's *Convivio* on the theme of Love. But Cato, who is the authority in this realm of Purgatory, berates Dante and the others. He calls them laggards who need to hurry on with their journey.[103] Cato's rebuke is important because it shows the underlying moral deficiency of the inhabitants in this realm of Ante Purgatory. Robert Hollander says that the rival to Casella's song is the song that the people on the boat sang as they were on their way to Purgatory, i.e., Psalm 113. In that psalm, there is the admonition that God, not false idols, is what will bring people deliverance. Praise should be given to God. He delivers all who trust in him out of their misery because his love is the source of all goodness. Hollander's point is that when one contrasts Psalm 113 with Casella's song of love, it is

> clear that Casella's song cannot be taken as innocently or only slightly inappropriate amusement. It is absolutely the wrong thing, wrought by a Dante who retrospectively berates his previous divagations from Beatrice and from God.[104]

Cato's rebuke is proper, and Dante will more fully understand how he squandered his time in his earthly life chasing after carnal love. Instead, he should have been spending time seeking the one most important Love. Dante conveys the idea of Ante Purgatory as a place for waiting during his encounter with the character of Belacqua in *Purgatorio* IV. Dante has prepared us for the nature of waiting in the earlier part of the canto when he discussed two ways in which one processes time. If we see or hear a "thing" that concentrates our soul, "time passes and we're not aware of it"

---

103. Robert Hollander argues that Cato's rebuke of the crowd is more than just reproving them for wasting time. In the *Convivio*, Dante explains that Lady Philosophy, as influenced by Boethius, assuaged his love for Beatrice. In Purgatory, however, philosophy must give way to theology. Hollander phrases it quite entertainingly, saying, "Boethius's Lady is still considered expert in the affairs of the world, but is specifically replaced by Beatrice, in the dress of Thomist schoolmarm, with respect to things of Heaven" (Hollander, "*Purgatorio* II," 354). In other words, a song about love and Lady Philosophy is inferior to the idea of theological love, i.e., love for God, to whom one aspires in Purgatory.

104. Hollander, "*Purgatorio* II," 356.

(*Purg.* IV, 9). Dante's reference to a thing that concentrates the senses is critical because when one is engaged with the senses, time passes freely. In contrast, however, if one focuses on the passing of time itself, one is bound and not free. The contrast, between one who is engaged and free, and the other who hears time passing and is bound, is an important distinction. It has a bearing on the idea of waiting. Dante's use of the phrase "hears the passing of time" relates to the person who is not engaged but passive. Dante personifies that abstract quality during his first meeting with Belacqua. Before Dante meets Belacqua, he reports seeing people "resting in the shade behind the boulder / as men will settle down in indolence to rest" (*Purg.* IV, 104–5). The indolence of resting as passive is characteristic of Ante Purgatory, and one can read a Levinasian theme into Dante's description of these characters. One can construe their passivity as being enclosed in themselves in their indolence. Perhaps they are still in trauma as a result of newly emerging out of the *il y a*.

Prior to the encounter with Belacqua, Virgil instructs Dante on the nature of their climb up the mountain in Purgatory. Virgil tells Dante that it will be steep in the beginning, but it will become easier, and he will be able to rest as he nears the top. Dante then hears words directed to him that say, "Perhaps / you'll feel the need to sit before then" (*Purg.* IV, 98–99). Dante, the character, tells Virgil, "just look at him. / He shows himself more indolent / than if sloth had been his very sister" (*Purg.* IV, 109–11). Dante's focus is on Belacqua's indolence, and he waits to receive a response from Belacqua. He sarcastically tells Dante that if he is so energetic, then he should commence up the hill. Then later, once Dante realizes with whom he is speaking, Belacqua tells Dante why he is so passive. Belacqua can think of no reason for him to start climbing since he would not be let into Purgatory Proper anyway. He will not be let in until he completes his penance in Ante Purgatory. Those in Ante Purgatory do not have any agency to improve their state. An inhabitant in Purgatory Proper knows that they must work on their penance. But in Ante Purgatory, the inhabitants have no real motivation for movement or working on their penance since they cannot of their own accord gain entrance into Purgatory Proper. Ante Purgatory is a zone in between. Souls are not experiencing the pain of the *Inferno*, and yet their work of purification has not begun. They do not have the insight that will provide them a vision of their ultimate redemption. Walter A. Strauss speaks about Ante Purgatory as a place where "the resignation to long waiting merely conceal[s] the pathos of the soul in idle expectation as it withdraws, unmotivated in its own lethargy."[105] Therefore, Belacqua's initial passivity is understandable in the realm of Ante Purgatory. Since movement within Ante Purgatory cannot get them into Purgatory proper any faster, beings do not rush to get on with the climb. One might make a comparison between the *il y a*, Ante Purgatory, and Purgatory proper. The waiting resembles a subject who is not yet aware that they have, in Levinasian terms, become hypostasized. Their lack of energy appears like a lethargy left over from the *il y a*. They have not yet accustomed themselves to being a full-fledged subject. They are half alive—half immersed in the anonymity and impersonality of the *il y a*, and half born as a subject. Waiting is perhaps a hangover from the timelessness of the *il y a*. Other writers have compared the lethargy of the characters in Ante Purgatory to life on earth. Some modern writers have used the idea of waiting passively for an event to happen in their own texts. Samuel Beckett has a character in his stories named Belacqua Shuah whose life is perpetually in a state of incertitude.[106] Yet, Ante Purgatory has other characteristics that are more than just waiting.

The character flaws of the inhabitants of Ante Purgatory change from the pure indolence of *Purgatorio* I to the more active vices of *Purgatorio* II where Dante presents those who were violent in their earthly lives and or were excommunicated from the church. In *Purgatorio* II, Dante meets Manfred (ca. 1232–1266) who was the illegitimate son of the emperor Frederick II of the House of Hohenstaufen. In 1252 Manfred assumed the kingdom of Sicily. Manfred was at odds with Pope Innocent IV who wanted political power in Italy. Because of their conflict, Manfred was excommunicated by Innocent IV (1243–1254) in 1254. When Pope Alexander IV (1254–1261) succeeded Pope Innocent after his death, Alexander IV excommunicated Manfred when they could not negotiate a settlement regarding restoring Sicily to papal authority. After Alexander IV, Pope Urban IV (1261–1264) tried to negotiate with Manfred again regarding Sicily. Unable to achieve

---

105. Strauss, "Dante's Belacqua and Beckett's Tramps," 251.

106. One example is Beckett's story "Dante and the Lobster" from a collection of his short stories (Beckett, *More Pricks Than Kicks*, 9–22). In the story, Belacqua spends his entire day in self-absorption and indolence. The last lines of the story involve Belacqua's concern about a live lobster that is put to death in a boiling pot. He objects that it should have to end its life that way. His aunt tells him that they feel nothing. Belacqua tries to reassure himself that death will be quick. His last lines in the story are "Well thought Belacqua, it's a quick death, God help us all. It is not." Belacqua's uncertainty is not just about the lobster but also about his own life and the prospect of an endless state of anguish.

a settlement with Manfred, Urban aligned himself with Charles, count of Anjou (1226–1285). Urban persuaded Charles to launch a crusade against Manfred and the Saracens. Urban excommunicated Manfred in 1261. In 1266 the Angevin army killed Manfred at the battle of Benevento. When Dante meets Manfred in *Purgatorio* III, Dante describes him as "blond, handsome and of noble aspect" (*Purg.* III, 106). Manfred fits the bill as a physical example of elite beauty. Yet his body also carries wounds, a cleft on his eyebrows and a wound on his chest. Manfred explains that his body was ripped apart during combat. As he was dying, he asked God to pardon him. He admits that his sins were horrible, but a God of infinite goodness forgave him. He realizes that even though he was repentant at the end of his life, he will need to spend thirty years waiting outside of Purgatory Proper for every year of excommunication.[107]

In *Purgatorio* V, Dante meets many violent sinners. As Dante is walking with Virgil in Ante Purgatory, he meets a group of sinners who want to speak with Dante. An anonymous soul tells Dante and Virgil about their spiritual condition.

> Sinners to the final hour,
> We were all at the point of violent death
> When a light from Heaven brought us understanding
>
> so that, repenting and forgiving,
> we parted from our lives at peace with God,
> who with desire to see Him wrings our hearts. (*Purg.* V, 52–57)

The sinners that we meet not only died a violent death but were engaged in sinful activities themselves. In *Purgatorio* VI, Dante changes tactics. The six characters that we meet at the beginning of the canto are those who were killed because of political fighting within Italy.[108] Yet Dante never has them verbalize any admission of guilt about why they are in Ante Purgatory. Most of them appear to have been just men who were killed by scheming political opponents. Still, it is unlike Dante to arbitrarily place men into places if he did not think they deserved it. We must assume that they were negligent in their contrition.

---

107. In *Purg.* III, 139–41, Manfred describes how the thirty-year rule applies. His time can be reduced by prayers of the faithful on earth.

108. Hollander in his notes identifies the six characters as Benincasa da Laterina, Guido de' Tarlati di Pietramala, Federico Novello, the son of Marzucco degli Scornigiani, Count Orso degli Alberti della Cerbaia and Pierre de la Brosse. See Dante Alighieri, *Purgatorio*, 131–32.

What are we to make of the violent perpetrators and seemingly innocent victims that are in Ante Purgatory, and how might we relate this to Levinas's modes of being? Most of the violent are rulers who held to no ethical code and whose primary goal in life was a quest for power through war. One way to examine them from a Levinasian perspective is to see what Levinas says about war in the Preface of *Totality and Infinity*. Levinas asks how we might know whether "we are not duped by morality."[109] Levinas says that war makes ethics seem derisory. For those who advance the notion of real politics, war is winning by any means possible. Levinas is invoking Hobbes who said that the natural condition of humans is a state of "war of all against all."[110] During Dante's time, Northern Italy did seem like a society engaged in a state of war of all against all. There were so many factions in play: the papacy, White Guelfs, Black Guelfs, Ghibellines, and state interests from the Holy Roman Emperor to the French monarchy. In *Purgatorio* VI Dante throws up his hands in exasperation and cries:

> Ah, Italy enslaved, abode of misery,
> Pilotless ship in a fierce tempest tossed,
> No mistress over provinces but a harlot! (*Purg.* VI, 76–78)

Dante's blistering rhetoric continues throughout the canto as he condemns all the rulers who provide no leadership and no peace. One can compare Dante's hot discourse about war to Levinas's cooler philosophical reasoning. Levinas's explanation of what happens to existents in war is that they completely lose their identity. They are sucked into a totality where "individuals are reduced to being bearers of forces that command them unbeknown to themselves."[111] Levinas states that in the political arena, the idea of a prophetic eschatology never wins arguments. He describes eschatology as that which "institutes a relation with being beyond the totality or beyond history, and not with being beyond the past and the present."[112] For Levinas eschatology arrests beings and "calls them forth to their full responsibility."[113] Levinas superimposes eschatology upon the totality of war and states that even with war, eschatology presupposes an encounter with an Other that is beyond history. Levinas goes so far as to say, "Only beings capable of war

---

109. Levinas, *Totality and Infinity*, 21.
110. Hobbes, *Leviathan*, 186.
111. Levinas, *Totality and Infinity*, 21.
112. Levinas, *Totality and Infinity*, 22.
113. Levinas, *Totality and Infinity*, 23.

can rise to peace."[114] Yet when Levinas talks about eschatology, as Robert Bernasconi points out, he is not speaking of a Christian eschatology, i.e., of the last judgment.[115] Rather it is "the judgments of all instants in time when the living are judged."[116] The totality which war imposes on existents is in the Levinasian model a cross between the *il y a* and the antipode to the mode of Interiority and Economy. In Levinas's mind, war is a force that assimilates humans into a collective. They lose their separate identities and become swept up by a force that steals their subjectivities. As a totality, it is similar to the *il y a* where hypostasis of the individual has not taken place. Yet war involves existents who are in the world. It involves the harnessing of material elements for armaments to defend a totality from a competing force's totality. It is the opposite of Levinas's idea of what Interiority and Economy should be. In that mode, Levinas recognizes that the world and its material elements are good. The existent has enjoyment from what they find in the world. And while they must labor to provide a dwelling for themselves, the labor is constitutive of the mode of Interiority and Economy itself. It is not a punishment that is imposed on the subject. In war, however, the totality compels the existent to work and to fight, and in the process, they must lose their personhood to become part of a group into which their identity is assumed. Levinas believes that he must neutralize the mixed nature of an impersonal totality and the perverse manipulation by the forces of war operating in the mode of Interiority and Economy. In order to do that, Levinas imagines a world of peace. In his essay "Peace and Proximity," Levinas imagines a governmental state that promotes

> peace on the basis of truth, which (marvel of marvels) commands men without forcing or combating them, which governs or assembles them without making them subservient, which can convince [*convaincre*] them with words without conquering [*vaincre*] them, and which masters nature's hostile elements by the calculations and practical knowledge of technology.[117]

In Levinas's ideal governmental state, each person is left by themselves. They are not formed into a totality. They live in cooperation and proximity with each other. He imagines humans outside in the elements but mastering those elements and, by implication, putting them to use for peace.

114. Levinas, *Totality and Infinity*, 222.
115. Bernasconi, "Different Styles of Eschatology," 7.
116. Levinas, *Totality and Infinity*, 23.
117. Levinas, "Peace and Proximity," 131.

Levinas describes "Peace as tranquility or rest"![118] The manipulation of the material elements of nature and the tranquility or rest is what the existent does in Levinas's mode of Interiority and Economy. Each existent exists in their own dwelling. They enjoy the gentleness of the dwelling while at the same time they are in proximity to each other in rest. Levinas warns that the peace from inside the dwelling cannot be a "bourgeois peace" with each person shut inside and rejecting that which is outside.[119] Rather, what is required is a "fraternal way of a proximity to the other."[120]

How does one reconcile Levinas's idea of peace, where one lives in fraternal proximity to the other, and Dante's violent rulers? Most of the rulers who are in Purgatory had little concern for the Other when they were alive, but later they had what we must assume is a legitimate conversion and contrition for their acts of violence. Ironically, Virgil, a pagan, expresses the mystery of a soul's reconciliation with God and tells Dante,

> Foolish is he who hopes that with our reason
> We can trace the infinite path
> Taken by one Substance in three Persons. (*Purg*. III, 34–36)

This way of knowledge does not allow us to understand how a formerly violent person becomes convinced of his sins. But perhaps the reader can understand how a violent person can become repentant through a thought experiment. Let us take the case of Manfred in Purgatory. When Dante encounters him, he appears with battle wounds on his forehead and his side. He relates that immediately before he died, he turned "in tears to Him who freely pardons" and asked for forgiveness (*Purg*. III, 121). Can the reader imagine Manfred at his death appearing before the Other, who is Christ? Imagine that it is Christ who utters the words that Levinas uses to succinctly summarize his ethics: "Do not kill me." Can the reader see the wounded Manfred encountering the wounded Christ at that moment? We must take Dante seriously when he says that Manfred was truly sorry for his sins. Is it possible for the reader to imagine that Manfred's experience at death was a transcendent experience so overwhelming that it completely shattered his own violent nature and he saw in Christ the naked Other with whom he must obey? Can one imagine that the complete alterity of Manfred's experience allowed him to be held hostage? Perhaps he came to realize that this

---

118. Levinas, "Peace and Proximity," 132.
119. Levinas, "Peace and Proximity," 136.
120. Levinas, "Peace and Proximity," 137.

brief interlude before death showed him how he should have lived his life as a hostage in substitution for the life of Christ who is the transcendent Other.

For those who do not qualify for Purgatory Proper because they were late in repenting (i.e., the heretical, the indolent, the violent, and the negligent), Ante Purgatory serves as a place of waiting. Those in the lower portions of Ante Purgatory can still feel the fearful emptiness between the time of death and the time that they arrive at Ante Purgatory. When Dante encounters the first inhabitants of Ante Purgatory, he depicts them as dawdlers, as those who are not inclined to movement and whom Cato needs to reprimand so that they can be on their way. Indolence is a characteristic of those found in Ante Purgatory. Manfred, however, is a different character who was prone to violent action and then repents late in life. He freely admits his guilt and is sorry for his sinful behavior. He appears to have grown spiritually. He exhibits a bit of the humility that is necessary to enter into Purgatory Proper.

3.9 LEVINAS AND PURGATORY PROPER

Dante ascends the mountain of Purgatory in the order of the seven vices, starting with the worst: pride; then envy, wrath, sloth, avariciousness and prodigality, gluttony, and lust. Christian theology establishes two primary objectives for a soul in purgatory. The first is to suffer for sins committed and the second is to become purified so that the soul can be worthy of transit to heaven. How can we compare Purgatory Proper to Levinas's mode of Interiority and Economy? If for the soul Purgatory is a place to expiate sinfulness, and for the subject Interiority and Economy is a mode of enjoyment, then are they not somewhat contradictory? Without a doubt, Dante and Levinas have different models in their respective states and modes. But I contend that it is possible to see similarities as well as differences for a soul or subject in these states or modes.

One way to approach it is to notice the nature of the respective portals that deliver a soul or subject into Purgatory Proper or hypostasis. In order to leave Ante Purgatory, St. Lucy, in the form of an Eagle, transports Dante in his sleep. When Dante awakens, he describes his psychic state:

> I awoke, the sleep gone from my eyes,
> And then went deadly pale,
> Like a man frozen in his terror. (*Purg.* IX, 40–42)

Purgatory

Dante emerges from Ante Purgatory in a frightened and confused state. Sleep was a reaction to the transition from Ante Purgatory to Purgatory proper. Levinas uses the opposite of sleep to describe the *il y a* as a state of insomnia:

> Insomnia is constituted by the consciousness that it will never finish—that is, that there is no longer any way of withdrawing from the vigilance to which one is held. Vigilance without end. From the moment one is riveted there, one loses all notion of a starting or finishing point.[121]

Even though Dante uses sleep as a metaphor while Levinas uses insomnia, one can construe a similarity between the two. The state before Purgatory Proper, i.e., Ante Purgatory, is a state where the soul has no agency. It may as well be asleep since it is helpless to change its position. It is by going through the portal from Ante Purgatory to Purgatory Proper that Dante wakes up. In the realm of Purgatory Proper, the self begins to take on agency. It is in Purgatory Proper that the self can begin actively working on its salvation. In the Levinasian framework, the *il y a* is a mode suspended without time. When Levinas uses the metaphor of insomnia for this mode he is also talking about a subject without agency. The subject is riveted there. It has no way of withdrawing from the mode. Thus in both Dante and Levinas, the self either out of sleep or insomnia emerges from a limited state or mode of existence. In Dante's case, he is deposited at Purgatory Proper's doorstep. In Levinas's case, the self occurs through the process of hypostasis. In either case, the subject comes into being with more freedom. The existent comes from existence "as present and 'I,' hypostasis is freedom."[122] Levinas considers hypostasis as freedom in being. In Dante's model, the soul comes into Purgatory Proper in its individuality. A soul puts itself in charge of its own atonement. God calls a soul to atonement, and it responds willingly. This is a necessary condition for its eventual encounter with God.

In the Levinasian model, the subject is in the world and finds itself in the material elements. One enjoys the world, in breathing, eating, and working. Labor is essential in this mode. Labor is not just a means to an end. Levinas explains, "We live from our labor which ensures our subsistence, but we also live from our labor because it fills (delights or saddens) life."[123] In Dante's Purgatory, the souls attend to the business of labor. In

---

121. Levinas, *Time and the Other*, 48.
122. Levinas, *Time and the Other*, 54.
123. Levinas, *Totality and Infinity*, 112.

Purgatorio XI in the tier of purgatory reserved for those who are expiating the sin of pride, Dante opens up with a variant of the Pater Noster. In it, he asks God,

> Give us this day the daily manna
> Without which he who labors to advance
> Goes backward through this bitter wilderness. (*Purg.* XI, 13–15)

In Purgatory Proper and in this tier of pride, labor is necessary for a soul's daily sustenance. Like Levinas, Dante provides an additional reason for one's labor. Where Levinas describes it as the way of filling life, in the Dantean framework, labor is a necessity for countering the damages caused by sin. In *Purgatorio* XI, those who committed the sin of pride must practice the countervailing virtue of humility. How Dante demonstrates humility is by having the inhabitants of this tier carry heavy stones as they are trudging up the mountain. In his travels, Dante meets Omberto Aldobrandesco. The Aldobrandesco's were a powerful Ghibelline family. Omberto tells Dante that he held all men in great scorn because of the arrogance he had from his family's elevated status. Omberto, however, takes responsibility for his sin and tells Dante,

> And for this pride, here must I bear this burden—
> Here among the dead, since I did not
> Among the living—until God is satisfied. (*Purg.* XI 70–72)

Dante's rationale for Omberto's labor is that he must do in Purgatory what he did not do while living. But if we examine Omberto through a Levinasian lens, we can say that his arrogance kept him suspended within himself from an ethical point of view. He was an existent, who although hypostatized, could not detach himself from his ego. Levinas describes how through hypostasis the ego has freedom. But the price of this freedom is the "*I* riveted to itself."[124] The I is shut up within itself. The way out for Levinas is light from the other, i.e., "Light is that through which something is other than myself, but already as if it came from me."[125] For the subject to experience the reality of transcendence, light is required to lead the subject away from itself. The object that the light illuminates appears to come from the self. Dante, in *Purgatorio* XII, describes how he and Virgil climb upward towards the light. He asks Virgil why he feels as if a weight has been lifted from him. Virgil responds,

124. Levinas, *Time and the Other*, 57.
125. Levinas, *Time and the Other*, 64.

> Your legs shall be so mastered by good will
> Not only will they feel no effort going up,
> But they will take delight in being urged to. (*Purg.* XII, 124–26)

Virgil is the light that brings Dante out of himself. Virgil brings light in two senses of the word. He leads Dante towards the light which illuminates Dante's path. And he helps Dante feel the lightness of the weight that he is carrying so that Dante's labor in the tier of pride takes on the aspect of Levinasian enjoyment. Levinas clarifies the idea of enjoyment, saying, "It is not correct to say that happiness is an absence of suffering."[126] Instead, "happiness is accomplishment: it exists in a soul satisfied and not in a soul that has extirpated its needs, a castrated soul."[127] For the souls in Purgatory Proper, the activity required to expiate one's sins is a form of happiness, even if suffering is part of that accomplishment.

3.10 LEVINAS AND EARTHLY PARADISE

Dante's transcendent encounter with the Other occurs with Beatrice in the Earthly Paradise. At the start of the *Divine Comedy*, Virgil explains to Dante how Beatrice came to understand and enact her role as Dante's moral and spiritual mentor. First, St. Lucy meets with Beatrice and implores her to help Dante. Lucy pleads with Beatrice saying,

> Do you not hear the anguish in his tears?
> Do you not see the death besetting him? (*Inf.* II, 106–7)

As the saint who personifies spiritual light and vision, Lucy understands the lack of light in Dante's desperate spiritual condition. Beatrice takes Lucy's entreaty seriously and visits Virgil in Limbo. She pleads with Virgil to help Dante and requests that he use his formidable persuasive skills

> and whatever else is needed for his safety,
> go to his aid, that I may be consoled
> I who bid you go am Beatrice. (*Inf.* II, 68–70)

Virgil and Beatrice become the guiding forces in Dante's life. Erich Auerbach comments that their love for Dante is so strong that they "leave their place in the predetermined and fulfilled scheme in order to carry out the

---

126. Levinas, *Totality and Infinity*, 115.
127. Levinas, *Totality and Infinity*, 115.

work of grace."[128] Virgil leaves his place in Limbo and Beatrice leaves her place in Heaven to help Dante. Beatrice understands that Dante's life, as pilgrim, has gone horribly wrong. At the beginning of the *Inferno*, fear locks Dante and immobilizes him. Three beasts (a lion, a wolf, and a leopard) block his path. They symbolize obstacles that prevent Dante from progressing in his spiritual life.[129] In the midst of his terror, Virgil comes to his aid. He tells Dante that he must follow him. He also intimates that he will not be with Dante for the entirety of the journey:

> You'll find a soul more fit to lead than I:
> I'll leave you in her care when I depart. (*Inf.* I, 122–23)

The "her" that Virgil references above is Beatrice. In the Earthly Paradise of *Purgatorio*, she will take over Dante's spiritual guidance. But first Dante must come into a new state of consciousness. One way of describing Dante's state at the beginning of the *Divine Comedy* is to look at it from a Levinasian framework. One might say that Dante's distress in the dark woods manifests an anterior anxiety from the unconscious memory of the *il y a*. At the beginning of the *Inferno*, Dante has little hope. Levinas's conception of the *il y a* provides an interesting antecedent mode to describe Dante's anxiety. One might say the confusion and fear that Dante experiences at the beginning of the *Inferno* can be likened to him emerging from that impersonal anonymity. At the beginning of the *Inferno*, Dante describes his subjective state with the infamous words, "I came to myself in a dark wood" (*Inf.* I, 2). Dante's language of coming to myself, "*mi ritrovai*" (literally, I found myself), analogizes Levinas's idea of the subject who through hypostasis comes into being.

When Dante finds himself lost in the woods, he is experiencing himself in a temporal mode of hypostasis. Dante does get sucked back into the darkness during his tour of hell. But he will emerge again in *Purgatorio* and become an existent in time. Giuseppe Mazzota states, "In *Purgatorio* we are given an existential sense of time, which is understood as future-oriented, as a projection into some kind of future, and, at the same time, a return to

---

128. Auerbach, *Dante*, 98.

129. Robert Hollander, in his notes to *Inferno* I, says that early Dante scholars interpreted the three beasts as the sins of lust, pride, and avarice. Later scholars, however, have disputed these interpretations. For a discussion of this, see Dante Alighieri, *Inferno*, 16–17. In a different interpretation, Giuseppe Mazzotta describes these beasts as "animal projections of our desires, of his [Dante's] desires, and that's all we can tell about them" (Mazzotta, *Reading Dante*, 30).

the past."¹³⁰ When Dante arrives in *Purgatorio*, he has an intimation that there will be a hopeful future. But Dante must overcome many obstacles. He tries to proceed on his journey, but he is stymied by the animal apparitions that he sees. These apparitions are representative of a self that has turned in on itself. Dante realizes that he has lost his way, but he does not know how to break out of himself. Levinas prescribes a solution to this impasse by saying, "It is necessary to begin with the concrete relationship between an I and a world."¹³¹ The subject must have a relationship with something exterior to itself. One way to have a relationship with something exterior is through being in the world. However, the ultimate event is a face-to-face encounter with an other. In the *Divine Comedy*, Dante finds a way out initially through an encounter with Virgil. With Virgil as his guide, Dante begins to dimly perceive the light. In the companionship of Virgil, he will gain self-consciousness as he traverses through *Purgatorio*. Virgil helps Dante move out of stuckness with the self. Levinas prescribes a further solution for relinquishing the focus on the self, which is being in the world's elements and encountering the Other.

The relinquishing of self-absorption and focus on the world is crucial for Levinas. The subject encounters the world as separate from itself. To become free from the self, the subject enjoys the world's elemental materiality. Enjoyment is not an intellectual matter. Rather, one affirms the world and "posit[s] oneself in it corporeally."¹³² In the world, the subject feels the physical elements on its body. To escape the world's elemental materiality and have time to recollect, the self establishes a dwelling, which is the home. The home is more than just an enclosure. For Levinas, "the privileged role of the home does not consist in being the end of human activity but in being its condition and in this sense its commencement."¹³³ The home provides a place of security and of gentleness that serves as a foundation for the self's being in the world. But one cannot shut oneself up in a home forever. A danger of being in the world and enjoying it is the possibility that the self absorbs the otherness of the world into itself, including the home. To do so would be making it into a totality, which is like the *il y a* from where the

130. Mazzotta, *Reading Dante*, 117. Mazzotta's explanation of a projection into the future is Dante's ongoing journey forward through Purgatory. Yet Dante's journey to the top of Purgatory ultimately leads him back to the Garden of Eden found in the symbolic beginning of time as recounted in Genesis.

131. Levinas, *Totality and Infinity*, 37.

132. Levinas, *Totality and Infinity*, 127.

133. Levinas, *Totality and Infinity*, 152.

self escaped. Levinas warns that "the separated being can close itself up in its egoism, that is, in the very accomplishment of its isolation."[134] For the self not to relapse into totality or darkness, it must change from enjoyment to the light of knowledge. The way one does this is by freeing oneself "from the very possession that the welcome of the home establishes."[135] Levinas says that change happens in the encounter with the Other as the feminine.

Levinas makes a distinction between two kinds of intimacy with reference to the familiar *thou* [tu] and the formal *you* [vous]. The vocation of the familiar feminine is "one who does not conquer."[136] The familiar feminine expresses gentility and provides a place of hospitality. Levinas describes it as "a coming to oneself, a retreat home with oneself as in a land of refuge."[137] By contrast, the formal feminine "reveals itself in a dimension of height."[138] An asymmetrical relationship exists between the self and the formal feminine Other, which is transcendent to the self. The Other's voice comes to the self from a realm outside of the self. It comes from a height as a teaching, and that teaching is the establishment of an ethical relationship between the self and the Other.[139] Levinas's encounter with the world and the Other is different from Dante's. Yet they both involve an aspect of the home and an encounter with the feminine.

In Purgatory, Dante journeys out of self-absorption through a voyage of purification from narcissism; then a return to an Edenic home, and an encounter with the feminine Other. Unlike in the *Inferno*, where the inhabitants are self-absorbed and tormented unwillingly, in Purgatory the characters strive to remove their narcissistic tendencies and take on penitence willingly. In Purgatory, the inhabitants begin to shed their false idols. Dante, the character, begins his journey with seven letter "P's" (for *peccatum* or sin) imprinted on his forehead. As he climbs higher in Purgatory, the process of purgation removes the sins of Dante, and his burden becomes lighter. Dante moves towards his primordial home, the home of the Edenic garden where he will meet the feminine, first in the form of Matelda and then later Beatrice.

---

134. Levinas, *Totality and Infinity*, 172.
135. Levinas, *Totality and Infinity*, 171.
136. Levinas, *Difficult Freedom*, 33.
137. Levinas, *Totality and Infinity*, 156.
138. Levinas, *Totality and Infinity*, 155.
139. Levinas, *Totality and Infinity*, 171–72. Levinas speaks to the encounter with the Other as a teaching of the ethical.

Purgatory

Dante's encounter with Matelda in *Purgatorio* is a meeting analogous to Levinas's feminine of the dwelling, i.e., the informal feminine. Dante encounters her in the highest realm of *Purgatorio*, which is the Earthly Paradise. Dante's entry into the Edenic setting is a returning home, i.e., humankind's home before the fall. When Dante first sees Matelda picking flowers and singing, he does not know who she is. Matelda addresses Dante intending to help to allay his confusion. She tells Dante that they are in a "place chosen for mankind as its nest" (*Purg.* XXVIII, 78). Matelda explains the protected nature of the place. In this locale, she informs Dante that the turbulent weather below will not affect them. In Eden, one is protected from the elements. Levinas describes the home as a place of protection as well. Dante finds a sense of peace in this Edenic garden. However, not long after Dante meets Matelda, who represents the naturalism of the world, he catches a glimpse of the supernatural as it enters the garden. He sees flashes in the sky and hears voices singing. He sees flames approaching and then he espies a procession coming towards him. The alterity of the vision baffles him. Dante's description of Beatrice's otherworldly procession is a far cry from the naturalism of Matelda. With Beatrice's entrance, the feminine familiar departs and the feminine formal arrives.

If Matelda can be thought of as an earthly Other, Beatrice represents the transcendent Other. When Levinas delineates the transcendental Other, he describes it as the one who "commands me as Master," the one who engages in a discourse "to call me to responsibility."[140] Beatrice acts as Dante's master. Dante describes her as "like an admiral who moves from stern to brow" urging men "on to better work" (*Purg.* XXX, 58–60). Beatrice expresses her unhappiness with how Dante conducted his life. In her address to the procession participants, she says that Dante could have lived a more ethical life, but "he set his steps upon an untrue way"(*Purg.* XXX, 130). In Beatrice's mind, Dante followed an unethical path. Giuseppe Mazzotta says that Beatrice's confrontation with Dante is warranted because she "asks the sleeping pilgrim to awake, to move out of the land of false shadows and make his moral decisions."[141] In the past, Dante's focus was on himself. Levinas portrays the other as "the Other [who] is the very locus of metaphysical truth and is indispensable for my relation with God."[142] In order to reconcile himself with God, Beatrice commands Dante to admit

---

140. Levinas, *Totality and Infinity*, 213.
141. Mazzotta, *Dante's Vision*, 149.
142. Levinas, *Totality and Infinity*, 78.

his sins. When Beatrice asks Dante why he did not continue to seek the ethical way of life, he tells her:

> Things set in front of me,
> With their false delights, turned back my steps
> the moment that Your countenance was hidden. (*Purg.* XXI, 34–36)

Dante admits that he fell back because he failed to see the face of Beatrice, as the face of the Other. Drew Dalton speaks about how the arrival of the Other requires a "response to the appeal of the Other solicited in the experience of shame."[143] For Levinas, the shame that the self experiences is the recognition that one pursued their own self-interest rather than their ethical responsibility. Dante admits his shame, saying,

> Remorse so stung me then
> that whatever else had lured me most to loving
> had now become for me most hateful. (*Purg.* XXXI, 85–87)

Dante now understands the false attractions that he pursued and admits his remorse. He concludes that his real self-interest and his ethical responsibility are ultimately the same. Through his encounter with Beatrice, Dante experiences an enlightenment. As a result of his shame and contrition, Dante can have the stains of his sins washed away by Matelda via Beatrice's request.

3.11 CONCLUSION

The remainder of *Purgatorio* outlines a shift in Dante's relationship with Beatrice. Beatrice's role will change from what Robert Hollander calls "moral preceptor" to "spiritual guide."[144] The role of the Other who calls Dante into an ethical life will move from Beatrice to God's reflection found in Beatrice's face. After Matelda washes Dante in the river, Dante looks at Beatrice and sees "Heaven with its harmonies reflected" (*Purg.* XXXI, 144). When he eyes Beatrice, he sees beyond Beatrice to a vision of heaven. But while Dante resides in Purgatory, he cannot see it directly for himself. Beatrice will help lead Dante into Heaven where Dante will be able to visualize it on his own. Beatrice, as Other, has enabled him to make progress. One of

---

143. Dalton, *Longing for the Other*, 132.

144. Hollander in Dante Alighieri, *Paradiso*, xxiii–xxiv. Hollander notes that Beatrice takes over the role of guide from Virgil at the beginning of *Paradiso*. Yet, the shift begins in the *Purgatorio*'s Earthly Paradise.

the last requests that Beatrice will make is for him to use this experience to help others like himself who are lost. She asks Dante to

> set these words down for those
> who live the life that is a race to death (*Purg.* XXXIII, 52–53)

Upon finishing his journey, Dante will become a teacher and his teaching will be the *Divine Comedy*. For contemporary readers who may find themselves lost in a deep dark wood, the *Divine Comedy* can become a school of learning. As an author who is removed from us by more than seven centuries, Dante's world today may seem remote. Perhaps twenty-first-century readers experience the alterity of Dante's medieval world. Yet that alterity can be a positive reason to read Dante. If Dante's alterity challenges a reader's existing presumptions, that can be a good thing. Mazzotta says that reading the *Divine Comedy* is "tantamount to transcending the confines of our own narrow vision" and "entering an imaginary disorienting space."[145] Perhaps that alterity can help us encounter the Other that calls our own life into question. Hopefully, Levinas's philosophy can serve as a contemporary lens through which one can understand Dante's vision.

---

145. Mazzotta, "Why Did Dante Write the Comedy?," 64.

4

Heaven

Hans Urs von Balthasar's Theory of Beauty and Dante's Heaven

4.1 INTRODUCTION

HANS URS VON BALTHASAR is the modern thinker who will be used to help illuminate the idea of Beauty in Dante's *Paradiso*. Balthasar brings several key ideas into play that give insight into *Paradiso* for a contemporary reader. He is important because as a Christian theologian he is knowledgeable and sympathetic to the theological ideas about Beauty that Dante illustrates in *Paradiso*. Yet as a twentieth-century theologian and philosopher, he can bring together both theology and modern philosophical aesthetics. Balthasar believes that modern aesthetics theory cut out theology from the discipline of aesthetics. Unlike modern theorists, Balthasar ties the idea of Beauty and God's Love together. In his article, "A Résumé of My Thought," he uses an analogy of how the love of a mother and a child for each other is like God's love for human beings. He states, "The infant is brought to consciousness of himself only by love, by the smile of his mother. In that encounter, the horizon of all unlimited being opens itself for him."[1] The beauty of the smiles that mother and infant share allows the infant to see

---

1. Balthasar, "Résumé of My Thought," 471.

that even though it exists apart from her, the child is one with her in love. The infant recognizes that love and being are good, true, and beautiful. Beyond this intuitive idea of Beauty, Balthasar also posits philosophical and theological ideas of Beauty.

Balthasar's ideas about beauty can be divided into beauty's inner dynamics and its outer dynamics. The theory of the Analogy of Being and how the interactions of the Trinity are understood as a form of aesthetic beauty comprise the inner dynamics. Beauty's Form and the aesthetics of God's glory comprise the outer dynamics. The theories of the analogy of being and the interactions of the Trinity are two driving forces in *Paradiso*, and Balthasar's aesthetics can illuminate them. These inner dynamics help produce external beauty's Form and Glory. All four aspects of Balthasar's work are inextricably bound to Love, which is a manifestation produced by the internal dynamics and the external dynamics. The analogy of being and the interactions of the Trinity are hidden but dynamic. Their signs are manifest by the external Forms of beauty and the exempla of glory which are united in love. Dividing Balthasar's aesthetics into inner and outer is a means of speaking about them systematically. Yet, in no way can these conceptions be isolated from each other. Balthasar is neither a systematic theologian nor a systematic philosopher. His writings are symphonic, and his themes move in and out together in rhythms—where the elements of his thoughts often coincide and blend with each other. Because Balthasar's output concerning these topics is prodigious and *Paradiso* is a complex text, it will be necessary to narrow the scope and define how this chapter will proceed.

The process of examining Beauty in Dante's *Paradiso*, as illuminated by Balthasar's theological and philosophical ideas, will consist of several steps. The first step will be to examine the idea of heaven based on scripture and the writings of several Christian theologians up through the Middle Ages. In no way is this meant to be a comprehensive history of heaven. The history provided is meant to give a flavor of how Christianity imagined the idea of heaven and its beauty. After that, I will discuss Balthasar's aesthetics, which consists of the inner dynamics and outer dynamics of beauty. For the inner dynamics, I will explore the analogy of being and the relationship among the persons of the Trinity. I will examine the analogy of being in terms of the relationship between creature and God. How this will be discussed is to review the understanding of predication which describes the attribute of a thing. That concept will explain how Balthasar understands the person of Christ as mediator between God and creature. Through Christ, God reveals the Transcendentals of the Good, the True, and the Beautiful to God's creatures. In *Paradiso*, Dante manifests the Good, True, and Beautiful as well, and I will demonstrate how Balthasar's conception of the analogy of being applies to Dante. Additionally, I will provide a historical context to Balthasar's conception of the analogy of being. The context has two sources. The first is a response to Karl Barth's denigration of the concept as a constraint on God's freedom. And the second is a response to Deleuze's critique that the Analogy of Being is static and lacks dynamism. I intend to show that in both Dante and Balthasar the analogy of being is dynamic and not a constraint on God. Additionally, I will show how dynamism is an attribute that characterizes the relationships among the persons of the Trinity.

This discussion of the Trinity is divided into two forms: the economic (exterior) Trinity and the immanent (interior) Trinity. The immanent Trinity describes the relationship between the divine persons, while the economic Trinity describes how the Trinity is manifest to humans. I will explain how Balthasar's conception of the Trinity differs from Augustine's and Aquinas's conceptions as well as from another modern theory (i.e., Karl Rahner's conception of the Trinity). Ultimately, I will show how Martin Buber's idea of the "Thou" influenced Balthasar's concept of the Trinity as dialogic in nature. Also implicit in Balthasar's theory is the kenotic nature of God, i.e., the self-emptying and giving from one person of the Trinity to another. Based on Balthasar's conception of the inner Trinity, I will examine certain passages in *Paradiso* that show how Dante's idea of the immanent Trinity compares to Balthasar's. Likewise, I intend to describe Balthasar's conception of the economic Trinity. The economic Trinity is how God's creatures see the energies of God and not God's essence. This is because no human can penetrate the essence of God. One of the ways creatures come to know God's truth is through scripture. In *Paradiso*, Dante makes multiple references to truth as revelation from scripture. I will show how Balthasar understands scripture as Logos and how it compares to Dante's understanding. The inner dynamics of the analogy of being and the Trinity lay the groundwork for the outer dynamics of beauty as the Form and as the glory of God.

The Form of beauty is Balthasar's conception of how beauty is made obviously manifest to God's creatures. Balthasar's critique is that contemporary theorists diminish beauty in favor of either professional aesthetics or scientism, both of which separate Beauty from the True and the Good. Philosophical aesthetics mainly focuses on Beauty without any relationship to God (Good). Scientism speaks mainly about the True without any relationship to Beauty. Balthasar wants to bring the three transcendentals together and to recognize it by looking at what he describes as beauty's Form. Balthasar speaks explicitly about Dante concerning how he used the form of the vernacular to convey beauty to his medieval readers. Rather than write for the schooled elite, Dante conveyed a form of beauty to the masses. Further, Balthasar states that Dante's form of beauty is rooted in historicism. Rather than writing strictly in a timeless or mythological way, Dante takes Greek and Roman culture and incorporates it into his Christian worldview, thus creating a form that achieves a symphonic mix of ancient and medieval Christian culture. A contribution that Dante makes that goes beyond ancient and classical culture is to claim Christ as the exemplar of beauty. Christ's Form is not only spiritual beauty but also eros as beauty. Eros for Dante and Balthasar is a force so powerful that the creature is willing to undergo suffering to become worthy of that love. In Dante's world, the person whom he personifies as being most worthy of this love is Beatrice. Dante's entire journey is learning how to channel the romantic love that he has for Beatrice into an eros that requires him to make a spiritual transformation. Dante enlarges his conception of love from a love of Beatrice to a love that encompasses the entire world. Ultimately Dante understands love as modeled by Christ who gave his life because he so loved the world.

The last section of this study deals with God's glory as an external manifestation of Beauty. God's glory illuminates itself to God's creatures. And reciprocally, God's creatures delight by responding to God's illumination. When God manifests Godself to creatures, the result is usually a sense of awe so powerful that it momentarily overwhelms the creature. This happens throughout *Paradiso* where Dante successively becomes vanquished by the supernatural light that shines upon him from the upper reaches of the heavens. Additionally, the glory that Dante perceives in *Paradiso* is often a result of the education he gets from Beatrice and St. Bernard. Thus, glory becomes more discernible through a dialogical exchange between Dante and the heavenly beings whom he meets in the various realms of *Paradiso*.

Dante logically lays out the various realms of *Paradiso* in an orderly and rational conception of the universe over which God presides. To a certain extent, Balthasar will criticize Dante for his overreliance on Scholasticism, particularly in his final encounter with God. Balthasar's major critique of *Paradiso* is that Dante does not explicitly recognize Christ's passion as a form of God's glory. Additionally, because Dante foregrounds his love for the feminine in the form of Beatrice, it convinces Balthasar that *Paradiso* is essentially a Marian aesthetic work. While that may be true, Dante's journey takes him past Beatrice and Mary to an encounter with the Divine. Still, Balthasar's point is valid in that Dante in *Paradiso* places Christ on the cross in the background. Christ's passion is more intimated than explicated in *Paradiso*. Still, if one imagines, as Dante did, that the final goal for creatures is to meet the Divine face-to-face, then Dante's ending is the only ending one could imagine. By the time Dante reaches *Paradiso* he has passed the places of torment and penance. Rather than encountering Good Friday as the final destination, Dante chooses to imagine the glory of Easter Sunday as the creature's goal. At that moment, Dante loses, at least temporarily, his human senses and has a brief encounter with what can be thought of as union with God. Dante never loses his own individuality, even while experiencing a vision of God's transcendent glory.

4.2 HEAVEN: A CHRISTIAN HISTORY IN RELATION TO DANTE'S PARADISO

The Bible and many Christian theologians describe heaven in various ways. Heaven appears in the book of Revelation when an angel carries the writer to a new Jerusalem:

> And he carried me away in the Spirit to a mountain great and high, and showed me the Holy City, Jerusalem, coming down out of heaven from God. It shone with the glory of God, and its brilliance was like that of a very precious jewel, like a jasper, clear as crystal. (Rev 21:10–12)

Revelation depicts heaven as a Holy City on a great height above the earth. It shines with a brilliance of light that is so stunning that it appears like a reflection of precious minerals. These two attributes of heaven, i.e., as a place above and flooded with light, are consistent with how Dante will depict *Paradiso*.

Another of heaven's attributes is encountering God in God's full glory. Gregory of Nyssa is noted for his ideas concerning the beatific vision, which is the final destination of a faithful Christian. Gregory believes that the project of seeing God is a dynamic process. While a creature cannot see God in

God's entirety, the creature can see God in a way because "each sublime idea brings God into view."[2] Gregory employs the notion of the analogy of being by saying that "you possess in yourself what you seek. . . . God is certainly in you."[3] For Gregory, striving for perfection was an eternal process. In his treatise *On Perfection* he writes, "For this is truly perfection: never to stop growing towards what is better and never placing any limit on perfection."[4] Hans Boersma comments, "Gregory's notion that participation allows for continuous (eternal) growth is an answer to the problem that a more static view of the beatific vision would seem to entail."[5] Boersma is saying that the beatific vision is better explained as eternal growth rather than a static existence. Augustine does not necessarily endorse a dynamic movement in Heaven although there will be activity. In the *City of God*, Augustine relates how eternal life will be a continuous exhortation of God's glory:

> Who can measure the happiness of heaven, where no evil at all can touch us, no good will be out of reach; where life is to be one long laud extolling of God, who will be all in all; where there will be no weariness to call for rest, no need to call for toil, no place for energy but praise.[6]

Augustine mentions that all will be singing "a great hymn of praise to the supreme Artist who has fashioned us" and who "will ravish our minds with spiritual beauty."[7] Augustine goes on to explain that there will be "ranks of saints" that are graded according to their "merited honor and glory," but there will be no envy because each person is rewarded according to what they could ever have conceived.[8] Dante will also rank people in various realms of heaven. However, like Augustine, he will relate that all are satisfied with their place in heaven.[9]

Besides heaven's brilliant manifestations of God's glory, the idea of love between God and creature is important. Bernard of Clairvaux, who

---

2. Gregory of Nyssa, *Homilies on the Beatitudes* 6.141.17–18, 69.
3. Gregory of Nyssa, *Homilies on the Beatitudes* 6.144.2–4, 70.
4. Gregory of Nyssa, "On Perfection," 122.
5. Boersma, "Becoming Human in the Face of God," 141.
6. Augustine, *The City of God* 22.30.
7. Augustine, *The City of God* 22.30.
8. Augustine, *The City of God* 22.30.
9. In *Paradiso* III, 70–72, Dante asks the character Piccarda if she desires a higher place in heaven. She answers, "Brother the power of love subdues our will / so that we long for only what we have / and thirst for nothing else."

appears in Dante's *Paradiso*, discusses the nature of that love. In his text *On Loving God*, Bernard states, "In the heavenly Fatherland no sorrow nor sadness can enter."[10] Bernard will propose a four-step treatise on love whereby the person first loves himself for his own sake. Next is loving God for the creature's own sake. The third step is to love God for God's sake. The final stage is not something that a person can perform with their own will. The last stage is a gift from God. The person at this stage loves himself for God's sake. At this stage, the person will experience the kind of love that he experiences in heaven with God. Balthasar will agree with Bernard that God first initiates love with the human. In Balthasar's conception, the last transformation happens through Christ:

> In order to appropriate its new "nature," transformed as it is by Christ (μεταστοιχείωσις), humanity must become conscious of its new center and carry out in him and through him that supreme synthesis of death and life. . . . The Christian must himself pass away through Christ, by means of his attitude of nothing less than a free assimilation to Christ by the "putting to death" of the old nature and handing over the whole self to God with Christ.[11]

Like Bernard, Balthasar believes that Christ transforms the creature through love, and in that transformation, the creature hands itself over to God completely. This is not as surprising as it might seem because God makes humans in God's image. Through the recognition that our being is analogous to God's essence, God's love transforms us.

4.3 INNER DYNAMICS OF BEAUTY

4.3.1 Analogy of Being

4.3.1.1 Introduction to the Analogy of Being

Underlying Balthasar's aesthetics is the idea of the analogy of being. One way to understand the analogy of being is to put it into contrast with how Heidegger conceives being. Heidegger's being is the unveiling of what is, as it is in the world. Being is the experiencing of what is present. Being is not a transcendent beyond as in a transcendent God. This would be onto-theology. Balthasar has another understanding of being when he speaks

---

10. Bernard of Clairvaux, "On Loving God," 14.
11. Balthasar, *Presence and Thought*, 153.

of the analogy of being. Balthasar's being is the unveiling of a relationship between the creature and the divine. Unlike Heidegger's concept of being, the analogy of being is relational. Balthasar credits Aquinas with a superior understanding of Being compared to Heidegger. Balthasar says that Heidegger's understanding of being is a "de-essentializing of reality." He states of Heidegger:

> When being is no more than just being "there," something simply posited in a colorless, valueless way, it is robbed of its transcendental fulness, is in itself neither true nor good nor beautiful and this immediately affects the natures to whom it gives its "thereness."[12]

In contrast to those like Heidegger who would reduce being to "thereness," Balthasar claims that the metaphysics of Aquinas is a celebration of the

> reality of the real, of that all-embracing mystery of being which surpasses the powers of human thought, a mystery pregnant with the very mystery of God, a mystery in which creatures have access to the participation in the reality of God.[13]

Glenn Morrison advises that Balthasar drew from Aquinas to show "how the structure of the relation between Being and beings points to the freedom and power of God to offer the creature the possibility to participate and share in divine Being."[14] In *Theo-Drama III*, Balthasar relates how God shows up in creation.

> Being, in its hierarchical stages and degrees of interiority (existence, life, feeling, thinking and loving) simply cannot be anything but a trace, an image of eternal, triune Being; and the more vibrant, communicative, and fruitful it is, the more clearly it manifests this relation.[15]

In the above passage by Balthasar, he is using the word "trace" to indicate that within existents, no matter how insubstantial, God exists. God may exist only as a trace because of the enormity of God's Being compared to a human being. But still, a substance of God exists in the trace. One may note the difference between Balthasar's understanding of trace in the passage above versus the idea of trace in postmodern theory. In the postmodern

12. Balthasar, *Glory of the Lord*, 4:405.
13. Balthasar, *Glory of the Lord*, 4:407.
14. Morrison, *Theology of Alterity*, 83.
15. Balthasar, *Theo-Drama*, 3:525.

paradigm, being is immanence and a transcendent God has abandoned its creation. What is left is merely a trace of God who is vacated from being. Balthasar speaks to the idea that in modernity, unlike in antiquity and Christianity, the *theos* is removed from being:

> Post-Christian thought, which rejects such a presence as "Christian" presumption, will also want to reject antiquity's openness to being in all its totality (or like Heidegger exclude the *theos* because it is a Christian element). Thus it will narrow the true and the good within a purely anthropological perspective, to plain "interest."[16]

Balthasar is proposing that humans and God have an analogous relationship. God has not vacated his presence. And since God in the Christian tradition is trinitarian in the godhead, Balthasar sees the human being as a trace of the trinitarian godhead's being. If the being of the creature is analogous to the Being of God and God is trinitarian, then the analogy of being and the trinitarian nature of God are woven together. In relation to Dante, the trinitarian conception of God is important because, in the culmination of the last canto of the *Divine Comedy*, Dante experiences a vision of God that is threefold in nature. Dante, at the apex of the Empyrean, tries to relate his vision by saying,

> In the deep, transparent essence of the lofty Light
> there appeared to me three circles
> having three colors but the same extent
>
> and each one seemed reflected by the other
> as rainbow is by rainbow, while the third seemed fire,
> equally breathed forth by one and by the other. (*Par.* XXXIII, 115–20)

At the highest stage of *Paradiso*, Dante experiences the vision of Being in its truest form, and that Being is three in person. The idea of God as trinitarian will be discussed later, but first I will examine Balthasar's conception of the analogy of being in relation to predication.

4.3.1.2 Analogy of Being and Predication

In Catholic theology, one can more easily grasp the analogy of being by understanding an aspect of medieval theology called predication. Predication is the act of defining the properties of a thing through affirmation or denial.

---

16. Balthasar, *Theo-Drama*, 3:424–25.

Predication can be either univocal, equivocal, or analogical. If a predication is univocal, then words mean that one thing is like another in exactly the same way. For example, the words "Beautiful," "Good," and "True" describe God's essence not as a relation nor negation but as a trait that God is like. Yet one could not say that a person is good like God is good. God's goodness and a human's goodness are not univocal. If God's goodness and a human's goodness were univocal then God would cause an effect (i.e., a being) that is the same as God is. On the other hand, the term equivocal means that words could have different meanings. An example of an equivocal predication is the word "crane," which could be predicated of either a tall wading bird or a machine to lift heavy weight. This predication is equivocal because "crane" can mean more than one thing. Creatures and God are not equivocal "because if that were so, it follows that from creatures nothing could be known or demonstrated about God at all; for the reasoning would always be exposed to the fallacy of equivocation."[17] If humans and God are equivocal, Aquinas asks, then how can one say that humans are an image of God? Thus, if a creature is neither univocal nor equivocal, how can one explain the relationship between a creature and God? Aquinas answers that the relationship is an analogous one, "and in this way some things are said of God and creatures analogically."[18] Since beings and God are neither equivocal nor univocal, then they are analogical. The analogy of being runs as an undercurrent throughout Balthasar's work; however, in *Theo-Drama III* he goes into detail in the section titled "*Analogia Entis* in Christology."

In *Theo-Drama III*, Balthasar discusses how Christ mediates between the divine and the creature. He states that if one were only to consider God and the creature, then "between the divine and the created natures there is an essential abyss. It cannot be circumvented."[19] Balthasar maintains, however, that the person of Jesus can help narrow the abyss between God and humans, and that should create in us a sense of astonishment. Yet Balthasar holds out the caveat that "even Christ's unique graces (of his hypostatic union and of his position as Head of the Church and of creation) cannot and will not abolish the difference between created and uncreated natures."[20] As such, humanity and God cannot cross the abyss. Balthasar's answer, however, is found in Christ's trinitarian mission. According to Balthasar,

17. Aquinas, *ST* I, 13.5.3.
18. Aquinas, *ST* I, 13.5.3.
19. Balthasar, *Theo-Drama*, 3:220.
20. Balthasar, *Theo-Drama*, 3:222.

"the Father commissioned him [Jesus], in the Holy Spirit, to reveal God's nature and his disposition toward man."[21] Christ in his revelation reveals not only the full truth of humanity but also the truth of God. And if God, as Balthasar states, is the Good, the True, and the Beautiful, then Jesus is the one who is the consummate artist revealing those qualities. According to Balthasar, the highest instance of "that gracious self-communication of God to a creature ... reaches its peak in the beatific vision."[22] Dante experiences the vision of God at the end of *Paradiso*. Yet he also sees glimpses of it earlier. For example, at the beginning of *Paradiso*, Beatrice tries to explain to Dante what he is experiencing. She tells Dante,

> All things created have an order
> In themselves, and this begets the form
> That lets the universe resemble God. (*Par.* I, 103–5)

Beatrice's instruction to Dante introduces him to the mystery of how an infinite God is analogous to the finite universe. Balthasar glosses this section of *Paradiso* by saying that "the order of the cosmos is itself an expression of divine love and is loved by individual beings for its likeness to God."[23] As an example, in *Paradiso* XXIII, Dante, the pilgrim, hears a paean of love sung to Mary by an angel: "I am angelic love and I encircle / the exalted joy breathed from the womb" (*Par.* XXIII). As a faithful Christian, Dante would know that creation ultimately comes from God out of love, and the form of God's creation resembles God's beauty. Balthasar would add that the form of God's creation resembles God analogously. The context within which Balthasar developed his theory helps us to understand why the analogy of being was so important to Balthasar.

4.3.1.3 Barth and the Critique of Analogy of Being

The early church fathers influenced Balthasar's conception of the analogy of being. Also important to him was his dialogue with contemporaries Karl Barth and Eric Przywara. Przywara was a fellow Jesuit while Barth was a renowned Swiss Protestant theologian. Balthasar and Karl Barth had an ongoing exchange concerning the analogy of being. Because of the respect that Balthasar had for Barth, and because of the vehemence with which

---

21. Balthasar, *Theo-Drama*, 3:225.
22. Balthasar, *Theo-Drama*, 3:229.
23. Balthasar, *Glory of the Lord*, 3:69.

Barth opposed the concept, Balthasar felt compelled to address the issue. Barth expressed his opposition, saying,

> I regard the doctrine of the analogy of being as the invention of the Antichrist and hold that precisely because of this doctrine one cannot become a Catholic. At the same time, I believe that all other reasons that one can have for not becoming a Catholic are shortsighted and frivolous.[24]

Barth criticized the analogy of being by accusing the Catholic Church

> of possessing a systematic principle that is not in itself Christ the Lord but an abstract theory—namely, the analogia entis—from which one can determine the relation between God and creatures in advance, according to a prior philosophical understanding (i.e., of natural theology), so that the revelation of God in Jesus Christ appears ultimately as the fulfillment of an already existing reality and knowledge.[25]

Barth's concern is that the analogy of being would put God into a preexisting system and would allow humans to be on the same level as God. That would result in a univocal relationship between creature and God. Balthasar utilizes Przywara's conception of the analogy of being to counter Barth. He quotes Przywara where he states that if analogy was

> like a formula of the creaturely realm . . . then it would become the absolute starting point of an absolute metaphysics, from which we would be able to derive everything, including the deepest mysteries of theology. But it is only the expression for how the restless potentiality of the creaturely is unfolded as thought.[26]

Further on in Balthasar's book on Barth, *The Theology of Karl Barth*, Balthasar covers Barth's later evolution to a different form of analogy. Barth is willing to admit a relationship between creature and God. However, Barth's analogy is an analogy of faith that emphasizes revelation and Christ's centrality. In defense of a Catholic understanding of analogy, Balthasar counters Barth's analogy of faith. Like Barth, Balthasar believes that theology is the content of revelation as the divine Logos itself. Theology as Logos expressed through revelation is what Balthasar will call a top-down

---

24. Balthasar, *Theology of Karl Barth*, 49.
25. Barth quoted in Balthasar, *Theology of Karl Barth*, 37.
26. Przywara quoted in Balthasar, *Theology of Karl Barth*, 255.

approach. But Balthasar adds that theology must work from below as well. Theology from below

> needs all the forms of the worldly logoi of truth to present its inexhaustible fullness: the abstract and general as well as the concrete and individual. Theology must work from below, where, as Newman loved to show, all the truths of cultures and peoples are gathered up by the Church and made serviceable to theology. But theology also works from above where the divine Logos wants to enrich all logoi in his mission to the world and lead them back to the Father in himself. But in any case, Catholic theology will burst the confines of any specific and limited structure of thought.[27]

Balthasar's counter to Barth is that the Logos is not just top down. Logoi also consist of truths that individuals on the ground express. When creatures congregate together and engage with each other, the church's understanding of truth enlarges. Balthasar believes that when the church is speaking polemically it must immerse itself in the dialogue of a specific epoch to make itself clear. The church's teaching is dialogical in nature. It cannot be limited to one epoch in history. Yes, the church must protect the totality of revelation as a *depositum fidei*.[28] Yet the understanding of revelation will never be a closed. The understanding of revelation is never finished. The openness of the church's expressive means of revelation and the principle of the analogy of being was not only rejected by Barth. The philosopher Gilles Deleuze critiqued the analogy of being differently.

4.3.1.4 Deleuze and the Critique of Analogy of Being

Deleuze's primary opposition to the analogy of being is that in his conception it is a static model. In *Difference and Repetition*, Deleuze argues:

> In effect, the genus in relation to its species is univocal, while Being in relation to the genera or categories themselves is equivocal. The analogy of being implies both these two aspects at once: one by which being is distributed in determinable forms which necessarily distinguish and vary the sense; the other by which being so distributed is necessarily repartitioned among well-determined beings, each endowed with a unique sense. What is missed at the

---

27. Balthasar, *Theology of Karl Barth*, 253.
28. Balthasar, *Theology of Karl Barth*, 253.

two extremities is the collective sense of being [*être*] and the play of individuating difference in being [*étant*].²⁹

Analogy functions to preserve religious language from two opposing errors: on the one hand, the error of presumption (of assuming that our words mean the same thing when applied to God and creatures), and on the other hand, the error of agnosticism (of assuming, whether on the basis of skepticism that our words when applied to God have an ambiguous reference). The analogy of being says that creaturely being does have some likeness to God but God is wholly different from God's creation.

For Deleuze, analogy's problem is that at each polar side of analogy (i.e., the univocal and equivocal) not much dynamism exists. How this relates to Balthasar's conception of the analogy of being and its theological implications is that critics of the analogy of being misconstrue what it means, especially in the theological and philosophical considerations. Eric Przywara states that the analogy of being

> signifies that what is decisive in "every similarity, however great," is the "ever greater dissimilarity." It signifies, so to speak, God's "dynamic transcendence," i.e., that God is ever above and beyond [*je-über-hinaus*] everything external to him and everything that can be conceived.³⁰

The contribution that the analogy of being brings to theology is its dynamic quality. It is not static as Deleuze has described it. Michael Hanby states that the dynamism of the analogy of being is a dynamic middle that "does not ground itself, [because] each pole being dependent upon the other—and thus on the Wholly other."³¹ John Betz describes the analogy of being as the "dynamic ontological tension between essence and existence."³² Betz continues his explanation that the essence of the creature, unlike God's essence which is to exist, is precisely not identical to its existence. Instead, "essence and existence are related in the creature in such a way that the essence of the creature is never fully given . . . but always on the horizon of its existence as something to be attained."³³

---

29. Deleuze, *Difference and Repetition*, 303.
30. Przywara quoted in Betz, "Beyond the Sublime," 10.
31. Hanby, "Creation as Aesthetic Analogy," 368.
32. Betz, "After Barth," 59.
33. Betz, "After Barth," 60.

Dante exhibits the ever-expanding dynamism that exists in the analogy of being by his character's continual unfolding from hell to the tiers in heaven. An example from *Paradiso* exemplifies the idea of movement forward by a creature towards God. Dante tells Beatrice that he is intrigued by the lightness of his own body in *Paradiso*. Beatrice as teacher uses this opportunity to explain certain metaphysical topics to Dante, saying that,

> All things created have an order
> in themselves, and this begets
> the form that lets the universe resemble God. (*Par.* I, 100–102)

Beatrice tells Dante that all existents have an analogous relationship with God because their form resembles God. The "order" that Beatrice refers to, however, is not a one-size-fits-all order. Rather, it is dynamic. She goes on to say:

> In that order, all natures have their bent
> according to their different destinies
> Whether nearer to their source or farther from it
>
> They move, therefore, toward different harbors
> upon the vastness of the sea of being,
> each imbued with an instinct that impels it on its course. (*Par.* I, 109–14)

Beatrice says that God impels each existent's movement. Even though their movements are not the same, their movements always bring them forward. Dante's metaphor of an existent traveling on the "vast sea of being" is similar to Betz's description of analogy of being, i.e., where the creature's movement is always on the horizon of its existence as something to be attained.[34] The movement between creature and God is a movement of participation in Being. The creature will experience freedom in this movement. Beatrice tells Dante that sometimes a creature will deviate from its intended course.

> So sometimes a creature, having the capacity
> to swerve, will, thus impelled, head off another way
> in deviation from the better course. (*Par.* I, 132)

---

34. This is a phrase attributed to John Damascene as an explanation of "I Am Who Am" (i.e., Being itself): *Damascenus quod non significat quid est deus, sed significat quoddam pelagus substantiae infinitum, quasi non determinatum* (Aquinas, *Scriptum super primum Sententiarum* d. 8, q.1, a. 1, resp. 4).

Heaven

The creature has freedom of will to go its own way. It can swerve onto a different path, even though that path is inferior to the one directed by God. Yet Balthasar assures us that "opening to the horizon of truth, means opening to ever more truth, ever more intelligibility" and that "openness is an 'always more,' is an *a priori* constituent of truth's essence."[35] Thus, the inner mechanism of the analogy of being consists of a dynamic participation that is never static but always in movement. One aspect of the dynamic movement in the analogy of being is the creature's constant endeavor to conform itself in an analogous relationship to Christ.

Balthasar's idea of the analogy of being helps to explain how Christ's mission to sacrifice his life is in relationship with the creature's mission to conform itself to Christ. Balthasar's explanation for Christ's death will be different from how Beatrice explains the reason for Christ's death. In *Paradiso* VII, Beatrice explains to Dante why Christ needed to become human. She tells Dante that because of the sin of Adam, "man could never offer / satisfaction, for he could not descend as deep / into humility by latter-day obedience" (*Par.* VII, 97–99). Beatrice's argument is that only Christ as God could redeem humans because as mere creatures, they could never provide enough satisfaction for Adam's primal sin. Similarly, Aquinas, among several explanations that he gives for Christ's death, states, "It was fitting for Christ to die. First of all to satisfy for the whole human race, which was sentenced to die on account of sin. . . . So Christ resolved to die, that by dying He might atone for us."[36] Balthasar, however, will provide a different answer which incorporates the analogy of being between humanity and the divine. Balthasar explains that even though the Father truly abandons Christ on the cross,

> this "infinite distance," which recapitulates the sinner's mode of alienation from God, will remain forever the highest revelation known to the world of the diastasis (within the eternal being of God) between Father and Son in the Holy Spirit.[37]

While the idea that the Father truly abandons his son on the cross feels harsh, it is in fact a necessity. To understand why is to know that Christ cannot give himself freely on the cross if the Father does not give the son freedom. Brandon Gallagher explains it as part of the dynamics of the Trinity.

---

35. Balthasar, *Theo-Logic*, 1:227.
36. Aquinas, *ST* III, 50.1.co.
37. Balthasar, *Theo-Drama*, 3:228.

> The Father in begetting the Son *is* by His giving of Himself, His free letting be of the Son. The Son in turn *is* Himself by letting himself be generated, and hence the Father is dependent on His son's response.[38]

In order for the Father and the Son to be themselves, they must be free to mutually give themselves to each other. Thus abandonment is actually mutual freedom to give of themselves. In the above passage, Balthasar is saying that when God abandons Christ at his crucifixion, that abandonment is the most profound revelation of Christ's identification with humans. Balthasar says that Christ's alienation from God recapitulates the distance between creature and God. Thus, Christ's freedom to give himself because of the Father's letting be is similar to the relationship that creatures have with God. God gives creatures the freedom to abandon themselves to God as the father gives himself totally to the creature through Christ. By implication, Christ's resurrection offers hope to creatures that they too will be resurrected with Christ. Balthasar's argument is not the substitution-atonement argument of Beatrice and Aquinas (i.e., that Christ had to come and atone for humanity because humans could not redeem themselves). According to Balthasar, Christ became incarnate because it was his mission to do so. And as part of that mission, the human being's analogous relationship to God could be realized more fully. Balthasar's position is that part of the mission of Jesus is the "relationship between the incarnate Word to *human nature as a whole*."[39] For Balthasar, the analogous relationship between humans and Christ is not a passive one. Rather, "when conscious subjects . . . become persons in him, they are automatically allotted a combat role in the task of world liberation."[40] Also, because Christ takes away the sins of humans in his passion, we are given something in exchange and that givenness moves us "from alienation to authentic personal being."[41] Finally, Christ's mission also allows us to analogously participate in the being of Christ. Balthasar quotes various church fathers about this issue. Athanasius writes, "Just as the Word became man by taking flesh, we men are divinized by being taken into the flesh of the Word."[42] Balthasar also references Hilary of Poitiers, who writes, "The Word became flesh so that, through the incarnate Word,

38. Gallaher, *Freedom and Necessity*, 180.
39. Balthasar, *Theo-Drama*, 3:231.
40. Balthasar, *Theo-Drama*, 3:231.
41. Balthasar, *Theo-Drama*, 3:231.
42. Athanasius quoted in Balthasar, *Theo-Drama*, 3:238.

flesh should become one with God the Word."[43] And finally, he quotes from Theodore of Mopsuestia, who states, "When Christ was crucified, our whole nature was somehow crucified with him; subject to death, our whole nature rose with him."[44] Therefore, Balthasar places less stress on the idea that Christ became incarnate and died because humans were unworthy due to their being marked with the sin from Adam. Balthasar, as opposed to Beatrice's address to Dante in *Paradiso* VII, is emphasizing that the mission of Christ allows humans to analogously join in Christ's being. Balthasar speaks to the idea that through Christ's obedience to be baptized by John, he is in solidarity with all of humanity.

> Jesus's descent into the river is at one and the same time solidarity with all who confess their guilt . . . and—as solidarity—obedience to the voice of God which sounds forth from the prophet's voice, and thus obedience incarnated in history.[45]

Therefore, through baptism Christ sets an example for all others to become free from their sinfulness and become a participant in Christ's life. Through Christ incarnate, humans become elevated in their being which allows them to catch glimpses of the divine in their lived lives. Finally, Christ's death and resurrection allow humans to have the promise of their own resurrection. Thus, the analogy of being is not a static idea that imprisons God and God's creatures. This idea of dynamic movement is also a concept that is implicit in the *Divine Comedy* and in Balthasar's notion of a trinitarian God.

4.3.2 Trinity

One can discuss the concept of the Trinity from two perspectives—the economic Trinity and the immanent Trinity. While going too deeply into the theology of the Trinity is beyond the scope of this study, it is necessary to discuss briefly what is meant by the economic Trinity and the immanent Trinity so that it becomes clear how Dante is exhibiting the distinction in the *Divine Comedy* and how Balthasar is using it in his work. The economic Trinity is how humans understand God. The term economic comes from the Greek word *oikonomia* and refers to God's action in the world. The immanent Trinity refers to the inner actions of the three persons in one

---

43. Hilary quoted in Balthasar, *Theo-Drama*, 3:238.
44. Theodore of Mopsuestia quoted in Balthasar, *Theo-Drama*, 3:238.
45. Balthasar, *Glory of the Lord*, 7:56.

God. Gilles Emery explains the economic Trinity as "the action by which the Trinity reveals and communicates himself, particularly the incarnation of the Son and the sending of the Holy Spirit."[46] As a historical event, Christ as Logos revealed the Trinity to the world. From revelation, humans know that Christ died on the cross and gave himself up in kenosis to the Father. Also recorded in revelation is that at Pentecost the Holy Spirit came to the apostles. The words and events of the economic Trinity are those which are available to humans, and which make known God's plan for human salvation. On the other hand, Emery, who following Athanasius and other theologians through the centuries, describes the immanent Trinity as "the life of the Trinity itself in its eternal being."[47] The immanent Trinity details the always already relationships of the three persons in one God. Where knowledge of the economic Trinity is based on human experience, the immanent Trinity is *a priori* to human experience. To understand the immanent Trinity better, I want to show how Augustine and Aquinas understood the immanent Trinity and how that understanding appears in Dante. After that, I will discuss how Balthasar conceives the immanent Trinity and how that compares to Dante's conception.

4.3.2.1 *Immanent Trinity: Augustine, Aquinas, and Dante*

Augustine in *De Trinitate* explicates an idea of the immanent Trinity. When Augustine speaks of the immanent Trinity, he speaks of the mind which produces knowledge and love. Although Augustine states that these three are one and of one substance, he stipulates the order of the three as first mind, then knowledge, and then love. He states: "And so there is a certain image of the Trinity: the mind itself, its knowledge, which is its offspring and love as a third."[48] As we will see later, Balthasar critiques Augustine on this issue. At this point, however, I will examine Aquinas's conception of the Trinity.

In the *Summa Theologia*, Thomas Aquinas speaks of the inner dynamics or processions among the persons of the Trinity. Aquinas's notion is that the processions are not physical but mental movements. And because they are mental movements, they are more perfect. He writes:

---

46. Emery, *Trinity*, 159.

47. Emery, *Trinity*, 159. Note that Emery chooses to use the words "theology" for "immanent trinity" and "economy" for "economic trinity."

48. Augustine, "On the Holy Trinity" 9.12.18.

> Whatever proceeds by way of outward procession is necessarily distinct from the source whence it proceeds, whereas whatever proceeds within by an intelligible procession is not necessarily distinct, indeed, the more closely it is one with the source whence it proceeds.[49]

Aquinas argues that mental movements are more perfect than physical movements. Using a human example, if humans move something outside of themselves, e.g., a cup, the result of the movement (i.e., the cup) is outside of the human who moves it. However, if a person thinks of something, the resulting thought is one with the source of the thought. Because mental movements are not physical, it allows Aquinas to propose the idea that the processions among the trinitarian persons are closely tied to the source from which they proceed. Aquinas states that the "divine Word is of necessity perfectly one with the source whence He proceeds, without any kind of diversity."[50] According to Karen Kilby, the problem with Aquinas's description of procession is that

> in God we precisely *cannot* think of difference between that which proceeds and that from which it proceeds: divine simplicity requires the denial of this. Thomas is presenting us with a procession that is so perfect that we in fact have no idea why it could not also be called "not a procession."[51]

Ultimately, Kilby argues that Aquinas's explanation of this issue is not developed to "make sense" of the nature of procession, i.e., how a procession could be one with the source. Rather, Aquinas is using a manner of grammatical expression about God that will always be beyond human understanding. The reason for this is precisely due to the fact that this is the mystery of the Trinity as understood by the church, and that is that the three persons are the same God. An example appears in *Paradiso* II where Beatrice instructs Dante about the optics of light's reflection.

Dante and Beatrice find themselves in the realm of the Moon. The light here is not as clear as what Dante will experience as he progresses higher through the circles of *Paradiso*. In the realm of the Moon, Dante cannot see well and tells Beatrice that "It seemed to me that we were in a cloud" (*Par.* II, 31). He is confused by the spots on the moon and asks whether they are

---

49. Aquinas, *ST* I, 27.1.2.
50. Aquinas, *ST* I, 27.1.2.
51. Kilby, "Aquinas," 420.

due to different densities of matter. Beatrice implies that Dante's theory is wrong because the common human error that burdens him is due to his human senses and this is where "reason's wings fall short" (*Par.* II, 57). Beatrice's explanation is best summed up in James Miller's article "Three Mirrors of Dante's *Paradiso*." Miller explains that while human knowledge is uncertain, Beatrice's true "knowledge depends on the experience of boundless certainty that grace reserves for the soul directly illuminated by God."[52] Thus, as an illuminated soul, she knows better than Dante and can help him understand it. She encourages Dante to create an experiment. She suggests that he take three mirrors and place two at equal distance apart and place the third on the side between the two. Then she tells Dante that he should put a light behind him that will shine out and reflect on all three mirrors. The result will be that all three mirrors reflect Dante's image but the one further out will be smaller. Yet Beatrice assures him that even though the smaller one is further away, it shines with equal brightness. Several theories exist about the reason Beatrice poses this experiment to Dante. Scholars explain it from various angles—i.e., from a medieval physics perspective, from a spiritual perspective, from a narratological structural perspective, and combinations thereof.[53] While Beatrice is certainly providing Dante with her version of medieval physics, her dialogue is more than that. She tells Dante,

> I shall now reshape your intellect
> thus deprived, with a light so vibrant
> that your mind will quiver at the sight. (*Par.* II, 109–11)

Beatrice is providing Dante not only a physics lesson but an apprehension of the triune God. Even though the reflection in one of the mirrors looks smaller, within the Trinity all are co-equal. The light that shines from behind Dante is a light furnished from a human perspective. But Beatrice tells Dante that the true light comes from above:

> And the heaven made fair by all these lights
> takes its stamp from the intellect that makes it turn
> making of itself the very seal of that imprinting. (*Par.* II, 130–32)

In the above passage, the lights in the sky receive their knowledge from the intellect (i.e., angels) from above. The intellect makes a seal on that

---

52. Miller, "Three Mirrors," 263.

53. In addition to the Miller article, see Tate, "Symbolic Imagination"; Tharn, "Medieval Christian."

which lies below it. Beatrice is telling Dante that ultimately a higher light shines down on the heavens. And that higher light will become clearer as he progresses further into heaven's circles. Dante is prefiguring the trinitarian vision that he will ultimately see at the end of his journey. Beatrice is setting the foundation for Dante to understand what he will see when he comes face to face with the triune godhead. At this point, the best he can hope for is a mirror analogy that lays the groundwork for what he will ultimately encounter. Dante does not have enough spiritual knowledge yet to understand how all persons in the Trinity reflect each other's light. To sharpen the understanding of the immanent Trinity, it will be helpful to see two more modern conceptions of it. The next section includes both Karl Rahner's and Balthasar's conception of the immanent Trinity. The reason for including Rahner's conception is because it will present a contrast to Balthasar's conception and hence increase the understanding of Balthasar's ideas.

4.3.2.2 Immanent Trinity: Rahner, Balthasar, and Dante

Karl Rahner saw a problem with the scholastic treatment of the Trinity. His critique is that to understand the use of "'three persons' correctly . . . we must always return to the original experience of salvation history."[54] What Rahner is intimating is that the immanent must be known through the creaturely experience of the economic Trinity in people's lives. In accentuating the complementarity between the immanent Trinity and the economic, Rahner writes with emphasis that "*the 'economic' Trinity is the 'immanent' Trinity and the 'immanent' Trinity is the 'economic' Trinity.*"[55] One of Rahner's primary theories about the immanent Trinity is that only one consciousness resides in God and it is shared by the three persons. Yet Rahner believes that there is a problem with using the concept of person. He states that the concept of person is, "at any rate, not *absolutely* constitutive of our knowledge in faith about Father, Son, and Spirit as the one God. This faith can exist without reference to this concept."[56] He explains the Trinity by writing that "the one God subsists in three distinct manners of subsisting." Rahner wishes to emphasize the term three "distinct manners of subsisting" to describe the one God's self-communication. Rahner believes that a

54. Rahner, *Trinity*, 105–6.
55. Rahner, *Trinity*, 22 (emphasis in the original).
56. Rahner, *Trinity*, 104.

> "distinct manner of subsisting" would then be an explanatory concept, not for a person, which refers to that which subsists as distinct, but for the "personality" which makes God's concrete reality, as it meets us in different ways, into precisely this one who meets us thus.... The single "person" in God would then be: God as existing and meeting us in this determined distinct manner of subsisting.[57]

Rahner uses the phrase "distinct manner of subsisting" as a way of describing our experience of the Trinity in salvation history. His concern with the word person is that in modern times it has taken what he calls an "anthropocentric turn" with a confusing idea of subjectivity.[58] Jordan Matthew Miller observes that "Rahner's concern is that essential unity, and thus the monotheistic faith of Israel (which Jesus also shares as a faithful Jew), is compromised by a doctrine that affirms three subjectivities."[59] Rahner wants us to know that God's knowledge includes three distinctions of only one real consciousness.[60] Rahner returns to what he calls his basic axiom, which is that "without our experience of the Father, Son and Spirit in salvation history, we would ultimately be unable to conceive at all of their subsisting distinctly as the one God."[61] Thus Rahner stresses the singular essence of God while allowing God to meet the creature in the "subsisting manner" of the Father, or of the Son, or of the Holy Spirit. Rahner privileges the economic Trinity over the immanent Trinity, because for humans the internal workings of the Trinity are perhaps impossible to understand. Rahner's position is in contrast to Balthasar's concerning the immanent Trinity.

Balthasar disagrees with Rahner's tendency to play down the distinctions between the persons of God. Jordan Matthew Miller states that Balthasar "argues that the distinction of the Father from the Son, which distinction *is* the Spirit, is the root of the distinction between God and creatures, and that this is the meaning of the [New Testament] teaching that all creatures exist through the Son."[62] Balthasar believes that Rahner's

---

57. Rahner, *Trinity*, 109–10.

58. Rahner adds that the concept of person invokes the idea one's relational nature. In the conventional idea of the person, nature is multiplied. However, when one returns to the original experience of salvation history, we experience the father as God, the son as God and the spirit as God.

59. Miller, "You Loved Me Before," 389.

60. Rahner, *Trinity*, 107.

61. Rahner, *Trinity*, 111.

62. Miller, "You Loved Me Before," 309–10. Miller lists a number of places where

theology does not account for the relationship of love that exists between the persons of the Trinity. Balthasar in *Theo-Drama V* quotes Aquinas saying, "If according to our faith, we assume the procession of the Divine Persons . . . this procession must be the cause and ground of the procession of creatures."[63] Also, Balthasar sees the interdependency between the economic Trinity and the immanent Trinity through Christ, the Holy Spirit, and revelation. He states that

> There is, however, no access to the trinitarian mystery other than its revelation in Jesus Christ and the Holy Spirit. No claims about the immanent Trinity can afford to lose their footing in the New Testament. Otherwise, they will plunge into a void of abstractions without pertinence to this history of salvation.[64]

Balthasar requires that one must work backward from Christ and revelation and the economic Trinity to the immanent Trinity. But he will not go as far as Rahner to claim that the immanent Trinity and the economic Trinity are one and the same. Additionally, Balthasar attends to an important aspect of the Trinity that Rahner does not emphasize.

When Balthasar speaks of the immanent Trinity, he talks about Love as the reason for the Father giving himself away to his Son. Balthasar critiques Augustine's view of the Trinity because it focuses on the being of the Trinity, "in the form of *mens, notia, amor* [mind, awareness, love]" and that "love (as a third) here can follow only on the mind's self knowledge."[65] Balthasar's critique is that Augustine's notion of the Trinity is more of an "I" and as such would confine the Trinity to self-love rather than charity for all. Balthasar looks to Richard of St. Victor and later Bonaventure to seek

---

this can be found in Balthasar's corpus: "The begetting of the Son and the procession of the Spirit are the precondition and the basis for creation—creation is not only similar to the begetting, it is one with the begetting but in an analogous way" (Balthasar, *Theo-Drama*, 5:61); "The act of the free coming-forth of the world is based on the Father's act of begetting within the Godhead" (*SC*, 108); "Being totally dependent on divine freedom, the world can receive its possibility and reality nowhere else but in the eternal son, who eternally owes his divine being to the Father's generosity. If the Son is the Father's eternal Word, the world in its totality is created by this word (John 1:3), not only instrumentally but in the sense that the Word is the world's pattern and hence its goal" (*Theo-Drama*, 2:261); "The world can only be created within the Son's generation" (*Theo-Drama*, 4:326); "A world that is full of risks can only be created within the Son's [generation]" (*Theo-Drama*, 4:327).

63. Aquinas quoted in Balthasar, *Theo-Drama*, 5:63.
64. Balthasar, *Theo-Logic*, 2:125.
65. Balthasar, *Theo-Logic*, 2:38.

a corrective to Augustine. For Richard of St. Victor, God is love and God must have a beloved equal to God. Additionally, for love to be complete, the two persons must have a third common object of love. Balthasar quotes Richard of St. Victor:

> When two love each other, exchanging the gift of their heart in intense longing, and love flows from the one to the other and from the other to the one and thus case tends in an opposite direction toward a diverse object, there is indeed love on both sides, but the partners do not yet love with each other [*condilectio*]. We cannot say that they love each other until the two love a third in harmonious unity, lovingly embracing him in common [*socialiter*], and the affection of the two surges forth as one in the flame of love for the third.[66]

The affectionate relationships through which Richard St. Victor and Balthasar describe the Trinity are different from how Aquinas describes the immanent Trinity.

Brendan McInerny states that Balthasar differentiates himself from Aquinas who posits that the relationships between the persons are characterized by necessity. McInerny describes Aquinas's trinitarian relationships as "intramental acts of God's self-knowing and self willing [that] must produce 'subsistent relations,' identical to the essence but distinct according to their relation and known in their relation of opposition to one other."[67] Aquinas's position emphasizes the Trinity and its three persons. Instead of being intra-person focused, Balthasar adopts what he calls a "dialogic" focus. Martin Buber's concept of "I-Thou" greatly influenced Balthasar. In fact, Balthasar claims that Buber

> attains, without realizing it, a unique *imago Trinitatis*: spirit reigns between the I and the Thou, who are pure relation to each other, but each one, incommunicable in his core (as the Other), nonetheless (and precisely for this reason) communicates all that he has.[68]

Balthasar marks his transition from Buber's I-Thou to the three person God by noticing Buber's emphasis on the "inter" "spirit" between the I and the Thou. Therefore, Balthasar sees Buber as coming close to his idea of the Trinity and emphasizing the relations between the persons. But Balthasar

---

66. Richard of St. Victor quoted Balthasar, *Theo-Logic*, 2:41.
67. McInerny, *Trinitarian Theology*, 21.
68. Balthasar, *Theo-Logic*, 2:54–55.

says that Buber's limitation is inherent in his Judaism because, in Judaism, God remains in expectation whereas Christianity believes in the historic revelation provided by Christ.[69] Balthasar's emphasis on Love between the persons of the Trinity is not static but dynamic.

Balthasar focuses on the dynamic movement generated by the Father out of gratuitous love for the Son and the Holy Spirit. The Father is the Father through this giving of himself. Balthasar claims that the Father

> remains the eternal Father only insofar as he has eternally given over to the Son all that is his, including the divinity. The same applies, analogously, to the Father and the Son in connection with the production of the Holy Spirit, who otherwise could not be the coeternal God."[70]

The idea of giving himself eternally is something that Balthasar claims corresponds to "thought's incapacity to exhaust God" and thus God remains to humans an inexhaustible mystery. God's love for the Son and the Son's reciprocation of love to the Father "is so inconceivable that its fruitfulness gives rise to the Holy Spirit" and "he is the objectivized fruit of the triune love."[71] Thus the Holy Spirit proceeds from the Father and the Son. Yet Balthasar goes even further in explaining the relationships of the Trinity. Balthasar emphasizes God's kenosis within the Trinity. Balthasar states, "The Father's self-utterance in the generation of the Son is an initial 'kenosis' within the Godhead. . . . For the Father strips himself, without remainder, of his Godhead and hands it over to the son; he 'imparts' to the Son all that is his."[72] Balthasar's emphasis is upon the movement of the kenotic giving of the Father that is based upon love. The kenosis of the Father "simultaneously includes the Son's self-givenness . . . and his filial thanksgiving (Eucharist) for the gift of consubstantial divinity. The world can only be created within the Son's 'generation.'"[73] McInerny's explanation concerning the Father's kenotic movement is that if "the Son is the perfect image and expression of the Father, then the kenotic incarnation of the Son indicates that the Father is the source of the kenosis."[74] Balthasar's conception of the Trinity, which is a dynamic procession among the persons, is

69. Balthasar, *Theo-Logic*, 2:55.
70. Balthasar, *Theo-Logic*, 3:136.
71. Balthasar, *Theo-Logic*, 2:140.
72. Balthasar, *Theo-Drama*, 4:323–24.
73. Balthasar, *Theo-Drama*, 4:326.
74. McInerny, *Trinitarian Theology*, 31.

based on kenotic love. The Eucharist brings the fruitfulness of the Son to the world. Balthasar's conception of the Trinity allows us to take a look at one of Dante's passages on the Trinity found in *Paradiso* X, which is the first canto in the realm of the Sun.

Paradiso X is the canto of the theologians. This is where Dante meets wise and holy men. Dante fittingly begins canto X with a description of the Trinity. For the purpose of the *Paradiso* passage below, I am using Teodolinda Barolini's translation because it provides a clearer idea of what Dante is doing in reference to the Trinity. Dante opens up the canto with these words:

> Gazing upon His Son with that Love
> One and the Other breathe eternally,
> the Power—first and inexpressible—
>
> made everything that wheels through mind and space
> so orderly that one who contemplates
> That harmony cannot but taste of Him. (*Par.* X, 1–6)[75]

Dante's words reflect his notion of the immanent Trinity. Barolini states that Dante, rather than commenting on the Trinity, actually performs the Trinity.[76] Barolini correctly identifies that the word "Power" in verse three is the subject of the first three verses. These six verses might be paraphrased as:

> By the Power of God's Love, which is primal cause and incomprehensible, the Father gazes upon his Son and through the Father and the Son, the Holy Spirit breathes forth eternally. Through the Father's Love, everything is created (whether in Heaven or below), moves in an orderly realm. Anyone who contemplates the Trinity cannot help but be in communion with the Triad God.

The activating power in the above verses is the power of God's love. And that movement of love breathes forth the Holy Spirit. Thus, in one way, Dante's words reflect Balthasar's concept of the Trinity, but in other ways, they do not. Dante's verses do resemble Balthasar's conception of the love that the Father has for the Son. The Father gazes on his Son, and through the Father and the Son, the Holy Spirit breathes forth into the world. Balthasar and Dante are certainly in alignment with the power of God's Love as a dynamic

---

75. Dante Alighieri quoted in Barolini, "*Paradiso* 10."

76. Barolini states that Dante by using the participle "Guardando" (Gazing) provides a "living" value and hence a performative feel to the verses.

among the persons of the Trinity. However, at least in this passage, Dante does not reflect on the Father's kenosis. This is a crucial point for Balthasar's conception of the Trinity. In Dante's passage above, kenotic passion does not move the Father to empty himself. Rather, the Father instead gazes, somewhat serenely, upon the Son. The Father's power is less a power of pathos borne by love and more an implicit knowledge of himself and the power of his loving gaze. What Dante brings to this passage is how that power not only is activated within the Triad persons but also how it moves forth into creation. The power is not the kenotic power of the Father but instead is a power that sets about the orderly activation of the world. Dante would agree with Balthasar that the procession of the Divine Persons is the cause and ground of the procession of creation and its creatures. In the passage above, Dante brings an additional insight to the understanding of the Trinity. He suggests that God's harmonious power is so apparent that the person "who contemplates / that harmony cannot but taste of Him."

One way of approaching what Dante means is to utilize Kilby's suggestion that a better way to understand the immanent Trinity is through contemplation. Kilby suggests it would not be difficult to engage in contemplation *of* the Trinity, as one who contemplates outside of the Trinity. Instead, one should find a place of contemplation within the Trinity, so that one is "by grace, involved with, taken up into, the life of the Trinity."[77] Hence, as Dante implies in the passage above, the only way one might understand the Trinity is to contemplate within it, rather than to use the analytic mind. To bypass the notion of the analytic mind, Dante associates the idea of contemplation with the human sense of taste. Further on in the canto, Dante addresses the reader again, telling them:

> Stay on your bench now, reader,
> thinking of the joy you have tasted,
> if, well before you tire, you would be happy.
>
> I have set your table. From here on feed yourself,
> For my attention now resides
> In that matter of which I have become the scribe. (*Par.* X, 22–27)

What can we make of Dante's use of the words "taste" and his reference to being at a table where the readers can "feed" themselves? The idea of taste and food is certainly not unknown in the realm of revelation. Psalm 34

---

77. Kilby, "Aquinas," 426.

("Taste and see that the Lord is good") is certainly one of the most known references. Likewise in Proverbs, we read:

> Wisdom has built her house;
> She has set up its seven pillars.
> She has prepared her meat and mixed her wine;
> She has also set her table. (Prov 9:1–2)

Dante in verse six of *Paradiso* X is using taste in order to drive both an artistic and a theological understanding of God.[78] As an artist, Dante must have known that his writing had to move out of the realm of the intellect and into the realm of the senses in order for it to have a felt effect on his readers. In fact, in *Paradiso* X, verses one through six, Dante moves the reader outward in a three-step process. The first three verses are a meditation on the power of love within the immanent Trinity.

> Gazing upon His Son with that Love
> One and the Other breathe eternally,
> the Power—first and inexpressible. (*Par.* X, 1–3)

Thus, the first three verses speak about the relationships among the immanent Trinity. Verses four and five, however, are a movement from the immanent Trinity to the economic Trinity which "made everything that wheels through mind and space / so orderly that one who contemplates" (*Par.* X, 4–5). In verses four and five, Dante speaks about how that love that exists within the Trinity is manifested in the orderly world. Finally, in verse six, Dante's meditation ends with a realization that the human "cannot but taste of Him" (*Par.* X, 6). Verse six is communicative of the Son who enters into the world and whom creatures can receive in the sacrament of the Eucharist.

Now that Dante has set up the idea of contemplation of the Trinity and how its love created the orderly world, in *Paradiso* X verses twenty-two through twenty-seven, he moves past meditation. This is where Dante lets the readers know that he accomplished his initial meditative work on the Trinity. Dante, the artist, sets the table and tells his readers, "From here on feed yourself" (*Par* X, 25). The reader feeds on the contemplative fruit of Dante's induced meditation. Dante as artist-priest has conducted his ceremony to bring the taste of the Triune God to the reader. The readers can stay and continue their contemplation (i.e., "feed yourself") but now Dante must move on and continue the narrative, "For my attention now

---

78. "That harmony cannot but taste of him" (Dante Alighieri *Par.* X, 6).

resides / In the matter of which I have become the scribe" (*Par.* X, 26–27). Dante's meditation on the Trinity and feeding is a reference to the effect of contemplation upon God by the person. Dante, in effect, shows his readers Christ in the form of a mystogogical use of the taste sense. This is one of the hallmarks of Christ's mission to bring the incarnational taste of God to humans. And mission is central to Balthasar's conceptions of Christology. Dante emerges out of the immanent Trinity and is ready to move on and meet Balthasar in the Economic Trinity, where God's creation lives, moves, breathes, and tastes.

4.3.2.3 *Economic Trinity*

Balthasar's theology of the economic Trinity emphasizes Christ's expression of Logos to creation. Balthasar states, "Jesus is the Word, the Image, the Expression and the Exegesis of God."[79] One of the outward expressions of God as Trinity is revelation itself. Balthasar states that the "finite intellect has no means, either inside or outside itself, to get an immediate glimpse of God; it remains dependent upon the sign language of the things through which God speaks to it."[80] One of the ways that God speaks with language is through scripture. For Balthasar, "Scripture is the Logos objectified and made the norm of all ages by the Holy Spirit in the context of the Incarnation."[81] As revelation, scripture is what allows humans to participate in God's truth. The reason scripture can do so is that it is

> precisely in this revelation that the creature, by God's liberality, acquires a share in God's truth, and God reveals his truth precisely by granting participation in this way. God thus equips the creature to be a relative center of truth, which is then able for its own part to know truth and to express something of it.[82]

Therefore, scripture allows the human person to know the truth of God. It allows one to participate in the body of truth and through that common participation enact the church. An example of how revelation fits into Dante's excursion in *Paradiso* is found in canto XXIV where Beatrice asks Peter to test Dante on his faith. Peter asks Dante several questions, the

---

79. Balthasar, *Glory of the Lord*, 1:29.
80. Balthasar, *Theo-Logic*, 1:234.
81. Balthasar, *Theology of History*, 100.
82. Balthasar, *Theo-Logic*, 1:232.

first of which is about Dante's definition of faith. Dante answers by quoting Hebrews 11: 1, whereby "faith is the substance of things hoped for, the evidence of things that are not seen." Peter's final question to Dante is what Dante believes and how he came to such a belief. Dante answers with a discourse that is a variant of the Nicene Creed. Dante's reply to Peter is that he believes "in one God / one and eternal" (*Par.* XXIV, 132–33). He goes on to tell Peter that he can prove his belief via scripture, "through Moses and the Prophets and the Psalms / Through what the Gospel says and what you [Peter] wrote" (*Par.* XXIV, 136–37). Then Dante goes on to recite his belief in the Trinity: "I believe in three eternal Persons, I believe / these are a single Essence, at once threefold and one" (*Par.* XXIV, 139–40). Dante's explication aligns with Balthasar's idea that scripture, as a form of revelation, is the Logos objectified and propagated by the Holy Spirit. Dante describes the truth of the gospel as something imprinted in his mind that is a spark that shines like a star in heaven (*Par.* XXIV, 142–47). When Dante finishes his conversation with St. Peter, he describes Peter's joy in the form of an avatar; a light that circles Dante three times. Peter's appearance as an avatar of light is just one of the manifestations of the form that Dante uses to express love and beauty. Throughout his theological aesthetics, Balthasar stresses the need for humans to understand God's beauty in a comprehensible form.

4.4 OUTER DYNAMICS OF BEAUTY

Among the three transcendentals of Truth, Good, and Beauty, Balthasar believes that since the Enlightenment, Beauty has been neglected. In the modern world, science has been dominant in representing the transcendental "Truth." Meanwhile, philosophy has focused on the "Good." But "Beauty" has either been minimized or has lost its grounding. Balthasar objects to the aestheticization of beauty. By that, he means that beauty has become unmoored from the True and the Good.[83] Previously, there was a bond between the beautiful, true, and good and Christian revelation. However, today professional aesthetics relegates the beautiful to a separate field. Balthasar states that "beauty can be loved for the sake of joy and virtue for

---

83. Balthasar, *Explorations in Theology*, 1:95. Balthasar believed that philosophers like Schleiermacher, Schelling, Hegel, and Schopenhauer moved the beautiful away from truth, whereas before the two were inseparable. He states that the beautiful became independent from religion and tied to materialism.

the sake of noble deeds, but this is not satisfactory."[84] Balthasar is saying that beauty and virtue are fine in themselves. But they need something more to elevate them into transcendentals. According to Balthasar, Dante's answer, "already in outline in the *Canzoniere* and developed in the *Convivio* and the *Comedy*, sees in beauty the expressive form of the good and the true."[85] Balthasar's project is to bring beauty back to its proper place by restoring its integral relationship with the good (which includes ethics) and the true (which is not just philosophy but a marriage of philosophy and theology). Two of the ways that Balthasar conceptualizes the outer dynamics of beauty are through the Form and God's glory. The next section will discuss the nature of the form and Christ as eros of the form.

4.4.1 The Form

4.4.1.1 Nature of the Form

For Balthasar, the expression of beauty through form can be characterized in three ways. First, beauty's power to transform depends not only on its display but also on its reception. Additionally, beauty is not the exotic province of the elite. Beauty is a gift to all of humankind. Finally, beauty is a combination of the earthly and the transcendent. Balthasar is expansive when he speaks about how beauty is expressed through form. He contends that the world contains inexhaustible forms of beauty. True beauty has a transcendental origin "only when the impact from above is truly felt."[86] Also at issue is whether the receiver of that impact "is open and receptive to the beauty in question [and] whether the times are propitious for the manifestation of the beauty in things."[87] Therefore, the form of beauty must tap into a transformative space that is larger than the immanent world, and the receiver must be ready to see and understand the form. Still, beauty cannot be merely a shower of beneficence that rains down on creatures. Balthasar states that "a transcendence of beauty alone is not viable."[88] Balthasar claims

---

84. Balthasar, *Glory of the Lord*, 3:103.
85. Balthasar, *Glory of the Lord*, 3:103.
86. Balthasar, *Explorations in Theology*, 1:104.
87. Balthasar, *Explorations in Theology*, 1:104.
88. Balthasar, *Explorations in Theology*, 1:107. Balthasar says that to keep beauty on only theological grounds would prevent it from being incorporated into the essences of subjects and objects.

that beauty is just "idle talk when divorced from the sense of a divine summons to change one's life."[89] Balthasar claims that Beauty supports a person to be "conscious of sharing in the continual transformation from the darkness of this world into the light of the next."[90] Beauty is more than purely individual grace "coming down from above on a lost world" since beauty is also grace bestowed "on the world so that, filled with divine power, it may—groaningly and in pain—struggle through into the light of eternity."[91] Thus beauty is a transformative power that is given to creatures through grace so that they can renovate their lives in conformance with God's truth. Given that the Form of beauty is important to Balthasar, how then does Dante display the Form in the *Comedy*? Balthasar claims that Dante does that through the use of the vernacular and by placing the *Comedy* within human history.

Balthasar states that Dante's use of the vernacular is one of the ways that he made the Form of beauty available to all Italians. Where Latin was the language of the nobility, Italian was the language of the servant. Balthasar asserts that Dante is aware that Latin is the language of the imperial court, but Dante "does not want to be a professional; he wants to be the legislator of a living culture" and "to that end he makes use of all the learning of his age, but such learning is at the service of his action, not vice versa."[92] By writing in the vernacular, Dante allows the masses to perceive his form of Beauty so that it transforms them. Therefore, for Dante and Balthasar, beauty is transformative when divinely inspired and can be received properly. Beauty need not be elitist because true Beauty is expansive and meant for all. For Dante and Balthasar, beauty combines both the heavenly and the earthly.

At the beginning of *Paradiso* in canto one, Dante asks for divine inspiration so that he can properly depict the union of heaven and earth for those who would read the *Comedy*. To create a conception of that union, Dante paints a vision that is part physical (i.e., literally related to medieval physics) and part divine (an acknowledgment of God's glory). He describes it as follows:

> The lamp of the world rises on us mortals
> at different points. But, by the one that joins

---

89. Balthasar, *Explorations in Theology*, 1:107.
90. Balthasar, *Explorations in Theology*, 1:109.
91. Balthasar, *Explorations in Theology*, 1:109.
92. Balthasar, *Glory of the Lord*, 1:15.

Heaven

four circles with three crossings, it comes forth

On a better course and in conjunction
with a better sign. Then it tempers and imprints
the wax of the world more to its own fashion. (*Par.* I, 37–42)

In Hollander's notes to this passage, he explains that the lamp of the world is the Sun. It rises each day at different points along the horizon. At a particular point on the horizon, four circles intersect. The circles are the horizon, the equator, the zodiac, and the colure of the equinox. The intersections of the circle form three crosses.[93] Dante's verses describe how God causes movement that affects physical creation. According to Aristotle, all natural bodies are capable of movement and that movement is either circular or straight. Since the movements of God are eternal, God's movements are circular.[94] On the other hand, the movement of a straight line is up and down and hence having a limit or end. Therefore, a vertical line is a symbol of the material world. Next Dante brings numerology into the picture. Usually, the number four deals with the material world, as indicated by the four seasons, the four elements (earth, air, fire, water), and the four parts of the body—head, trunk, legs, and arms.[95] On the other hand, the number three is usually associated with the eternal: Plato divides the soul into three parts (rational, appetitive, spirited), Euclidean geometry posits three dimensional space, and Christianity has a triune God as well as three transcendentals (Beauty, Truth, Good). When Dante makes straight lines (crossings) equal to three and the circles equal to four, he inverts the numbers belonging to the eternal and the physical. Dante performs the inversion in order to position the material in the eternal and the eternal in the material. Dante is forming a union of heaven and earth. The three crossings, as represented by the cross of Christ, are symbolic of Christ's supreme love for humanity where he offers himself up for its redemption. The incarnational or material aspect of the three crosses (Christ as human), embedded in the four circles (the eternal) unites humans and God through the kenosis of Christ. Balthasar references Bonaventure who declares, "The eternal God bends down in humility (*humiliter se inclinans*) when he raises

---

93. See Hollander's notes in Dante Alighieri, *Paradiso*, 24.

94. "The activity of God is immortality, i.e., eternal life. Therefore the movement of God must be eternal. But such is the heaven, viz. a divine body, and for that reason to it is given the circular body whose nature it is to move always in a circle" (Aristotle, "On the Heavens" 2.3.286b10–286b11, 473).

95. Dudley, *Numerology*, 25.

up the clay of our nature into the unity of his Person."[96] The passage above with its pronounced geometry of lines and circles is a prefiguration of the impossible geometry contained in the last canto of *Paradiso*. In *Paradiso* I, Dante, the character, is still in the process of learning. His geometric configuration in *Paradiso* I, although difficult, is possible to comprehend. However, when he finally arrives at the vision of God in canto XXXIII, the geometry of squaring the circle will be beyond comprehension. In *Paradiso* I, Dante unites the metaphysical realms of heaven and earth. Dante's character will understand more as he progresses through *Paradiso* and arrives at a true essence that is no longer conceptualized through the eyes or the mind. The essence that Dante encounters will be what he describes as the Love that moves the sun and stars.

4.4.1.2 *Christ and the Eros of Form*

Balthasar in his text *Love Alone is Credible* discusses the meaning of Love and its importance in Beauty's Form. According to Balthasar, Love is an "unconditional assent to and readiness for God's will, whether this will has expressed itself yet or not; love is an *a priori* Yes to whatever may come."[97] Balthasar compares Dante favorably to other Christian theologians in his writings on love. He says that Dionysius and Bonaventure found divine Eros in the cosmos but no personal Eros. And Augustine confessed personal Eros without it being theological. But with Dante "there appeared for the first time in Christian theology, the theme of individual, personal and fateful love."[98] Balthasar credits Dante for his demonstration of the long sweep of ever purifying love, starting with the *Vita Nuova* and ending in the *Comedy*. Balthasar is quite clear that in the *Comedy* the person who expresses this love most completely is Beatrice. Balthasar effusively praises how Dante demonstrates love via Beatrice. For Balthasar, Beatrice is not just an abstract symbol but "a young Florentine girl of flesh and blood."[99] Balthasar insists on Beatrice's incarnational presence. But like Mary, mother of God, Beatrice has a transcendental quality. Balthasar states, "Beatrice's purificatory and redemptive power in the end remains unique; she alone leads from Eros to Agape, or rather she is the Eros that is transfigured

---

96. Bonaventure quoted in Balthasar, *Glory of the Lord*, 2:353.
97. Balthasar, *Love Alone is Credible*, 125.
98. Balthasar, *Glory of the Lord*, 3:31.
99. Balthasar, *Glory of the Lord*, 3:32.

into agape."[100] Balthasar understands the incarnational and transcendental nature of feminine Love in Christian theology as starting with Mary who assents to God's desire that she will become the mother of God. Within the *Comedy*, it is Mary who directs St. Lucy to speak with Beatrice and intercede with Virgil to help Dante lost in the woods. When she swiftly comes to Dante's aid, Beatrice emulates revelation's depiction of Mary who gives immediate assent to God at the Annunciation. She embodies the idea of immediate and intuitive agape love. In contrast, Balthasar allows that it will take Dante a long journey through Hell, Purgatory, and Heaven before he understands love. Still, Balthasar praises Dante:

> The principle is established for the first time and never again so magnificently: [that] for the sake of infinite love, it is not necessary for the Christian to renounce finite love. On the contrary, in a positive spirit, he can incorporate his finite love into that which is infinite—but at the cost of terrible sufferings of course, as Dante shows us.[101]

Dante's "terrible sufferings" are a result of his own misconceptions about love. Throughout the *Comedy*, Beatrice insists that he must give up his old ideas concerning love and change his attitude. Beatrice's adamancy reaches its peak in *Purgatorio* when she dresses down Dante for his deviation from the true path of love. In *Paradiso*, Dante's relationship with Beatrice changes, and Beatrice becomes more of a gentle teacher rather than the admiral figure who first appeared in *Purgatorio*.[102] Beatrice believes that her instructions to Dante constitute time well spent. Her confidence that Dante has learned what he needs to know about love is exemplified when she recommends that St. John question Dante about his conception of love.

In *Paradiso* XXIV, XXV, and XXVI, saintly figures in heaven question Dante on the theological virtues of faith, hope, and love. St. Paul tests Dante on faith, St. James on hope, and St. John on love. John is the disciple at the last supper who reclines at Jesus's side and "whom Jesus loved" (John 13:23). A curious event happens when Dante meets St. John in *Paradiso* XXV. As he is trying to behold St. John who appears as a bright flaming entity, Dante loses his sight. Some scholars have interpreted the nature of Dante's blindness as a form of via negativa, i.e., a way towards God without

---

100. Balthasar, *Glory of the Lord*, 3:36.
101. Balthasar, *Glory of the Lord*, 3:32.
102. Dante describes Beatrice during their meeting in Purgatory as "Just like an admiral who moves from stern to prow" (Purg, XXX, 58).

the use of the light of the senses. Dante tries to look for Beatrice, but he realizes he cannot see her. John instructs Dante that his loss of sight is only temporary and that he should not worry,

> For the lady who guides you through
> This holy place possesses in her glance
> The power the hand of Ananias had. (*Par.* XXVI, 10–12)

The reference to the "hand of Ananias" alludes to St. Paul's blindness encountered on the road to Damascus. Paul ultimately had his blindness restored by Ananias. In the passage above, St. John signifies that Beatrice's love for Dante is so strong that she can restore his spiritual sight. In response to St. John's words, Dante answers that he is unafraid about his vision loss and that Beatrice can heal him "as soon or as late as she wishes" (*Par.* XXVI, 13). Thus, Dante has proven that he has faith and hope—both of which he expresses in his answer concerning Beatrice's power.

Now St. John will test him on love. For that examination, John asks Dante about his soul's goal. Dante answers that

> The good that satisfies this court
> Is the alpha and omega of whatever scripture
> Love teaches me in loud or gentle tones. (*Par.* XXVI, 16–18)

Dante's answer signifies that he will accept anything that Love teaches him, whether it comes loudly or softly. Balthasar glosses Dante's passive response by saying that some had suspected Dante of Averroism, charging him with a view of human nature as passive as wax and only waiting for God's imprint.[103] Balthasar, however, objects to this idea and states that Dante addresses more than just one side of love's dialectic. Love is not an either/or situation. Love is not just "Eros (striving upwards) or Agape (condescending)" because love transcends that opposition, and the understanding of love is made clearer "in the successive stages of the work."[104] Thus Balthasar sees that Dante's love is not just pure passivity in the captivity of condescending Agape. Grace does pour down from heaven, but the lover also extends himself upward through his own efforts. Therefore, both are necessary as part of the dialectic. And Dante, the writer, will make that clearer

---

103. Balthasar, *Glory of the Lord*, 3:37. Balthasar says that there is a misconception about Dante, and he has been seen as implying that "all good activity originates from Heaven, while the human heart . . . is again and again compared to a passive 'wax' which can at most contribute a greater or lesser pliability to the form."

104. Balthasar, *Glory of the Lord*, 3:37.

through his responses to St. John's questions. As an example, St. John is not satisfied with Dante's answer about love and tells him, "It is clear you need to sift / with a finer sieve" (*Par.* XXVI, 22–23). Dante responds and says that he learned love through "philosophic reasoning" (*Par.* XXVI, 25). He states that knowledge that is Good kindles love, and the more knowledge is good, the more love it kindles (*Par.* XXVI, 28–30). Dante credits his understanding to "him who demonstrates to me the primal love / of all eternal substances" (*Par.* XXVI, 38–39). The "him" of whom Dante speaks is Aristotle.[105] In addition to divine intuition, Dante includes philosophical wisdom as a source for understanding love. Thus philosophical truth becomes another method to understand love.

Dante then lists two other ways to understand love. He credits the "truthful Author" who spoke to Moses saying, "I will make all My goodness pass before you" (*Par.* XXVI, 42). Thus Dante invokes revelation from the Old Testament as a source of divine truth which expresses the good. Dante then tells John that it was "your [John's] own great message, which, more than any other herald, / proclaims the mystery of this high place on earth" (*Par.* XXVI, 44–45). In his response, Dante invokes the New Testament as a source of knowledge that provides the message of love.[106] Thus, Dante has invoked Aristotle, the Old Testament, and the New Testament concerning the nature of Love. It would have seemed that by this time, John would have been satisfied with Dante's answer. Instead, St. John presses Dante further, asking him to name the "chords that draw you to Him" and to "declare the many teeth with which this love does bite" (*Par.* XXVI, 49–51). Dante enlarges his answer with an answer that goes beyond just himself. He replies:

> all those things
> the bite of which can make hearts turn to God
> converge with one another in my love.
>
> The world's existence and my own,
> The death He bore that I might live,

---

105. Dante Alighieri, *Paradiso*, 715. In Hollander's notes he states that "Aristotle is the nearly unanimous opinions of the commentators, who are divided only about the precise passage . . . explaining how the spheres' love for the God head set the universe in motion."

106. Dante Alighieri, *Purgatorio*, 716. Hollander states that Dante's commentators split between whether Dante is referencing John's gospel or the Apocalypse, both of which were attributed to St. John during Dante's time.

And that which all believers hope for as do I. (*Par.* XXVI, 55–60)

Dante's love is for himself and the entire world which enfolds him within his own love. Additionally, Dante understands the impact of Christ's sacrificial love wherein Christ died so that Dante might live. Thus Dante's love comes from his acceptance of Christ's love demonstrated through the crucifixion, and he sees that love manifested in the church (i.e., "all believers"). Finally, Dante acknowledges the journey that has taken him "from the sea of twisted love" to "the shore where love is just" (*Par.* XXVI, 62–63).

Thus Dante's examination by St. John on love and Dante's replies are extremely comprehensive. Love is more than just intuitive illumination descending from God. The understanding of God is multifaceted. Philosophic reasoning can be used to understand love as truth. We know what is true because it is good. We can also understand God's love through revelation—both the New and the Old Testaments. Additionally, we are knowledgeable of not just our own love but how our love is intertwined with all of God's people, and especially in communion with the church. Finally, we understand God's love through the witness of Christ's death and resurrection. All share in Christ's love so that all might have divine life. Dante's answer substantiates what Balthasar will define as love. Balthasar believes that Christian thought became too mixed with Platonic Western metaphysics such that it overemphasized the vertical dimension (i.e., love between God and creature) and diminished the horizontal dimension (i.e., love of one's neighbor). Also, Christ's mission was "the abolition of the Law which divided the Jews from the Gentiles."[107] Thus in Christ one finds a single figure who can unite heaven and earth, human with human, Jew with Gentile. With the arrival of Christ in history.

> No longer does God content himself with intervening from Heaven on the side of the poor man (who in truth is the sinner): now he crosses over to him as a man. And he does not do this in an act of condescension, by distributing alms among the poor: the crossing-over takes place down below, on the level of the poor themselves, when he takes upon himself the burden of all their poverty.[108]

Balthasar's description of Christ's kenotic love is more extensive than Dante's answers to St. John about love. But it contains Dante's essential elements. Dante knows love through philosophical reasoning and revelation.

---

107. Balthasar, *Glory of the Lord*, 7:442.
108. Balthasar, *Glory of the Lord*, 7:443.

But even more importantly, he knows love because of Christ's willingness to undergo death to bring about the unification of heaven and earth. In summary, Dante answers that we can know love because it is good, true, and beautiful. Love is not merely a single relationship between God and creature, but it is manifested throughout creation of all to all within God's realm. Love is the most important Form of beauty, and an attribute of that Form is God's glory.

4.4.2 God's Glory

4.4.2.1 *God's Illumination and the Human Response*

For both Dante and Balthasar, God's glory consists of two actions. The first is how the Godhead reveals Its illuminative glory to creatures, and the second is that creatures praise God for the revelation of illumination. God's glory can be related through a dialogical approach whereby those humans who are more advanced attempt to communicate it to another human. Another way is through a demonstration of God's power. According to Balthasar, those who have seen God's glory revealed to them are so overpowered that "the deeper a creature is allowed to encounter God's glory, the more this creature will want to extol this glory as being exalted over itself and over all creation."[109] Balthasar's explanation about why a creature like Dante would want to extol God's glory is because he is so grateful to have received God's grace that he wants to share it with others. We saw that Dante opens *Paradiso* by praising God's glory.[110] Dante discusses the difficulty of praising God's glory because the person who has seen heaven and returns "can neither show nor tell what he has seen" (*Par.* I, 6). Still, Dante wants to do his best to try. However, for Balthasar, God's radiance of glory is almost impossible for a human to explain.

The reason that Balthasar gives for the impossibility of a human to explain God's glory is because dialogical form cannot explain it. That form of communication is for humans and was part of Christ's mission during his time on earth. For Balthasar, communication of God's glory to one of his creatures "can occur only by virtue of a primary sense of being overawed by the undialogical presupposition of the dialogue that has started, namely,

---

109. Balthasar, *Glory of the Lord*, 6:10.

110. "The glory of Him who moves all things / pervades the universe and shines" (*Paradiso* I, 1–2).

the divinity or glory of God."[111] As an example, when Dante is traveling through the different realms of heaven he is often in communication with Beatrice. That kind of communication is dialogical in nature. For instance, Dante asks in *Paradiso* II why dark spots appear on the Moon. Beatrice instructs Dante and answers his questions. Then Beatrice tells Dante,

> Observe well how I pass along this way
> To the truth you seek, so that in time
> You may know how to ford the stream alone. (*Par.* II, 124–26)

The reason that Beatrice offers dialogical instruction is so that Dante can later understand God's glory and ultimately reach the pinnacle of God's illumination on his own. That is the only way one can experience God's glory. Another example of the difference between dialogical exchange and God's glory is a reference made in *Paradiso* XXII during Dante's conversation with Benedict. Benedict gives Dante a list of the problems that beset the extant earthly church. The monasteries are more concerned with money. Usury is prevalent among the faithful, etc. After Benedict tells Dante how far the people of God have strayed, he tells Dante that God can intervene in the present:

> Still, the sight of Jordan driven back and of the sea
> that opened it at the will of God were greater wonders
> to behold than would be His intervention here. (*Par.* XXII, 94–96)

Benedict's point is that the dialogical method necessary for rectifying the church's sins (i.e., exhorting humans to be more ethical and devout in their lives) would be less effective than a demonstration of how God parted the Jordan (Joshua 3–4). In his description of how God makes his glory manifest through sensory perception, Balthasar speaks to God's power. He states that "the overwhelming sensory signs by which God proclaims his presence point initially, in an elemental way, to power."[112] While God has exhibited many manifestations of power in revelation (e.g., storms, lightning, fires, etc.), Balthasar reminds us that, "Yhwh, however, was never a nature-god but rather a God who led, chose, and instructed."[113] Here Balthasar is contrasting God as ruler over nature with pagan gods whose power was used only for their own benefit. Instead, Yahweh directs power for the benefice of his creatures. A parting of the Jordan's waters was not a trick of nature.

---

111. Balthasar, *Glory of the Lord*, 6:11.
112. Balthasar, *Glory of the Lord*, 6:54.
113. Balthasar, *Glory of the Lord*, 6:55.

Rather it was to benefit the Israelites who were God's chosen. After Dante relates how glorious God's power was in parting the waters, he ascends the stairs of heaven. Dante describes how quickly he can ascend compared to his laborious climbing of steps on earth. Dante is impressed not only with the power related in the Old Testament story but also at God's power in making the laws of gravity less onerous for him in *Paradiso*. He exclaims God's glory stating,

> O glorious stars, O light made pregnant
> With a mighty power, all my talent,
> Whatever it may be, has you as a source. (*Par.* XXII, 112–14)

Dante's short ode to God's glory reinforces Balthasar's claim that a reciprocal relationship occurs between the manifestation of God's eminent glory and the desire for creatures to proclaim it of their own.

Yet Power manifested through an earthly means is not the only way that Dante depicts God's glory. Balthasar notes that Dante, in *Paradiso*, arranges the cosmos in a manner that is "permeated with divine energies, [that] is understood in a Christian way. Its entire aesthetic power of expression serves to support a Christian theological aesthetic."[114] One example that Balthasar cites is while Beatrice is leading Dante from the realm of the Heaven of the Stars to the Primum Mobile. Dante describes how he was looking up at his destination, but Beatrice asks him to look down "and see how wide a circle you have traveled" (*Par.* XXVII, 78). When he looks down, Dante can see an all-encompassing view from where he came. He describes his view beyond the heavens as panoptic:

> So that on the one side I could see, beyond Gades,
> the mad track of Ulysses, on the other, nearly
> to the shore where Europa made sweet burden of herself.
>
> More space of this small patch of earth
> could I have seen, had not the sun, beneath my feet,
> now moved a sign and more away. (*Par.* XXVII, 82–87)

The scale of Dante's view is incomprehensible. Balthasar describes the immensity of it by saying,

> Here is a journey through space to induce vertigo, following the revolutions of the concentric spheres, astronomically exact, and

---

114. Balthasar, *Glory of the Lord*, 3:69.

soaring out of space, for the sphere of crystal, which is pure invisible transparency, adjoins what is beyond space.[115]

Balthasar's description of Dante's journey as inducing vertigo attests to its cosmological extravagance. But Balthasar questions if Dante, in making his ascent so far flung, runs the risk of losing its spiritual sense. He rhetorically asks whether Dante's cosmological description "hinders, rather than helps, the development of an authentically Christian theological aesthetic."[116] Balthasar's answer, however, is that Dante works with the materials available to him, which are pure light, and love and blessedness.[117] Additionally, Balthasar goes on to speak of the other forms of sensory experiences that Dante utilizes to provide a sense of God's glory. He cites *Paradiso* X where the teachers of wisdom dance around Dante and *Paradiso* XVIII where the souls spell out the first words of the book of Wisdom (*Diligite Justitiam*, Love Justice). Balthasar goes on to cite many other choreographic manifestations that are shocking to the senses in their movement and sound.[118] Ultimately, however, Balthasar experiences a bit of disappointment with Dante. He says that with Dante's overabundance of sensory shocks "there is a certain embarrassment, even emptiness."[119] He believes that the assault on the senses is perhaps overkill. He even concludes that the threefold examination of Dante on faith, hope, and love "succeeds only in being boring."[120] Balthasar states that Dante describes the cosmological heavens by relying too much on abstract Scholastic theology. Yet Balthasar does grant Dante credit in his depiction of Beatrice. He mentions how human Beatrice's cries are for Dante when she comes to the *Inferno* to ask Virgil to assist Dante. Even so, Balthasar asserts that Dante's journey in *Paradiso* XXVII from the Heaven of the Stars into the Primum Mobile has too much of the ethereal Neoplatonism in it. For Balthasar's tastes, Dante is not earthly enough and lacks human emotionality. Balthasar ends his discussion of *Paradiso* with the following:

> It can therefore be said that ultimately his Paradise has a Marian form. Christ stands higher [than Mary], dwelling in the heart of

---

115. Balthasar, *Glory of the Lord*, 3:70.
116. Balthasar, *Glory of the Lord*, 3:71.
117. Balthasar, *Glory of the Lord*, 3:72.
118. In addition, Balthasar cites the martyrs in the sphere of Mars coming together in the shape of a cross and in the sphere of Saturn the contemplatives forming Jacob's ladder.
119. Balthasar, *Glory of the Lord*, 3:73.
120. Balthasar, *Glory of the Lord*, 3:73.

the Trinity. Only "in the mirror and enigma" of supreme rapture can man have an inkling of him as the humanly incomprehensible "quadrature of the circle"—the dazzling glorious identity of God and man. His [Christ's] triumphal procession through the eighth heaven makes only a faint impression, and if his outline is to be seen in the great living image in Mars, the cross formed of souls, it is only an image to which Dante is not prepared to concede the full presence. The cross of Christ, in all its reality, is met nowhere in the *Divine Comedy*.[121]

In the next section, I will address Balthasar's critique which encompasses two principal areas. The first is that Dante's encounter with God in *Paradiso* overly relies on the sensation of vision and progressive illumination that results from it. The other critique is that *Paradiso* is a form of Marianism, and it does not foreground Christ, especially the kenotic idea of Christ Crucified.

4.4.2.2 *God's Glory Perceived as Vision*

The ultimate experience of Dante in the *Comedy* is the vision of God which occurs at the end of *Paradiso*. In that vision, God reveals God's full glory. It is the culmination of the long journey that Dante begins in the *Inferno* and ultimately completes in *Paradiso*. Dante's journey is an accumulation of knowledge and experience as his soul becomes purified enough to have an encounter with the divine. Dante's conception of the vision of God and Balthasar's idea of seeing the image of God are quite different. To understand the differences I would like to discuss four aspects of Dante's vision. First, Dante's vision is progressive in nature, requiring preparation and purification. Complete purification is not an instantaneous event that happens out of God's gratuity. Additionally, Dante's vision is strongly associated with the sense of sight, which is privileged over other sensory phenomena. Third, the experience of the vision is passive in nature. But although the experience is passive, God's illuminative light completely overwhelms the creature. Finally, how Dante arrives at his vision is ultimately Marian. However, the vision is Marian in the Catholic sense of Mary as an intercessor between humans and God.

In contrast to Dante, Balthasar believes that an encounter with God is a participatory event between the creature and God. Participation is not a single event like Dante's vision of God but an unfolding of the creature into

---

121. Balthasar, *Glory of the Lord*, 3:82.

God's presence. Second, no strict boundary endures between heaven and earth. Rather, reciprocity between heaven and earth prevails. Heaven is not only the future but also the present. Additionally for Balthasar, a vision of God is not only a vision but also a hearing. The Word of God always influences us—not just Christ's visual form but also his words. Finally, Balthasar agrees with Gregory Palamas that although one may think that they see God, what they really experience is God's energies and not God's true essence.[122] This is because God is infinite and the creature will never truly comprehend God, at least not until the resurrection of the flesh at the end of this world.[123]

To understand how Dante presents his ideas about how a creature encounters the Divine, I want to examine cantos thirty through thirty-three of *Paradiso*. Canto thirty is where Dante crosses over from the Primum Mobile to the Empyrean. Dante notices that he has crossed over and records Beatrice's annunciation that they have gone

> from the largest body to the Heaven of pure light
>
> light intellectual, full of love,
> love of true good, full of joy. (*Par.* XXX, 39–41)

Beatrice tells Dante that they have gone from the Primum Mobile, the largest body of matter, "maggior corpo" (39) in *Paradiso*, and entered into the Empyrean which is a spiritual sphere of light. The progressive nature of the light's intensity will increase as Dante travels higher. Dante privileges the visual sense by describing the "faville / sparks" (64) that settle on the "fiori / flowers" (65) and how he seemed "come imbrïate da li odori / as though intoxicated by the odors" (67). The sparks are the angels in the Empyrean and the flowers are the souls in heaven. Dante is painting a visual picture that is attempting to explain the exorbitance of heaven using earthly images. Dante's language does a much better job representing the visual.

---

122. In John Cheng's article, he claims that Gregory Palamas (1296–1359) makes the distinction between God's essence (*ouisa*) and God's energy (*energeia*). Cheng writes: "The Ultimate reality and Meaning of the Palamite theology consists of the distinction between God's Essence and Energy. This is a way of expressing the idea that the transcendent God remains eternally hidden in his Essence, but at the same time God also seeks to communicate and unite Himself with us personally through His Energy" (Cheng, "Distinction between God's Essence and Energy," 60).

123. Balthasar's ideas concerning the creature's encounter with God are not from his comments on Dante found in *Glory of the Lord* (vol. 3). Instead, they are mainly in *Explorations in Theology* (vol. 4) and *Theo-Drama* (vol. 5).

When it comes to the sense of smell, he explains the activity of the angels "as though" there were intoxicating odors. In this example, Dante does not even try to describe the smell with a metaphor, a simile, or another literary device. Next, Beatrice tells Dante that, to understand what he is seeing, he "di quest'acqua convien che tu bei" / "must drink first of these waters" (73). In this passage, the drinking that Dante is doing is with his eyes. To paraphrase what Dante means is to say, "take this vision in with your eyes, as you would take water to quench the thirst in your body." Then Dante describes Beatrice as "il sol de li occhi miei" / "the sun of my eyes" (75). Thus does Dante accentuate the idea of sight. Beatrice tells him that his perception of what he is seeing is "acerbe" / "unripe" (79) because "che non hai viste ancor tanto superbe" / "your vision is not yet strong enough to soar" (81). Dante privileges sight because of the influence of classical philosophy and early to medieval Christianity.

Hans Boersma, in *Seeing God: The Beatific Vision in Christian Tradition*, validates why Dante emphasizes sight as the means for attaining the grace required to see the vision of God. He states, "Both the Hellenic and Christian traditions have often valued sight over speech."[124] As an example, Plato in the *Timaeus* states, "The sight in my opinion is the source of the greatest benefit to us, for had we never seen the stars and the sun and the heaven, none of the words which we have spoken about the universe would ever have been uttered."[125] Plato asserts that vision is one of the greatest gifts given to us by God and because of it philosophy developed.[126] Aquinas also describes sight as chief among the senses. In the *Summa Theologica*, he states that unlike animals who have their faces turned to the ground to procure food, humans have their faces "erect, so that by the senses, and chiefly by sight, which is more subtle and penetrates further into the differences of things . . . so as to gather intelligible truth from all things."[127] Aquinas goes on to add that the inferior parts of the body are lower to the ground and the superior parts are higher up, hence, by extension, giving special stature to the eyes and brains. Therefore, because of the emphasis on vision in ancient philosophical and Christian traditions, one can understand why Dante might make a vision of God the culmination of the *Divine Comedy*. And to a certain extent, Balthasar will agree that a vision of God plays an

---

124. Boersma, *Seeing God*, 249.
125. Plato, *Timaeus* 47a.
126. Plato, *Timaeus* 47b.
127. Aquinas, *ST* I, 91.3.

important part in Christian theology. Balthasar cites biblical verses emphasizing sight and the vision of God, including: "For now we see in a mirror, dimly, but then we will see face to face" (1 Cor 13:12), which describes how our vision of God will change once we attain infinite life.

Balthasar understands that vision is privileged in ancient culture and Christian theology. But he believes that the vision of God need not be the terminal point in one's encounter with God. Balthasar states, "One would do much better, therefore, to take the promise of Jesus to the Samaritan woman as the point of departure on earth for an understanding of what transcends it."[128] He favors a more participatory symbology with the living water of God. He quotes scripture, "Whoever thirsts, come to me; drink, whoever believes in me! As scripture says: 'Streams of living water will flow from within' [John 7:37]." The reason that Balthasar favors the idea of living water is not only because it changes the believer but "even more, in its recipients, it transforms itself into the gift that is to be given to others; only by being handed on can it be a true gift worthy of God."[129] Balthasar would prefer a gift that went beyond sight and that one person could give to another. Using the metaphor of a well with ever-fresh water provides an understanding of eternal transmission that can never be fully consumed. An additional critique that Balthasar has with perceiving God through sight is that God is an infinite Being with infinite freedom. Therefore, Balthasar questions how much a creature can truly perceive God through sight.[130] He states that an encounter with God

> can never be [as] an object totally available to our sight. If we wish to keep the metaphor of "vision," we must speak in dialectical terms of the highest presence of something that is beyond all that we can grasp.[131]

Balthasar wishes to move past the idea of sight as the predominant means of experiencing God's effulgence. But the idea that Dante fully grasped the experience of God at the end of the last canto of *Paradiso* is open to debate. Dante relates that his encounter with God was so overwhelming that his "exalted vision lost its power" (*Par.* XXXIII, 143). Thus, it could

---

128. Balthasar, *Explorations in Theology*, 4:441.

129. Balthasar, *Explorations in Theology*, 4:441.

130. Balthasar, *Theo-Drama*, 5:395. Balthasar states that the only way we can imagine this is as the opening-up of endless rooms. Still, the "visio Dei" is always an inadequate and one-sided portrayal of this open encounter.

131. Balthasar, *Theo-Drama*, 5:395–96.

be that Dante is agreeing with Balthasar and that his human vision failed him at the crucial moment. On the other hand, Dante does proclaim that as a result of his vision, his will and his desire were turning like revolving wheels coordinated with "the love that moves the sun and all the stars" (*Par.* XXXIII, 245). Can we understand Dante's vision as mostly passive (i.e., merging with the revolving wheels) or does it reflect Balthasar's idea of more active participation with the Divine in an infinite exchange?

In his article "The Final Image: *Paradiso* XXXIII," John Freccero postulates:

> Even in the Beatific vision when God becomes the soul's most intimate possession, the external world of suns and stars never ceases to exist. The dialectic between the human soul and God was for Dante never to be dissolved into its two polarities, as it was later in the Renaissance. Just as the individuality could not be totally absorbed into divinity, so God could not be completely reduced to the proportions of the human soul.[132]

Freccero's idea is that even in the Beatific Vision the creature continues to exist without a dissolution of the polarity between itself and the divine. It brings back the idea of the analogy of being where God and creature can never bridge the divide between them. Even in the divine vision, the creature and the divine are separate. As Betz explained, God's essence is to exist while the essence of the creature is "always on the horizon of its existence as something to be attained."[133] Balthasar would agree with Betz in this area. However, he would disagree with Dante's idea that the creature is in movement with God as if were part of a giant mechanical clock's movement. Balthasar states, "Since in God there is eternal life and hence 'eternal surprise,' we too shall experience this surprise."[134] Additionally since God's love and freedom "require something like 'super-times' and 'super-space' so that his love can expand infinitely, we too shall experience, beyond our transitory nature a kind of 'elasticity' of duration in which there will be a coincidence of the 'eternal here' and the 'eternal now.'"[135] Balthasar's insistence on God's freedom and the notion of time and place elasticity suggests that a mechanical clock is not the ideal metaphor for his vision

---

132. Freccero, "Final Image," 27–28.

133. Betz, "After Barth," 60.

134. Balthasar, *Theo-Drama*, 5:400. In this section of *Theo-Drama*, Balthasar agrees with Jan van Ruysbroeck's conception of God's freedom.

135. Balthasar, *Theo-Drama*, 5:401.

of God. As opposed to Dante's preference for sight and perhaps the idea of creaturely passivity at an encounter with the divine, Balthasar prefers exchange, movement, and improvisatory freedom. This would allow the infinite quality of God to determine the encounter rather than for the creature to conceive its terms. Balthasar states, "God's creativity challenges the creativity of creatures to move beyond itself."[136] In other words, God's creativity not only inspires creatures to focus on the relationship between creature and God but also impels the person to move beyond itself and develop relationships between creature and creature. In contrast to Balthasar's idea of freedom, improvisation, and elasticity, Dante's vision of God is a progressive illumination.

Throughout *Paradiso*, Dante persists in the idea of ongoing enlightenment that step by step leads him onto a vision of God. Tamara Pollack explains:

> The vision of God in which the *Commedia* terminates is the vanishing-point of the entire poem, the ineluctable yet ungraspable punto which draws the gaze but remains itself invisible; every canto converges towards it and it orients each step of the journey.

Throughout the *Comedy*, Dante is on a steady movement towards his vision of God. In the *Divine Comedy*, Dante's progression is a matter of ever refined purification that makes him worthy to have an encounter with God. Even focusing exclusively on the *Paradiso*, one can see Dante transformed as he progresses from one realm of heaven to another with Beatrice and Bernard leading him on. Beginning in *Paradiso* I, Dante shows the transformative power of Beatrice's gaze:

> As I gazed on her, I was changed from within,
> As Glaucus was on tasting of the grass
> That made him consort of the gods in the sea
>
> To soar beyond the human cannot be described. (*Par.* I, 67–70)

Glaucus is a character of Ovid's *Metamorphoses* who began life as a mortal fisherman. By eating an herb he became immortal. Dante uses the word *trasumanar* (a Dante neologism meaning to soar beyond the human or to transhumanize) to indicate the changing nature of his spiritual condition. Dante's reference to Glaucus is not meant to indicate that Dante becomes a god himself. Rather, he uses a mythological figure to indicate the spiritual

---

136. Balthasar, *Explorations in Theology*, 4:443.

transformation that Dante is experiencing. He is progressing in his spiritual path by his fixed attention on Beatrice who is leading him on his journey. Yet Dante indicates that his journey towards God is more than just his or Beatrice's own doing. In his mercy, God offers man the path towards everlasting life. Dante indicates the power of Christ:

> More bountiful was God when He gave Himself,
> Enabling man to rise again, than if,
> In His sole clemency, he had simply pardoned.
>
> All other means fell short of justice
> Save that the Son of God
> Should humble Himself by becoming flesh. (*Par.* VII, 115–20)

Although Dante follows Beatrice in his ascent throughout most of the *Paradiso*, what makes Dante's ascent possible is Christ's descent. This idea ties into Balthasar's conception that the creature is in a participatory event with God. And through the creature's relationship with Christ, it "comes to participate in the natural indissolubility of the love between the Father and the Son and in the Holy Spirit."[137] Through the triune God, God and creature reach a hypostatic union. As such, Dante's rise through the realms of the afterlife is an ascent in response to Christ's kenotic love, a love that exists within the triune Godhead. According to Balthasar, the Father performs a kenotic act in the utterance of the Son as "the Father strips himself, without remainder, of his Godhead and hands it over to the Son; he 'imparts' to the Son all that is his."[138] The surrender of the Father to the Son and the subsequent thanksgiving to the Father by the Son together breathes forth the Spirit. This love is the foundation upon which Dante builds the *Comedy*. The kenotic love within the Trinity is what undergirds Beatrice's love for Dante and is that which Dante wants to return to Beatrice. Beatrice's love for Dante is buttressed by the triune love of the Godhead, while the form of that love shows up through Mary, who beckons St. Lucy, who contacts Beatrice. Since Mary is the initiator who sets Dante's journey into motion, Balthasar does have a point when he claims that *Paradiso* has a Marian form. Thus, it would be worthwhile to understand how Balthasar thinks about Marianism and how it shows up in *Paradiso*.

---

137. Balthasar, *Glory of the Lord*, 1:480.
138. Balthasar, *Theo-Drama*, 4:323.

4.4.2.3 *Paradiso as Marianism*

In his text *Mary for Today*, Balthasar begins his meditation on Mary by referencing Revelation 12, which forms the context for Mary as the church. Balthasar's image of Mary is the "woman clothed with the sun, with the moon under her feet and a crown of twelve stars on her head" (Rev 12:1). In Revelation 12, the woman is pregnant and about to give birth, but a giant red dragon who wishes to devour her child opposes her. She escapes and gives birth to the messiah and afterward, a tremendous battle occurs between the angels and the dragon. The angels defeat the dragon and hurl it to the earth. The dragon still pursues the woman and her child, but she is given wings so that she can escape to the wilderness. The dragon who is enraged at the woman's escape continues to wage war against the rest of her children who keep the commandments. According to Balthasar's reading of this passage of Revelation, the wilderness was a place of refuge where God fed and cared for the woman, just as God cared for Israel in the desert. Ultimately God led Israel into the promised land. But according to Balthasar, the church today has no promised land until "the other side of history: a new heaven and a new earth."[139] In the meantime, the church consists of the woman's children who fight the demons and keep God's commandments. Balthasar claims that Mary cares for her children because

> she lives in them, as her children live through and in her. Hence their fate is hers: exposed to the rage of the serpent and, if they fight [they are] protected and nourished by God.[140]

Mary is still available to her children through the church. Balthasar's genesis story of the church can be related to Dante's genesis story beginning with the *Inferno*. Dante is lost in the wilderness. Demons are pursuing him in the form of animals. He is one of the Holy Mother's children who is trying to keep the commandments but feels overwhelmed by the forces of evil attacking him. Ironically, Virgil, a pagan, arrives to help him. Yet the original source of help is from Mary, via Lucy, via Beatrice.[141] These feminine figures offer to help Dante out of the wilderness. Just as Mary escapes from the red dragon to the wilderness, she will initiate help for Dante so that he can find his way out of the darkness. Balthasar explains that the church has always been thought of as feminine. Even before the church, the Jews

---

139. Balthasar, *Mary for Today*, 12.
140. Balthasar, *Mary for Today*, 12.
141. Balthasar, *Mary for Today*, 12.

considered the synagogue as feminine and as a bride or wife of Yahweh.[142] Balthasar makes a distinction between the masculine ministerial offices of the church and the church as the bride of Christ. Balthasar's reasoning to link the church with Mary and the feminine is because of her undivided faith in God that began with a simple "yes" to become the mother of Christ. Dante echoes this yes when he accepts help from Virgil. With Dante's acceptance, he will have his faith strengthened and perfected throughout his journey in the afterlife. The Church Triumphant echoes the praise that the angel Gabriel offers Mary at the Annunciation in *Paradiso* XXIII where Dante describes the angels who praise Mary:

> And, like a baby reaching out its arms
> to *mamma* after it has drunk her milk,
> its inner impulse kindled to outward flame,
>
> all these white splendors were reaching upward
> with their fiery tips, so that their deep affection
> For Mary was made clear to me. (Par XXIII, 121–26)

The motherly affection that Mary generates is similar to Balthasar's words at the beginning of this chapter where he ties together the idea of beauty and love. The effect of the angelic lights who are united in love for their holy Mother is just like Balthasar's description of a child who "is brought to consciousness of himself only through love."[143] The smile from the child's mother brings joy to the child. Mary's smile is an indication of the love she has for all her children. The virgin's love for her child Jesus prefigures the announcement of God's love for his son at Christ's baptism. In love, Mary unifies the Church Triumphant. Bernard manifests that love in *Paradiso* XXXIII when he sings a hymn of praise to Mary.

Bernard's song opens up *Paradiso* XXXIII. He calls Mary both "Virgin Mother" and "daughter of your Son" (*Par.* XXXIII, 1). Dante's first line is wrought with two paradoxes. First is the use of the words "virgin" and "mother" together and second is the idea of a woman being the daughter of her son. The use of the word virgin, although often pro forma when speaking of Mary, should not be tossed aside here as merely a customary way of

---

142. Balthasar and Ratzinger, *Mary the Church at the Source*, 111. Balthasar explains that in the New Testament the church was also considered feminine. He cites 2 Corinthians 11:2 where Christ is pledged as the church's bridegroom and hence the church as the bride of Christ.

143. See footnote 1 above [x-ref], Balthasar, "Résumé of My Thought," 471.

addressing Mary. According to Balthasar, virginity is not something that one takes upon their own unless God gives its grace to them. With virginity bestowed by God, one gives up a certain kind of fecundity, only to be given a greater fruitfulness.[144] Of course, Mary's fruitfulness is the birthing of Christ. And since Mary is the daughter of God the Father and also the mother of Jesus (who is one with the triune God), she is the daughter of God's son. Using these two paradoxes, Dante can show glory not only to Mary but to God as well. In St. Bernard's prayer to Mary, he asks for Dante that "the highest beauty be displayed to him" (*Par.* XXXIII, 33). In the display of beauty, Dante's vision can become clearer with Mary's help. When Mary directs her gaze upwards, Bernard signals to Dante that he should follow Mary's gaze. Upon doing so, Dante's sight "rose higher and higher through the ray / of the exalted light that in itself is true" (*Par.* XXXIII, 54). After Dante follows Mary's gaze, his vision departs from Mary, and he follows his own inclinations. The remainder of the last canto is Dante's unfoldment into a vision of God. Therefore, Dante does follow Mary's lead. But if we want to know more about how Balthasar thinks about Mary's role in the *Divine Comedy*, it will be necessary to further examine his basic tenets on Marianism.

Balthasar cites three fundamental conclusions of what he calls the "Marian or catholic fundamental act." First, Mary's yes is that which founds the church. The yes of Mary is the "consent that goes along with everything that God is doing in the world."[145] Second, the yes is an act that is beyond childhood. The yes is an act of faith that allows the faithful "to act within the unlimited, universal, catholic mission of Jesus Christ."[146] Thus, the faithful are not acting alone. Instead, Christ unifies them. Finally, according to Balthasar, saying yes is an act that happens before anyone has an idea where their actions will take them. And "this Yes is the sole, nonnegotiable prerequisite of all Christian understanding, of all theology and ecclesial wisdom."[147] Only by saying yes, by being inside God's kingdom, can Christian truth be revealed. Thus, if Balthasar declares that Dante's *Paradiso* is Marian, we may agree with him. Dante gives his yes to Virgil that he will

---

144. To make his point, Balthasar speaks of St. Paul's virginity: "Paul, who could not yet know the extent to which his virginity had a Marian character, was very conscious of living it as a pregnancy linked with birth-pangs for his children" (Balthasar, *Mary for Today*, 26).

145. Balthasar and Ratzinger, *Mary the Church at the Source*, 165.

146. Balthasar and Ratzinger, *Mary the Church at the Source*, 165.

147. Balthasar and Ratzinger, *Mary the Church at the Source*, 165.

embark with him on his journey. Dante's yes will result in his authorship of the *Comedy*, which in its own way will help sustain the church. While throughout his journey, Dante may criticize the masculine clerical hierarchy, he is in partnership with the feminine ideal of the church. In a childlike fashion, Dante follows the direction of Virgil, Beatrice, and Bernard. He suspends his own will and agrees to their directions, even though he does not know where it will take him. As Dante finally reaches the end of his journey, he says yes to follow Mary's gaze. The vision that opens up for him is beyond anything that he could have ever imagined. The light pours down on him, and he loses the capacity to speak. If this is Marian, then *Paradiso* is Marian. But what is important to remember is that the final verses of *Paradiso* concern Dante's meeting with the ineffable triune God. The transcendent light has taken him captive in love. Like a bolt of lightning, the force strikes his mind. That which envelopes him is "the Love that moves the sun and all the other stars."

4.5 CONCLUSION

Being Marian does not exclude the triune God. The *Paradiso* is both Marian and trinitarian. The *Paradiso* is Dante's celestial vision, but it also deals with terrestrial life. Dante succeeds in showing the glory of God in various aesthetic forms. And Balthasar provides a way to understand those forms. Balthasar provides the theology which allows the Good to be reunited with the Beautiful and the True. With the ideas provided by Christian theology and enhanced by Balthasar, one can understand how the Forms of beauty are built upon the underlying structures of the Trinity and the Analogy of Being. The Love which the persons of God have for each other radiates within the immanent Trinity and spills out into God's love for humans. As humans are images of God, they share that love with others through their intimate relationship with God built upon the analogy of being. As children of God, we participate in the life of the Triune God. Although as humans our knowledge is imperfect, through the Forms of beauty we receive intimations of God's presence. The knowledge humans receive is not limited to the elite but is evident to everyone. God's Form reaches its zenith in Christ. Christ is the mediator in the analogy of being between God and humans. For Dante, the form's Glory becomes apparent as one matures spiritually. For Balthasar, the form invites humans to become fully participatory in the eternal life of God. For Dante, the Form is the *Divine Comedy*. In Dante's journey, he shines a light in the darkness to all those who will follow him. By his words, we can make our own yes to God. It is a yes that is incomprehensible to us initially, and we do it without knowing where it will take us. But it leads us step by step out of the darkness and into the light.

5

Conclusion

5.1 OBJECTIVE

RATHER THAN MERELY SUMMARIZING what has already been presented thus far, this concluding chapter will pursue the objective of determining where secular readers of this text might have their belief systems challenged. The reason for this objective is because the pressure points that the readers of this text experience could be beneficial to them, just like the cognitive dissonance that usually precedes a spiritual change. That event could happen if the ideas in the text upset a secular liberal mindset. The hope is that by reading this text the readers' spiritual frame will be enlarged so that it leads them to a deeper understanding of spirituality in their life. A further benefit of defining these aporias is so that more work can be done in the future to help make Dante more relevant to contemporary secular readers. To accomplish this, it will be necessary to better understand the belief systems that secular well-educated readers of Dante might have and why they have them. Once that is accomplished, it will be necessary to anticipate where contemporary readers of Dante might experience points of pressure concerning what has been presented in this text. Points of pressure will be identified by recapping the ideas presented in this text, but in a way that is more interesting than a mere rehashing of what already has been said.

Dante in Conversation with Contemporary Theorists

5.2 A CONVERSATION BETWEEN PAST AND PRESENT

The introduction to this text mentioned that my goal was to argue that Dante's *Divine Comedy* could still be used as a template for how one might have a spiritual experience via the intellect. To do that, however, Dante needed to be put into a more contemporary conversation. Since Dante wrote for a medieval readership that was predominately Catholic, the spiritual transformation that Dante describes in the *Divine Comedy* might not be appreciated by a readership that is contemporary and not religious. The imagined audience for this text is liberal and well-educated individuals who might consider themselves either spiritual and not religious, or secular, or agnostic. This would include those who were never religious, to begin with, as well as those who at one time might have been in a congregation but left it because it no longer spoke to them. This text argues that Dante could be made more accessible to this audience by putting him into conversation with contemporary theorists—i.e., French atheist philosophers, a Jewish philosopher, and a Catholic philosopher/theologian. The aim was to have these interlocutors either accentuate an idea of Dante's or to put Dante's idea into counterpoint. The objective was not to convert a reader to Dante's point of view, or the contemporary theorist's point of view. Rather, it was to enrich the reader's thinking by seeing Dante through different eyes. Additionally, the purpose was never to change a person's beliefs from religious to secular or from secular to religious. Rather, it was to enrich our secular moment through a conversation between past and present.

5.3 RELIGIOUS AND SPIRITUAL POLL DATA

The movement towards secularization in the United States is pronounced, as evidenced by two polling institutions' findings. In a General Social Survey poll, US respondents were asked the question, "How often do you attend religious services"? In 1972, 9 percent responded "never" while in 2022 the response climbed to 34 percent.[1] Another question asked US respondents, "Is the Bible the word of God"? In 1984 those who responded yes were 38 percent while in 2018 it was 29 percent.[2] Regarding ethics, a Pew Research poll conducted in 2014 asked US respondents if they believed in an absolute set of standards for right and wrong. Of those who attended religious

1. GSS, "How Often Respondent Attends."
2. GSS, "Feelings About the Bible."

Conclusion

services at least once a week, 49 percent believed that there was a set of absolute standards for right and wrong. However, for those who seldom or never attended, only 21 percent agreed.[3] In a related question, respondents were asked what their sources of guidance were for right and wrong. Of those who attend religious services at least once a week, 72 percent chose religion. However, for those who seldom or never attended religious services, only 7 percent chose religion.[4] An interesting sideline to the last question is that for those who seldom or never attended religious services, 73 percent chose "philosophy or reason or common sense" as a significant source of guidance. Those who had a college or post-college degree significantly chose "philosophy or reason or common sense" as a source of guidance concerning right and wrong.[5] Approaching the territory that Dante covers in his *Divine Comedy* (i.e., belief in heaven and hell), questions were posed to respondents about their beliefs in the afterlife. Of those who attended religious services at least once a week, 75 percent believed in the existence of hell, while for those who seldom or never attend religious services only 36 percent believed in hell. When it comes to education, those who were the least educated believed the most in hell, while the most highly educated believed least in hell (i.e., Educational Level Belief: High School or Less—65 percent; Some College—60 percent; College—48 percent; Post-graduate—40 percent).[6] Regarding the question about whether people believe in heaven, of those who attended religious services at least once a week, 87 percent believed in the existence of heaven, while for those who seldom or never attend religious services, only 49 percent believed in heaven. When it comes to education, those who were the least educated believed the most in heaven, while the most highly educated believed least in heaven (i.e. Educational Level—Belief: High School or Less—78 percent; Some College—73 percent; College—63 percent; Post-graduate—57 percent).[7] When the poll changed its questions from religious issues to spiritual issues, one finds that different education levels have approximately the same frequency of spiritual well-being. For the question of whether the respondents have weekly feelings of spiritual peace and well-being, the results were: High School or

3. PRC, "Belief in Absolute Standards for Right and Wrong."
4. PRC, "Sources of Guidance on Right and Wrong."
5. PRC, "Sources of Guidance on Right and Wrong Among College Graduates"; "Sources of Guidance on Right and Wrong Among Adults with a Post-Graduate Degree."
6. PRC, "Belief in Hell."
7. PRC, "Belief in Heaven."

Less—58 percent; Some College—60 percent; College—58 percent; Post-graduate—57 percent).[8] For the question of whether the respondents have weekly feelings concerning wonder about the universe, the results were: High School or Less—43 percent; Some College—47 percent; College—47 percent; Post-graduate—48 percent).[9]

 The poll data present the following implications. First, the United States is becoming a more secular country over time as fewer people attend religious services. Additionally, it shows that over time fewer people believe that the Bible is the word of God. Those who are the most educated and those who rarely attend religious services believe least that there are universal ethical standards and that hell and heaven exist. However, the data do show that people least likely to believe in religion turn to "philosophy or reason or common sense" as a source of guidance for the questions concerning right and wrong. Therefore, the hypothesis that twentieth-century philosophers could be influential as interlocutors of the *Divine Comedy* does have merit based on the poll data mentioned above. The findings also show that almost all respondents experience moments of spiritual well-being and a sense of wonder about the universe, regardless of educational level. These feelings of spiritual well-being and wonder about the universe indicate that while the population might be polarized when it comes to questions concerning religion, all respondents experience feelings of spirituality. Therefore, I believe that Dante in conjunction with Deleuze, Guattari, Levinas, and Balthasar can speak to that common sense of spirituality. The data above form a basis for which beliefs about religion and spirituality a secular, well-educated, contemporary reader would bring to a reading of the *Divine Comedy* and Dante's interlocutors. At this point, it will be fruitful to imagine how a contemporary reader might react to the ideas presented in this text. The reason for this is because it would show the pressure points where other work could be done in the future to relate Dante in a more contemporary way to modern readers.

 To understand the reaction that a contemporary reader might have to the ideas presented in this text and thus discern areas ripe for further exploration, the task will be to take the ideas expressed in the text and the data from the polls and filter them through concepts developed by the theorists of secularity. This will provide a basis for an understanding of why a reader might agree or disagree with the ideas that this text has brought

8. PRC, "Frequency of Feeling Spiritual Peace and Wellbeing."
9. PRC, "Frequency of Feeling Wonder About the Universe."

to the fore. For the afterlife states of heaven and hell, the secular theorists are sociologists who work in the academic field of religion and secularity. Therefore, to begin this walkthrough, it will be necessary to briefly review the idea of the afterlife in general and then proceed to discuss the states of hell, purgatory, and heaven from a secular perspective, in conjunction with what this text has discussed.

5.4 CONCEPTIONS OF THE AFTERLIFE

If we compare the medieval idea of the afterlife to a contemporary one, we will find much difference. Where the afterlife in the medieval era was a stark reality, our contemporary belief in the afterlife is not as strong. Using an educational metaphor, the medieval afterlife was a requirement while our contemporary belief in an afterlife is an elective. Dante's conception of an afterlife comes from a medieval Catholic metaphysical view. Hell is for the unrepentant egregious sinners. Purgatory is for those who had repented but need further purification. And Heaven is for those who lived an exemplary earthly life. While one might expect that a scientific and technological culture would reject the idea of afterlife states, remarkably a sizeable amount of the United States population believes in an afterlife.[10] When it comes to the afterlife, more people believe in the existence of heaven than in hell. Perhaps we can account for a greater belief in heaven by the theory that societies which provide existential security to their populace are more secular than others. Existential security allows people freedom of choice without feeling the threat of heresy. Peter Berger and Ronald F. Inglehart and Pippa Norris, who are sociological theorists of secularity, advocate for this idea.[11] It may be that because hell poses a greater threat than heaven, individuals who live in safe cultures will reject the threat of hell because of the safety of their secular environment. Still, a sizeable amount of people in our secular culture believe in both heaven and hell.[12] This indicates that

10. The statistics for belief in hell among that US population are 58 percent believe, 34 percent disbelieve, and 8 percent don't know/other. The statistics for belief in heaven among that US population are 72 percent believe, 21 percent disbelieve, and 7 percent don't know/other.

11. Among many publications from the three theorists mentioned above, the following are exemplary: Berger, *Sacred Canopy*; Inglehart and Norris, "Four Horsemen."

12. For belief in hell by education level, the statistics are: High School or Less—65 percent; Some College—60 percent; College—48 percent; Post-graduate—40 percent. For belief in heaven, the statistics are: High School or Less—78 percent; Some College—73 percent; College—63 percent; Post-graduate—57 percent.

the afterlife still has resonance for contemporary readers. We can further speculate why that is the case. Perhaps the notion that there is no continuation after death is an idea that people resist as too limiting. Perhaps there is a feeling that there needs to be an accounting for one's life on earth, with those who have lived charitable lives being rewarded and those who have lived selfish lives being punished. Nonetheless, the *Divine Comedy* and its focus on the afterlife would still interest a contemporary reader regardless of whether they have a religious affiliation or not. And although belief in the afterlife decreases as educational level increases, there is still a sizeable population among the college-educated who believe in an afterlife. As such, it is necessary to review the ideas presented in Dante's *Inferno* to see how a contemporary reader might perceive them.

5.4.1 Hell

Dante's depiction of hell presents a challenge to contemporary readers of the *Divine Comedy*. While the graphic novel quality of hell might appeal to those who enjoy being horrified by the grotesque, for many contemporary readers hell is a freakish fiction. The medieval Catholic conception of hell is that of a place of punishment that goes on eternally. The people who are sentenced to hell are those who have committed a mortal sin but have not repented from it or received absolution for the sin. A scene that was discussed in this text was the episode with Francesca and Paolo. Because of their adultery, Dante places them in hell, albeit in a circle of hell that is the second furthest away from its deepest depravity. Although Dante, the pilgrim, has sympathy for Francesca, Dante, the author, sentences her to hell for her sin. He does not prevent her from being punished. One can construct a secularist argument about why Francesca and Paolo are in hell by looking at the ideas of secular theorists Rodney Stark, Laurence Iannaccone, and Roger Finke, which have been dubbed as a "Supply Side" theory of secularization.[13] This theory postulates that in a pluralistic free society that does not have state control over religion, there can be many competing religious suppliers. Suppliers differentiate themselves and target a religious population segment to which they appeal. Individuals have the freedom to choose suppliers who have religious beliefs they deem satisfactory to their needs. However, if the state regulates suppliers, it provides few choices to the religious populace. In the medieval era, the state and the Catholic

---

13. Finke and Stark, "Religious Choice and Competition."

Conclusion

church combined to keep a monopoly on religious suppliers. As such, the church's theology deemed adultery to be a mortal sin and given that neither Paolo nor Francesca had an opportunity to repent and confess their sin, they were assigned to hell. Yet, it is likely that a contemporary reader will not abide by the idea that Francesca should suffer everlasting damnation because of an adulterous situation—especially since Francesca was forced into a politically arranged marriage. Dante's medieval society had few choices when it came to religious suppliers. Additionally, there is another secularist theory that is pertinent to the Francesca and Paolo episode. The theory postulates that as societies move from agrarian to technologically advanced, they move from pro-fertility norms to individual-choice norms. In a paper entitled "Cultural Change, Slow and Fast: The Distinctive Trajectory of Norms Governing Gender Equality and Sexual Orientation," the authors state that as a society becomes wealthier and moves from an agrarian society to a technologically advanced society, it shifts from materialist to post-materialist values.[14] Materialist values are defined as values that prioritize economic growth and maintaining the status quo. On the other hand post-materialist values are defined as concern for such issues as environmental protection and the expansion of individual rights within the population especially among minority communities. Implicit in the concept of post-materialist values is the acceptance of gender equality and divorce.[15] As individual freedom increases in a society, people feel safer expressing personal beliefs which may clash with their religious institution's beliefs. Most of the time they know that they will not be censored by their religious institution if they express beliefs contrary to that institution. Additionally, in a culture with more individual freedom, individuals are free to leave their religious institutions without suffering consequences. Thus economic and social forces that provide society with more choice can change the religious beliefs of a society.

The idea of cultural forces creating changes in the norms of a populace is very much in alignment with Deleuze and Guattari's idea of social machines. From the standpoint of Deleuze and Guattari, there are no transcendental ethical norms for Francesca to abrogate. Rather, there are

---

14. Inglehart et al., "Cultural Change, Slow and Fast."

15. Inglehart et al. argue that pro-fertility norms emphasized traditional gender roles related to reproduction. As societies become able to produce enough material items to avoid scarcity, pro-fertility norms shift to individual choice norms, which support gender equality and same-gender attraction. See Inglehart et al., "Cultural Change, Slow and Fast," 1314.

cultural machines that operate within a society (e.g., the courtly love system). Francesca enacted desires that went outside of the courtly love system. She lived in a medieval society that emphasized fertility and reproduction rather than individual rights. Francesca would be a sympathetic character to contemporary readers who live in a culture that deemphasizes reproduction and values individual choice for women. Deleuze and Guattari would not criticize Francesca's involvement with Paolo for ethical reasons. Rather, their critique would be that Francesca's behavior went against the dominant cultural machine and it ultimately crushed her. She failed to identify small movements of deterritorialization that would permit her some personal freedom. Where contemporary readers might find Francesca a sympathetic character, Deleuze and Guattari would see her as foolhardy. Her encounter with Paolo happened while they were reading about the romance of Lancelot and Guinevere. Her desires were fantasies, like the legendary romance she was reading, and she clung to them even when she met Dante, the character, in hell. Dante, the author, understands Francesca's fantastical naivete. And Deleuze and Guattari inject a philosophical realism into the situation, which I believe contemporary readers would find insightful. Deleuze and Guattari emphasize clear-sightedness and seeing the cultural formations for what they are rather than what one might wish they would be. They offer a corrective to judging a past culture using current cultural values—knowing the repressive force that social machines can generate and how they functioned in medieval culture. When one is operating within a highly coded culture, one must look for openings or lines of flight when the conditions present themselves. Dante, the author, implicitly understands Francesca's rash behavior. While Dante would blame her punishment on disordered desire, Deleuze and Guattari would see it as desire that did not find a productive insertion into a viable social machine. Thus, it may be true that a contemporary reader might find Francesca's placement in hell to be unenlightened because of various modern cultural factors—different beliefs concerning marriage, women's rights, and less restrictive moral codes concerning sexuality. However, Dante in conversation with Deleuze and Guattari can help a secular reader understand the episode more deeply and from a variety of perspectives.

CONCLUSION

5.4.2 Purgatory

The idea of purgatory as a place where a soul makes reparations for breaking the ethical code may be problematic for contemporary readers. Most Protestant and Evangelical denominations do not believe in purgatory, and even many practicing Christians may be less familiar with purgatory compared to heaven and hell. In *Purgatorio*, Purgatory Proper is arranged in the order of the seven deadly sins with pride being the worst human vice. Souls are sentenced to purgatory because they abrogated what Dante considered the universal ethical code as established by the ten commandments and other Christian canonical texts. As we saw in the Pew Research poll, however, contemporary readers mostly eschew a belief in a universal ethical code. Instead, they judge ethics according to each situation and the specific factors surrounding the situation. Therefore, they may not agree with Dante's structured purgatorial system with graded ethical steps through which Dante, the character, ascends. An aspect of Dante's traversal through Purgatory that might surprise contemporary readers is that he sees the journey as necessary to spiritually purify his soul. At each stage of purification, he begins to feel lighter and happier. What begins out of duty transforms into joy. Countering Dante's idea that greater spiritual purity leads to happiness is the secular theory that greater economic well-being leads to happiness. According to a Levinasian framework, economic security is good. Levinas believed that living in the world is enjoyable and using the materials of the earth to build a dwelling for oneself is an important enterprise. Therefore, to a certain extent, Levinas would agree with the secular theorists that economic security and living in the world is a pleasurable endeavor. Another factor that plays a dominant role in secularization theory is that democratization, political freedom, and societal tolerance for others unlike themselves create the conditions for happiness.[16] The word tolerance, however, has a passive connotation. For happiness to truly exist, the other must be not only tolerated but welcomed in society. Thus Levinas's conception of one's responsibility to the other can be tied into the idea that happiness is closely correlated to tolerance for others. Levinas's idea of responsibility, however, is much stronger than mere tolerance. Dante is also stern about correcting people in Purgatory who had been intolerant of others while they were alive. As an example, in the *Purgatorio* chapter of this text, the character Omberto Aldobrandesco was discussed. He was

---

16. Inglehart et al., "Development, Freedom," 264–85.

in the realm of Purgatory Proper for the most egregious vice, which is the sin of pride. Omberto needed to purify himself from his arrogance which came from the belief that his family's elevated social status made him better than others. Like Omberto, many of Dante's characters are in purgatory because of their self-centeredness and their desire to wield power. Often, they were political rulers or high-level clerics. Dante accuses them of denying political and religious freedom and tolerance for the other. What Dante and Levinas bring to the question of what drives social well-being and happiness is an ethical dimension that may not exist within the secular conversations on happiness. This brings a depth to the conversation that cannot be given justice by focusing solely on economic and sociological factors. Doing the right thing because it is ethical and ethics as first philosophy deepens the discourse on happiness that the secularists often overlook in their arguments. It would be interesting to see what opinions secular readers have concerning Dante's conception of purgatory as a place to purify one's selfishness and Levinas's call for a radical responsibility to the other. Is the idea of pursuing virtue at the expense of material happiness completely contrary to secularist sensibilities? Is the idea of responsibility to the other at odds with individual rights? These are points in question—and maybe in opposition to the secularist emphasis on pursuing one's freedom and striving for economic happiness. In purgatory, happiness is the result of rectifying one's selfish inclinations. However, in heaven happiness is a result of pursuing beauty.

5.4.3 Heaven

The idea that art and beauty can have a bona fide theological dimension could be problematic for secular readers of Dante. When Balthasar begins his multivolume work *The Glory of the Lord*, he speaks of the smile that the infant sees from its mother as the first encounter of beauty. Balthasar uses that example at the beginning of his corpus to emphasize that beauty cannot be divorced from the emotion of human love and ultimately divine love. As Balthasar sees it, the problem with contemporary aesthetics is that the Beautiful has been separated from the Good and the True—all of which is undergirded by love. Love and beauty, however, are hard to reconcile with the event of war. When the horror of the Holocaust was discovered in the mid-twentieth century, Theodor Adorno made his statement that "to

Conclusion

write poetry after Auschwitz is barbaric."[17] One might think of his statement as the obverse to Balthasar's treatise on beauty and art. For Adorno, the question is: given that the world is devoid of the good and the true, how can beauty be possible? Adorno believed that the beauty of poetry might not be possible because it would be destroyed or corrupted by the barbaric environment that contained it. Adorno, moreover, may be the opposite of Balthasar for a different reason. Adorno wanted to free art from its primitive religious and cultic origins so that art could advance and represent the human rather than the transcendent world. He believed that any desire to reunite art with religion was wishful thinking.[18] Yet, the conundrum for Adorno was that while he believed that art should be for the individual rather than for religious institutions, he believed that as society became less human and more barbaric, art's autonomy would be destroyed. Adorno's critique of art in a materialist culture (or as he phrased it, "the culture industry" was a critique of the commercialization of art. In a secular age devoted to the primacy of economics over art, an art object is converted into a commodity. Adorno's critique about how art has become commercialized is valid, but his solution to the problem would be illogical to Balthasar and Dante. Adorno believed that art was contaminated by revelation or religious topoi. Yet Adorno also believed that if every trace of revelation from art was eradicated, it would make the artwork "undifferentiated," by which he meant that it would be reduced to the status quo of an art piece of that genre. To escape the status quo, the artwork had to perform the impossible. It would somehow need to retain a trace of the force of revelation, but not so much that it would be corrupted by it. Adorno uses the term tour de force for an artwork that has performed the impossible. Adorno states that "Every artifact works against itself. Those that are a tour de force, a balancing act demonstrate something about art as a whole: They achieve the impossible."[19] According to Adorno, a successful work of art elicits a shudder in the viewer. He mentions Beethoven's *Ninth Symphony* as producing this kind of effect. Adorno translates this shudder into the words meaning "Thus it is,"—as if the audience for the musical piece would recognize the actual Truth in an aural experience. But that Truth is devoid of a theological dimension. Ironically, Adorno's desire to sever art from the "cultic" or the religious is carried out every day by visitors who are escorted by docents

---

17. Adorno, *Culture Criticism and Society*, 34.
18. Adorno, "Theses Upon Art and Religion Today," 677.
19. Adorno, *Aesthetic Theory*, 106.

to the Vatican or Catholic cathedrals throughout western Europe. In these groups, art is often explained only through its formal aspects by having the religious element vacated from the artwork. In our secular age, Beauty has been severed from the Good and the True. Still, for those who visit the Vatican and see the artwork on the ceiling of the Sistine Chapel, one cannot but wonder if many of the spectators experience a shudder. It is hard to believe that the shudder of the True is not related to the religious symbology of the artwork. In the *Divine Comedy*, Dante the character's last experience is stronger than a shudder. During his encounter with the Divine, he has a sensation like a bolt of lightning that strikes his mind. And as a result, his will and his desire revolve—"turning with / the Love that moves the sun and all the other stars" (*Par.* XXXIII, 144–45). Dante's encounter with the beauty of God has him merge his being with love. It is a love, as Balthasar would claim, one first experiences as an infant beholding the smile of one's mother. Adorno's translation of the shudder as "thus it is" can be viewed in the light of Mary's affirmation of "let it be done to me according to thy word" (Luke 1:38). More than just an understanding of the truth, however, Mary's affirmation is an emptying of herself—an expression of the kenotic love that is akin to the love that each person of the Trinity has for the others. It is an emptying of oneself so that the grace of another can be poured in. A contemporary reader of the *Divine Comedy* may understand that the shudder they feel when confronted with a magnificent work of art is not only an experience of beauty but also an experience of truth. Balthasar's reunification of the beautiful, the good, and the true can be a corrective to a secular culture that has lost the theological meaning of the beautiful. As Dante's interlocutor for heaven, Balthasar reaffirms that Dante's timelessness is a result of a hunger on the reader's part that often is not satisfied in the world today. Would secular readers of the *Divine Comedy* understand the shudder as more than an ancient feeling from a primitive cultic experience? Could it be that the reminiscence of our mother's smile could kindle an experience of love that fosters a desire for everlasting and divine beauty?

5.5 DANTE FOR OUR TIME

Dante's *Divine Comedy* is a text that was written over seven hundred years ago. How can something so remote from today still speak to our lives? To read it as a literary artifact is a noble scholarly pursuit. It can impart information about medieval culture, describe the history of Italy's city-states

Conclusion

and reflect the theology and philosophy of that era. The *Divine Comedy* is a publishing mill source for many academic books and papers that contribute to the ongoing dialogue on all things concerning Dante of the fourteenth century. But that is not the purpose of this text. What if through some scientific magic, we could bring Dante to life today and have him observe our contemporary culture? As he did in the fourteenth century, Dante would absorb the ideas and thoughts of the most interesting thinkers of our day and try to understand them in the architectonic framework of his artwork. Dante's goal was to demonstrate how a person can move from being lost in the dark woods to experiencing the light of the divine. He conceived that journey as being universal for all people. The *Divine Comedy* can be the illuminative path that shines in the darkness if one so chooses to understand it in that manner. But going alone into the dark woods is not advisable. In this text, I imagine Dante, Deleuze, Guattari, Levinas, and Balthasar walking along the path and discussing ideas. It is a conversation that today's secular readers will find fascinating. Each of the contemporary theorists had a desire to free people from suffering. However, they come at it in different ways. It is up to the reader to find the idea that sparks their imagination and helps them to move past obstacles and progress in their life. Dante wrote most of the *Divine Comedy* in exile from his beloved home in Florence. However, in his mind, he created a map of how everyone can find their true home if they desire to persist in the path that he constructed.

Bibliography

Adorno, Theodor. *Aesthetic Theory.* Edited by Gretel Adorno and Rolf Tiedemann. Translated by Robert Hullot-Kentor. Minneapolis: University of Minnesota Press, 1997.
———. *Culture Criticism and Society.* Translated by Samuel Weber and Weber Shierry. Cambridge: MIT Press, 1997.
———. *The Culture Industry: Selected Essays on Mass Culture.* Edited by J. M. Bernstein. London: Routledge, 2020.
———. "Theses Upon Art and Religion Today." *Kenyon Review* 7.4 (1945) 677–82.
Agamben, Giorgio. "Absolute Immanence." In *Introduction to the Philosophy of Gilles Deleuze*, edited by Jean Kalfa, 151–69. London: Continuum, 1999.
Allen, Sarah. *The Philosophical Sense of Transcendence Levinas and Plato on Loving Beyond Being*, Pittsburg: Duquesne University Press, 2009.
Aquinas. *Summa Contra Gentiles.* Translated by Charles J. O'Neil. Notre Dame: University of Notre Dame Press, 1975.
———. *Summa Theologica.* Translated by Fathers of the English Dominican Province. Benziger Brothers ed. 1947. Online. https://www.ccel.org/ccel/aquinas/summa/home.html.
———. "Quaestiones Disputatae de Veritate." Edited by Fr. Joseph Kenny, OP. *St. Isidore E-Book Library.* Online. https://isidore.co/aquinas/english/QDdeVer.htm.
Aristotle. "On the Heavens." In *The Complete Works of Aristotle: The Revised Oxford Translation*, edited by Jonathan Barnes, 1:447–511. 2 vols. Bollingen Series 71.2 Princeton: Princeton University Press, 1984.
Artaud, Antonin. "To Have Done With the Judgement of God [February 2, 1948]." *Surrealism-Plays.* Online. http://www.surrealism-plays.com/Artaud.html.
Atwell, Robert R. "From Augustine to Gregory the Great: an Evaluation of the Emergence of the Doctrine of Purgatory." *The Journal of Ecclesiastical History* 38.2 (1987) 173–86.
Auerbach, Erich. *Dante: Poet of the Secular World.* Translated by Ralph Manheim. Chicago: University of Chicago Press, 1961.
Augustine. *The City of God, Books XVII–XXII.* Translated by Gerald G. Walsh and Daniel J. Honan. Washington, DC: Catholic University of America Press, 1954.

Bibliography

———. *Confessions*. Edited and translated by Albert C. Outler. Grand Rapids: Christian Classics Ethereal Library, 1955. Online. https://www.ccel.org/ccel/a/augustine/confessions/cache/confessions.pdf.

———. "On the Holy Trinity." In vol. 3 of *Nicene and Post-Nicene Fathers*, Series 1, edited by Philip Schaff, 1–228. Translated by Arthur West Haddan. Buffalo, NY: Christian Literature, 1887. Revised and edited for *New Advent* by Kevin Knight. Online. http://www.newadvent.org/fathers/130113.htm.

Baker, Steve. *Postmodern Animal*. London: Reaktion, 2000.

Balthasar, Hans Urs von. *Explorations in Theology*. Translated by A. V. Littledale et al. 4 vols. San Francisco: Ignatius, 1989–1995.

———. *The Glory of the Lord: A Theological Aesthetics*. Edited by Joseph Fessio, SJ, and John Riches. Translated by Andrew Louth et al. 7 vols. San Francisco: Ignatius, 1982–1991.

———. *Love Alone is Credible*. Translated by D. C. Schindler. San Francisco: Ignatius, 2012.

———. *Mary for Today*. Translated by Robert Nowell. San Francisco: Ignatius, 1988.

———. *Presence and Thought: Essay on the Religious Philosophy of Gregory of Nyssa*. San Francisco: Ignatius, 1995.

———. "A Résumé of My Thought." *Communio* 15.4 (1988) 468–73.

———. *Theo-Drama: Theological Dramatic Theory*. Translated by Graham Harrison. 5 vols. San Francisco: Ignatius, 1988–1995.

———. *Theo-Logic: Theological Logical Theory*. Translated by Adrian J. Walker and Graham Harrison. 3 vols. San Francisco: Ignatius, 2001.

———. *A Theology of History*. San Francisco: Sheed and Ward, 1963.

———. *The Theology of Karl Barth: Exposition and Interpretation*. Translated by Edward T. Oakes. San Francisco: Ignatius, 1992.

Balthasar, Hans Urs von, and Cardinal Joseph Ratzinger. *Mary the Church at the Source*. Translated by Johannes Verlag. San Francisco: Ignatius, 2006.

Barolini, Teodolinda. "Dante and Francesca Da Rimini: Realpolitik, Romance, Gender." *Speculum* 75.1 (2000) 1–28.

———. "*Paradiso* 10: Multiple Truth and Intellectual Tolerance." *Commento Baroliniano*, Digital Dante, Columbia University Libraries, 2014. https://digitaldante.columbia.edu/dante/divine-comedy/paradiso/paradiso-10.

———. *The Undivine Comedy*. Princeton: Princeton University Press, 1992.

Beckett, Samuel. *Molloy*. New York: Grove, 1955.

———. *More Pricks Than Kicks*. New York: Grove, 1972.

Bell, Jeffrey A. *Philosophy at the Edge of Chaos: Gilles Deleuze and the Philosophy of Difference*. Toronto: University of Toronto Press, 2006.

Berger, Peter L. *The Sacred Canopy: Elements of a Sociological Theory of Religion*. New York: Anchor, 1990.

Bergo, Bettina. *Levinas Between Ethics and Politics: For the Beauty That Adorns the Earth*. Dordrecht: Kluwer Academic, 1999.

Bernard, of Clairvaux. "On Loving God." Transcribed by Paul Halsall. *Christian Classics Ethereal Library*, n.d. Online. https://ccel.org/ccel/bernard/loving_god/loving_god.xvii.html.

Bernasconi, Robert. "Different Styles of Eschatology: Derrida's Take on Levinas' Political Messianism." *Research in Phenomenology* 28.1 (1998) 3–19. https://doi.org/10.1163/156916498x00010.

Bibliography

Betz, John R. "After Barth: A New Introduction to Erich Przywara's Analogia Entis." In *The Analogy of Being: Invention of the Antichrist or Wisdom of God?*, edited by Thomas Joseph, OP, 35–87. Grand Rapids: Eerdmans, 2011.

———. "Beyond the Sublime: The Aesthetics of the Analogy of Being (Part Two)." *Modern Theology* 22.1 (2006) 1–50.

Boersma, Hans. "Becoming Human in the Face of God: Gregory of Nyssa's Unending Search for the Beatific Vision." *International Journal of Systematic Theology* 17.2 (2015) 131–51.

———. *Seeing God: The Beatific Vision in Christian Tradition*. Grand Rapids: Eerdmans, 2018.

Botterill, Steven. *Dante and the Mystical Tradition: Bernard of Clairvaux in the Commedia*. Cambridge: Cambridge University Press, 2005.

Burge, Ryan P. "Growth and Decline in American Religion over the Last Decade." *Religion in Public: Exploring the Mix of the Sacred and Secular* (blog), July 9, 2019. Online. https://religioninpublic.blog/2019/07/09/growth-and-decline-in-american-religion-over-the-last-decade.

Burggraeve, Roger. *Proximity With the Other: A Multidimensional Ethic of Responsibility in Levinas*. Bangalore: Dharmaram, 2009.

Cassell, Anthony K. *Dante's Fearful Art of Justice*. Toronto: University of Toronto Press, 1984.

Catholic Church. *Catechism of the Catholic Church*. New York: Image, 1995.

Certeau, Michel de. "Mysticism." *Diacritics* 22.2 (1992) 11.

Chanter, Tina, ed. *Feminist Interpretations of Emmanuel Levinas*. University Park: Pennsylvania State University Press, 2010.

Cheng, John. "The Distinction between God's Essence and Energy: Gregory Palamas's Idea of Ultimate Reality and Meaning." *Ultimate Reality and Meaning* 21.1 (1998) 56–75.

Cohen, Richard A. *Face to Face with Levinas*. Albany: State University of New York Press, 2012.

———. "Levinas on Art and Aestheticism: Getting 'Reality and Its Shadow' Right." *Levinas Studies* 11.1 (2016) 149–94. https://doi.org/10.1353/lev.2016.0020.

Colebrook, Claire. *Gilles Deleuze*. London: Routledge, 2001.

Dalton, Drew M. *Longing for the Other: Levinas and Metaphysical Desire*. Pittsburgh: Duquesne University Press, 2009.

Dante Alighieri. "De Vulgari Eloquentia." In *De Vulgari Eloquentia: Dante's Book of Exile*, translated by Marianne Shapiro, 47–90. Lincoln: University of Nebraska Press, 1990.

———. *De Vulgari Eloquentia: Dante's Book of Exile*. Translated by Marianne Shapiro. Lincoln: University of Nebraska Press. 1990

———. *Inferno*. Translated by Robert and Jean Hollander. New York: Anchor, 2002.

———. *Paradiso*. Translated by Robert and Jean Hollander. New York: Anchor, 2007.

———. *Purgatorio*. Translated by Robert and Jean Hollander. New York: Anchor, 2004.

Davies, Oliver. "Thinking Difference." In *Deleuze and Religion*, edited by Mary Bryden, 76–86. London: Routledge, 2001.

Deleuze, Gilles. *Difference and Repetition*. Translated by Paul Patton. New York: Columbia University Press, 1995.

———. *Empiricism and Subjectivity: An Essay on Hume's Theory of Human Nature*. Translated by Constantin V. Boundas. New York: Columbia University Press, 2001.

———. *Essays Critical And Clinical*. Minneapolis: University of Minnesota Press, 1997.

Bibliography

———. *Kafka: Toward a Minor Literature*. Translated by Dana Polan. Minneapolis: University of Minnesota Press, 1986.

———. *The Logic of Sense*. Edited by Constantin V. Boundas. Translated by Mark Lester and Charles Stivale. New York: Columbia University Press, 1990.

———. *Negotiations 1972–1990*. New York: Columbia University Press, 1995.

———. *Pure Immanence: Essays on a Life*. Translated by Anne Boyman. New York: Zone, 2012.

———. *Spinoza: Practical Philosophy*. Translated by Robert Hurley. San Francisco: City Lights, 1988.

———. *Two Regimes of Madness: Texts and Interviews 1975–1995*. Edited by David Lapoujade. Translated by Ames Hodges and Mike Taormina. New York: Semiotext(e), 2007.

Deleuze, Gilles, and Félix Guattari. *A Thousand Plateaus: Capitalism and Schizophrenia*. Translated by Brian Massumi. Minneapolis: University of Minnesota Press, 1987.

———. *Anti-Oedipus: Capitalism and Schizophrenia*. Translated by Robert Hurley. New York: Penguin Classics, 2009.

———. *What Is Philosophy?* Translated by Hugh Tomlinson and Graham Burchell. New York: Columbia University Press, 1996.

Deleuze, Gilles, et al. "What Is a Minor Literatuare." *Mississippi Review* 11.3 (1983) 13–33.

Driscoll, James F. "Terrestial Paradise." In vol. 14 of *The Catholic Enclyclopedia*, edited by Charles G. Herbermann et al., 519–20. New York: Robert Appleton Company, 1912. Transcribed for *New Advent* by Robert B. Olson. Edited by Kevin Knight. Online. http://www.newadvent.org/cathen/14519a.htm.

Dudley, Underwood. *Numerology: Or, What Pythagoras Wrought*. Washington, DC: American Mathematical Society, 1997.

Elliott, J. K. *The Apocryphal New Testament: A Collection of Apocryphal Christian Literature in an English Translation*. Oxford: Oxford University Press, 2005.

Emery, Gilles. *The Trinity: An Introduction to Catholic Doctrine on the Triune God*. Translated by Matthew Levering. Washington: Catholic University of America Press, 2012.

Finke, Roger, and Rodney Stark. "Religious Choice and Competition." *American Sociological Review* 63.5 (1998) 761–66.

Firey, Abigail, ed. *A New History of Penance*. Vol. 14. Leiden: Brill, 2008.

Freccero, John. "The Final Image: Paradiso XXXIII, 144." *MLN* 79.1 (1964) 14–27. https://doi.org/10.2307/3042718.

Gallaher, Brandon. *Freedom and Necessity in Modern Trinitarian Theology*. Oxford: Oxford University Press, 2016.

Garrigou-Lagrange, Réginald. *The Three Ways of the Spiritual Life*. Westminister: Newman, 1950.

General Social Survey (GSS). "Feelings About the Bible." *NORC at the University of Chicago*, n.d. Online. https://gssdataexplorer.norc.org/trends?category=Religion%20%26%20Spirituality&measure=bible&Measure%20Category=Word%20of%20god&Breakdown%20Label=Political%20affiliation%C2%B0.

———. "How Often Respondent Attends Religious Services." *NORC at the University of Chicago*, n.d. Online. https://gssdataexplorer.norc.org/trends?category=Religion%20%26%20Spirituality&measure=attend&Measure%20Category=Never&Breakdown%20Label=Total.

Gibbon, Edward. *The History of the Decline and Fall of the Roman Empire*. 11 vols. London: Tegg, 1827.

Bibliography

Gregory of Nyssa. *Gregory of Nyssa, Homilies on the Beatitudes: An English Version with Commentary and Supporting Studies*. Edited by Alberto Viciano and Hubertus R. Drobner. Translated by Stuart George Hall. Leiden: Brill, 1992.

———. "On Perfection." In *Saint Gregory of Nyssa Ascetical Works*, edited by Virginia Woods Callahan, 91–122. Fathers of the Church 58. Washington, DC: Catholic University of America Press, 1999.

Gurevich, A. Ja. "Popular and Scholarly Medieval Cultural Traditions: Notes in the Margin of Jacques Le Goff's Book." *Journal of Medieval History* 9.2 (1983) 71–90. https://doi.org/10.1016/0304-4181(83)90002-7.

Hanby, Michael. "Creation as Aesthetic Analogy." In *The Analogy of Being: Invention of the Antichrist Or Wisdom of God?*, edited by Thomas Joseph, OP, 341–78. Grand Rapids: Eerdmans, 2011.

Hobbes, Thomas. *Leviathan*. Edited by C. B. Macphearson. Harmondsworth, UK: Penguin, 1968.

Holland, Eugene W. *Deleuze and Guattari's Anti-Oedipus: Introduction to Schizoanalysis*. London: Routledge, 1999.

———. *Deleuze and Guattari's A Thousand Plateaus: A Reader's Guide*. London: Bloomsbury Academic, 2013.

Hollander, Robert. "*Purgatorio* II: Cato's Rebuke and Dante's Scoglio." *Italica* 52.3 (1975) 348–63. https://doi.org/10.2307/478438.

Houser, R. E., trans. *The Cardinal Virtues: Aquinas, Albert, and Philip the Chancellor*. Mediaeval Sources in Translation 39. Toronto: Pontifical Institute of Mediaeval Studies, 2004.

Inglehart, Ronald, et al. "Cultural Change, Slow and Fast: The Distinctive Trajectory of Norms Governing Gender Equality and Sexual Orientation." *Social Forces* 95.4 (2017) 1313–40.

Inglehart, Ronald, et al. "Development, Freedom, and Rising Happiness: A Global Perspective (1981–2007)." *Perspectives on Psychological Science* 3.4 (2008) 264–85.

Inglehart, Ronald, and Pippa Norris. "The Four Horsemen of the Apocalypse: Understanding Human Security." *Scandinavian Political Studies* 35.1 (2012) 71–96.

Ivanovic, Filip. "The Ecclesiology of Dionysius the Areopagite." *International Journal for the Study of the Christian Church* 11.1 (2011) 27–44.

Jamie Murray. "Deleuze & Guattari's Intensive & Pragmatic Semiotic of Emergent Law." *International Journal for the Semiotics of Law* 20.1 (2007) 7–32.

Johansen, Thomas Kjeller. "Plato's Teleology." In *Teleology: A History*, edited by Jeffrey K. McDonough, 14–38. New York: Oxford University Press, 2020.

Kilby, Karen. "Aquinas, the Trinity and the Limits of Understanding." *International Journal of Systematic Theology* 7.4 (2005) 414–27. https://doi.org/10.1111/j.1468-2400.2005.00175.x.

Lafferty, Roger Theodore. "The Philosophy of Dante." *Annual Reports of the Dante Society* 30 (1911) 1–34.

Larkins, Jeremy. *From Hierarchy to Anarchy: Territory and Politics before Westphalia*. New York: Palgrave Macmillan, 2010.

Le Goff, Jacques. *The Birth of Purgatory*. Translated by Arthur Goldhammer. Chicago: University of Chicago Press, 1984.

Lefebvre, Henri. *The Production of Space*. Translated by Donald Nicholson-Smith. Oxford: Wiley-Blackwell, 1992.

Bibliography

Levinas, Emmanuel. *Collected Philosophical Papers*. Translated by Alphonso Lingis. Dordrecht: Martinus Nijhoff, 1987.

———. *Difficult Freedom: Essays on Judaism*. Translated by Seán Hand. London: Athlone, 1990.

———. *Existence and Existents*. Translated by Alphonso Lingis. Pittsburgh: Duquesne University Press, 2001.

———. *Otherwise than Being or Beyond Essence*. Translated by Alphonso Lingis. Pittsburgh: Duquesne University Press, 1998.

———. "Peace and Proximity." In *Alterity and Transcendence*, translated by Michael B. Smith, 131–44. New York: Columbia University Press, 1999.

———. *Time and the Other*. Translated by Richard A. Cohen. Pittsburgh: Duquesne University Press, 1987.

———. *Totality and Infinity: An Essay on Exteriority*. Translated by Alphonso Lingis. Pittsburg: Duquesne University Press, 1969.

———. "The Trace of the Other." In *Deconstruction in Context*, edited by Mark C. Taylor, 345–59. Chicago: University of Chicago Press, 1986.

Lorraine, Tamsin. "Lines of Flight." In *The Deleuze Dictionary*, edited by Adrian Parr, 147–48. Edinburgh: Edinburgh University Press, 2010.

MacDonald, Michael J. "Losing Spirit: Hegel, Levinas, and the Limits of Narative." *Ohio State University Press* 13.2 (2005) 182–94.

Marder, Michael. "Anti-Nomad." *Deleuze Studies* 10.4 (2016) 496–503.

Mazzotta, Giuseppe. *Dante's Vision and the Circle of Knowledge*. Princeton: Princeton University Press, 1993.

———. *Reading Dante*. New Haven: Yale University Press, 2014.

———. "Why Did Dante Write the Comedy? Why and How Do We Read It?: The Poet and the Critics." In *Dante Now: Current Trends in Dante Studies*, edited by Theodore J. Cachey Jr. and Christian Moevs, 63–79. Notre Dame: University of Notre Dame Press, 1995.

McInerny, Brendan. *The Trinitarian Theology of Hans Urs von Balthasar: An Introduction*. Notre Dame: University of Notre Dame Press, 2020.

Message, Kylie. "Bodies Without Organs." In *The Deleuze Dictionary*, edited by Adrian Parr, 37–39. Edinburgh: Edinburgh University Press, 2010.

Miller, James L. "Three Mirrors of Dante's Paradiso." *University of Toronto Quarterly* 46.3 (1977) 263–79.

Miller, James Matthew. "You Loved Me Before the Foundation of the World: An Examination of Karl Rahner's Doctrine of Trinity and Comparison to That of Hans Urs von Balthasar." PhD diss., Fordham University, 2014.

Moore, Edward. *Studies in Dante. Second Series: Miscellaneous Essays*. Oxford: Clarendon Press, 1899.

Moreira, Isabel. *Heaven's Purge: Purgatory in Late Antiquity*. New York: Oxford University Press, 2010.

Morrison, Glenn. *A Theology of Alterity: Levinas, von Balthasar, and Trinitarian Praxis*. Pittsburgh: Duquesne University Press, 2013.

Murray, Jamie. "Deleuze and Guattari's Intensive and Pragmatic Semiotic of Emergent Law." *International Journal for the Semiotics of Law* 20.1 (2007) 7–32.

Perpich, Diane. *The Ethics of Emmanuel Levinas*. Stanford: Stanford University Press, 2008.

Bibliography

Pew Research Center (PRC). "Belief in Absolute Standards for Right and Wrong." *Pew Research Center: Religious Landscape Study*, 2014. Online. https://www.pewforum.org/religious-landscape-study/belief-in-absolute-standards-for-right-and-wrong.

———. "Belief in Heaven." *Pew Research Center: Religious Landscape Study*, 2014. Online. https://www.pewforum.org/religious-landscape-study/belief-in-heaven.

———. "Belief in Hell." *Pew Research Center: Religious Landscape Study*, 2014. Online. https://www.pewforum.org/religious-landscape-study/belief-in-hell.

———. "Frequency of Feeling Spiritual Peace and Wellbeing." *Pew Research Center: Religious Landscape Study*, 2014. Online. https://www.pewforum.org/religious-landscape-study/frequency-of-feeling-spiritual-peace-and-wellbeing.

———. "Frequency of Feeling Wonder About the Universe." *Pew Research Center: Religious Landscape Study*, 2014. Online. https://www.pewforum.org/religious-landscape-study/frequency-of-feeling-wonder-about-the-universe.

———. "Sources of Guidance on Right and Wrong." *Pew Research Center: Religious Landscape Study*, 2014. Online. https://www.pewforum.org/religious-landscape-study/sources-of-guidance-on-right-and-wrong.

———. "Sources of Guidance on Right and Wrong Among Adults with a Post-Graduate Degree." *Pew Research Center: Religious Landscape Study*, 2014. Online. https://www.pewforum.org/religious-landscape-study/sources-of-guidance-on-right-and-wrong/among/educational-distribution/post-graduate-degree.

———. "Sources of Guidance on Right and Wrong Among College Graduates." *Pew Research Center: Religious Landscape Study*, 2014. Online. https://www.pewforum.org/religious-landscape-study/sources-of-guidance-on-right-and-wrong/among/educational-distribution/college.

Picot, Jean-Claude, and William Berg. "Lions and Promoi: Final Phase of Exile for Empedocles' Daimones." *Phronesis* 60.4 (2015) 380–409. https://doi.org/10.1163/15685284-12341290.

Plato. Phaedo. In *The Collected Dialogues of Plato: Including the Letters*, edited by Edith Hamilton and Huntington Cairns, 40–98. Translated by Hugh Tredennick. Princeton: Princeton University Press, 2005.

———. Republic. In *The Collected Dialogues of Plato: Including the Letters*, edited by Edith Hamilton and Huntington Cairns, 575–844. Translated by Paul Shorey. Princeton: Princeton University Press, 2005.

———. Timaeus. In *The Collected Dialogues of Plato: Including the Letters*, edited by Edith Hamilton and Huntington Cairns, 1151–1211. Translated by Benjamin Jowett. Princeton: Princeton University Press, 2005.

Plotinus. "The Six Enneads." Translated by Stephen Mackenna and B. S. Page. *Internet Classics Archive*, n.d. Online. http://classics.mit.edu/Plotinus/enneads.mb.txt.

Pseudo-Dionysius. *Pseudo-Dionysius: The Complete Works*. Translated by Colm Luibheid. New York: Paulist, 1987.

Rahner, Karl. *The Trinity*. Translated by Joseph Donceel. New York: Seabury, 1974.

Rosenzweig, Franz. *The Star of Redemption*. Translated by Barbara E. Galli. Modern Jewish Philosophy and Religion: Translations and Critical Studies. Madison: University of Wisconsin Press, 2005.

Schneemelcher, Wilhelm. "Acts of Peter." In *Writings Relating to the Apostles, Apocalypses, and Related Subjects*, edited by Wilhelm Schneemelcher and Robert McLachlan Wilson, 271–321. Vol. 2 of *New Testament Apocrypha*. Louisville: Westminster John Knox Press, 1992.

Bibliography

Shaw, Robert. "Bringing Deleuze and Guattari Down to Earth Through Gregory Bateson: Plateaus, Rhizomes, and Ecosophical Subjectivity." *Theory, Culture & Society* 32.7-8 (2015) 151–71.

Singleton, Charles S. *Journey to Beatrice*. Dante Studies 2. Cambridge: Harvard University Press, 1958.

Smith, Daniel W. "Deleuze and the Question of Desire: Toards an Immanent Theory of Ethics." In *Deleuze and Ethics*, edited by Nathan Jun and Daniel W. Smith, 123–41. Edinburgh: Edinburgh University Press, 2011.

Smith, Jonathan Z. "Birth Upside Down or Right Side Up?" *History of Religions* 9.4 (1970) 281–303.

Strauss, Walter A. "Dante's Belacqua and Beckett's Tramps." *Comparative Literature* 11.3 (1959) 250–61.

Sugarman, Richard I. "Emmanuel Levinas and the Deformalization of Time." In *Logos of History—Logos of Life, Historicity, Time, Nature, Communication, Consciousness, Alterity, Culture*, edited by Anna-Teresa Tymieniecka, 253–69. Book 3 of *Logos of Phenomenology and Phenomenology of the Logos*. Analecta Husserliana 90. Hanover: Springer, 2006.

Surin, Kenneth. "Socius." In *The Deleuze Dictionary*, edited by Adrian Parr, 258–60. Rev. ed. Edinburgh: Edinburgh University Press, 2010.

Tate, Allen. "The Symbolic Imagination: A Meditation on Dante's Three Mirrors." *Kenyon Review* 14.2 (1952) 256–77.

Tharn, Tom A. "The Medieval Christian in 'Mirror-Mode': A Brief Sketch of the Mirror as Sacred Tool from Paul's 'In Aenigmate' to Dante's *Paradiso*." *Dulia et Latria Journal* 1 (2008) 33–46

Villani, Tiziana. "Gilles Deleuze: Philosophy and Nomadism." *Deleuze and Guattari Studies* 13.4 (2019) 516–27. https://doi.org/10.3366/dlgs.2019.0377.

Ward, Graham. "Kenosis: Death, Discourse and Resurrection." In *Balthasar at the End of Modernity*, edited by Lucy Gardner et al., 15–68. Edinburgh: T&T Clark, 2001.

Watson, Janell. "Intimacy Without Domestication: Courtly Love in a Thousand Plateaus." *L'Esprit Créateur* 44.1 (2004) 83–95.

Young, Eugene B., et al. *The Deleuze and Guattari Dictionary*. London: Bloomsbury, 2013.

Index

Acts of Peter, 47, 49
Acts of the Apostles, 49
Adam, 49, 91
Adorno, Theodor, 174, 175, 176
agape love, 9, 145
Aldobrandesco, Omberto, 102, 173
Alexander IV, 95
analogy of being, 8, 111, 112, 115, 116, 117, 118, 119, 120, 121, 122, 123, 124, 125, 127, 157, 163
Ananias, 146
Anaxagoras, 64
Ante Purgatory, 57, 58, 60, 67, 71, 72, 76, 77, 89, 91, 92, 93, 94, 95, 96, 97, 100, 101
Aquinas, 56, 64, 65, 66, 80, 81, 89, 90, 91, 112, 117, 119, 124, 125, 126, 128, 129, 133, 134, 137, 155
arborescent, 33, 46
Aristotle, 19, 143, 147
Artaud, Antonin, 38
assemblage, 43, 45, 50, 51, 52
Athanasius, 126, 128
Atilla, 21
Augustine, 19, 20, 36, 37, 42, 70, 71, 88, 112, 115, 128, 133, 134, 144

Barth, Karl, 112, 120, 121, 122, 123, 157
battle of Benevento, 96
Beatrice, 7, 8, 9, 42, 43, 56, 57, 59, 60, 80, 82, 83, 84, 85, 86, 92, 93, 103, 104, 106, 107, 108, 109, 113, 114, 120, 124, 125, 126, 127, 129, 130, 131, 139, 144, 145, 146, 150, 151, 152, 154, 155, 158, 159, 160, 163
Beckett, Samuel, 34, 95
becoming, 3, 4, 8, 16, 17, 35, 39, 40, 46, 47, 53, 54, 71, 76, 115, 121, 159, 168
becoming animal, 53, 54
becoming minoritarian, 39, 40, 46, 53
becoming woman, 17, 39, 40, 46, 53
Being in the World, 57, 59, 76, 77, 78, 105
Belacqua, 93, 94, 95
Bernard, 1, 2, 9, 113, 115, 116, 158, 161, 162, 163
Bernard, 2, 9, 115, 116, 158, 161, 162, 181
beyond being realm, 57
black holes, 52
Boccaccio, 41
body without organs, 4, 16, 17, 33, 38, 44
Bonaventure, 133, 143, 144
Boniface VIII, 48
Brutus, 23
Buber, 112, 134, 135

Cacciaguida, 84
Capaneus, 22
capital, 28, 30, 31, 32
capitalism, 3, 28, 30, 31, 32
capitalist social machine, 30, 32
caritas, 36
Casella, 92, 93

Index

Cassius, 23
Cato, 91, 92, 93, 100
Cave, 5, 57, 67, 69, 70, 71, 72, 73, 74, 75, 76, 77, 79, 80, 84
cave allegory, 5, 57, 67, 69, 70, 76, 77, 80, 84
Clement V, 48
Cleopatra, 21, 41
Constantine, 48, 49
Counter-Signifying, 50
courtly love, 42, 43, 44, 45, 46, 55, 172
cupiditas, 36

depositum fidei, 122
desire, 3, 9, 13, 14, 16, 17, 25, 26, 28, 35, 36, 37, 39, 40, 41, 42, 43, 44, 45, 49, 50, 53, 66, 78, 83, 96, 145, 151, 157, 172, 174, 175, 176, 177
deterritorialization, 14, 15, 28, 32, 45, 172
deterritorialize, 28, 45
diachrony, 56, 63, 67
Dido, 21
Dionysius, 20, 81, 144
distinct manner of subsisting, 132
dynamics of beauty, 8, 9, 111, 112, 116, 140, 141

Earthly Paradise, 6, 7, 56, 57, 59, 60, 67, 90, 91, 92, 103, 104, 108
Ecclesiastical Hierarchy, 20
Empyrean, 118, 154
equivocal, 119, 122, 123
ethics, 5, 6, 7, 19, 24, 25, 26, 35, 37, 41, 47, 55, 61, 62, 63, 97, 99, 141, 166, 173, 174
Eve, 79, 91
Exodus, 52

face of Christ, 14, 51, 53
face of God, 52, 115
face of the despot, 51
face-to-face, 62, 63, 105, 114
faciality, 14, 29, 40, 51, 52, 53, 54
faciality abstract machine, 53
Farinata, 21
first philosophy, 5, 174
Form of beauty, 9, 112, 113, 141, 142, 149

form of content, 50
form of expression, 50
Francis, 18, 48
Frederick II, 22

Gates of Dis, 21
genus, 122
Ghibelline, 102
Giancotto, 41
Glaucus, 158
Goethe, 81
good beyond being, 57, 58, 67, 68, 69, 73, 83, 84
Gratian, 88
Gregory of Nyssa, 7, 114, 115
Gregory Palamas, 154
Gregory the Great, 88

Hegel, 3
Heidegger, 5, 61, 116, 117, 118
hierarchy, 12, 15, 18, 19, 20, 21, 23, 24, 25, 29, 30, 31, 33, 34, 54, 55, 183
Hilary of Poitiers, 126
hypostasis, 6, 57, 59, 73, 74, 75, 76, 77, 79, 98, 100, 101, 102, 104
hypostatic, 74, 159

identity, 16, 26, 34, 35, 37, 39, 46, 48, 54, 83, 97, 98, 153
il y a, 6, 57, 58, 59, 73, 74, 75, 77, 80, 81, 90, 92, 94, 95, 98, 101, 104, 105
immanence, 3, 4, 12, 18, 23, 24, 31, 35, 44, 55, 118
immanent plane, 32
In exitu Israël de Aegypto, 92
inner dynamics, 8, 111, 112, 116
Innocent IV, 86, 95
Intelligible Realm, 57, 69
Interiority and Economy, 57, 73, 75, 80, 98, 99, 100
inversion, 49, 143
I-Thou, 134

Jonah, 52
Judas, 22, 23
judgment of God, 26, 38, 44

Index

Kant, 3, 35
kenotic, 8, 112, 135, 136, 137, 148, 153, 159, 176

Lancelot, 41, 45, 172
line of flight, 4, 14, 15, 33, 34, 44, 45, 46, 53, 54, 55
logoi, 122
logos, 8, 112, 121, 122, 128, 139, 140
Lucy, 100, 103, 145, 159, 160

Malebolge, 22, 47
Manfred, 95, 96, 99, 100
Marian, 114, 152, 153, 159, 162, 163
Marianism, 153, 159, 160, 162
Mary, 2, 114, 120, 144, 145, 152, 153, 159, 160, 161, 162, 163, 176
Matelda, 106, 107, 108
mixed regime of signifiance and subjectification, 51
modes of being, 6, 56, 57, 60, 62, 67, 73, 97
molar, 46
monarchy, 27, 31, 97

Neoplatonic, 20, 70
Neoplatonism, 12, 20, 23, 152
Neoplatonists, 20
Nicholas III, 48
Nineveh, 52
nomad, 15, 16, 32, 33, 50, 184
Novello, 42, 96

Odyssey, 61
orphic, 69, 74, 75
outer dynamics, 8, 9, 111, 112, 140, 141
Ovid, 158

Paolo, 3, 40, 41, 42, 43, 45, 46, 170, 171, 172
Parmenides, 61
Paul, 18, 145, 146
Peter, 47, 49, 139, 140, 169
Phaedo, 56, 64
Philip IV, 48
Pier della Vigna, 22

Plato, 5, 19, 54, 56, 57, 58, 60, 64, 65, 67, 68, 69, 70, 71, 72, 73, 74, 75, 76, 77, 78, 79, 80, 83, 84, 85, 91, 143, 155
Plotinus, 19, 20
post-signifying, 50, 51, 52, 53, 54
predication, 111, 118, 119
pre-signifying, 50
primitive, 27, 29, 50, 51, 73, 176
procession, 107, 129, 133, 135, 137, 153
production, 3, 27, 28, 29, 35, 135
progression, 16, 34, 56, 58, 60, 61, 67, 84, 158
purgatorial states, 56, 57
Purgatory Proper, 6, 7, 57, 58, 59, 60, 67, 71, 72, 76, 78, 83, 84, 90, 91, 93, 94, 95, 96, 100, 101, 102, 173, 174

regime of signs, 14, 29, 40, 50, 51, 52, 54
reterritorialization, 15, 44
rhizome, 15, 33
Richard of St. Victor, 133, 134

scholastic, 3, 131, 152
scientism, 113
Second Council of Lyons, 86
secularism, 1
self, 7, 12, 16, 17, 22, 33, 34, 44, 46, 57, 59, 61, 66, 75, 76, 77, 78, 79, 80, 81, 82, 85, 95, 101, 102, 104, 105, 106, 108, 112, 116, 120, 131, 133, 134, 135, 174
sensate realm, 57
signifying, 45, 46, 50, 51, 52, 53, 54
signifying and subjective programs, 45
Simon Magus, 47, 49, 52
Simoniac Popes, 40, 47, 49
simony, 49
smooth capital, 31, 32
social machine, 14, 29, 30, 31, 32, 43, 172
Socrates, 64, 67, 68, 91
species, 122
Spiritual Franciscans, 48
spiritual individualism, 1
states of being, 6, 56, 57, 58, 70, 73
striated capital, 31, 32

stuckness with the self, 57, 77, 105
subject, 6, 7, 13, 17, 28, 29, 33, 34, 35, 37, 38, 42, 43, 44, 59, 60, 63, 66, 67, 69, 74, 76, 77, 79, 80, 81, 82, 83, 85, 86, 88, 90, 95, 98, 100, 101, 102, 104, 105, 127, 136

teleology, 3, 56, 57, 64, 65, 66
teological, 56
Tertullian, 25
the Good, 5, 7, 8, 19, 20, 50, 57, 58, 62, 64, 65, 66, 67, 68, 69, 70, 73, 84, 90, 93, 112, 113, 118, 120, 140, 141, 146, 147, 163, 174, 175, 176
Theodore of Mopsuestia, 127
transcendent imperial machine, 30
transcendental empiricism, 35
trinitarian, 8, 118, 119, 127, 129, 131, 133, 134, 135, 163

True Beauty, 8, 141, 142
typology, 50

Ulysses, 15, 16, 23, 60, 151
univocal, 119, 121, 123
univocity of being, 13, 24
Urban IV, 95

Virgil, 7, 9, 21, 45, 53, 54, 60, 71, 74, 80, 82, 83, 84, 85, 92, 94, 96, 99, 102, 103, 104, 105, 108, 145, 152, 160, 161, 162, 163

white walls, 52

Zeus, 22